Business Ethics in the 21st Century

Issues in Business Ethics

VOLUME 39

For further volumes:
http://www.springer.com/series/6077

Norman E. Bowie

Business Ethics
in the 21st Century

 Springer

Norman E. Bowie
Carlson School of Management SMO
University of Minnesota
Minneapolis, MN, USA

ISSN 0925-6733
ISBN 978-94-007-6222-0   ISBN 978-94-007-6223-7 (eBook)
DOI 10.1007/978-94-007-6223-7
Springer Dordrecht Heidelberg New York London

Library of Congress Control Number: 2013935646

Printed on acid-free paper

Springer is part of Springer Science+Business Media (www.springer.com)

Dedicated to my family
Maureen, my wife of 26 years
Brian, son, his wife Christine, and
their children Alec, Kealyn, and
Ainsley Peter, son, his wife Christina, and
their children Larkin and Charles

Introduction by the Series Editors

'*Eminent Voices*' is a new sub-series within the *Issues in Business Ethics* book series. *Eminent Voices* aims to bring together the work of eminent business ethics scholars who have substantially contributed to the development of the field of business ethics over the course of their careers. Contributing scholars are invited to compile a collection of papers in which they reflect on the ways in which their thinking and careers have evolved in relation to developments within the field of business ethics. Authors are also invited to engage with their critics by revisiting earlier papers that gave rise to collegial criticism and reflecting on the development of important debates within the field. The series allows papers that did not really gain traction at the time of publication to be reintroduced and refined. It offers the opportunity for the author to restyle and expand papers that may have remained underdeveloped in earlier drafts, in order to solidify its main argument and harness its contribution to the field.

We are very proud that Prof. Norman E. Bowie accepted the challenge of becoming the first Eminent Voice in our series—an accolade that is certainly well-deserved. Norman E. Bowie is an important representative of the first generation of business ethicists that made business ethics flourish in the 1980s, defending a Kantian perspective in business ethics. One of his main publications was *Business Ethics: A Kantian Perspective*. He held the Elmer L. Andersen Chair in Corporate Responsibility at the University of Minnesota for 20 years. Upon becoming Professor Emeritus in 2009, he received the first life-time achievement award in scholarship presented by the Society for Business Ethics.

University of Tilburg   Wim Dubbink
De Paul University, Chicago   Mollie Painter Morland

Preface

I completed a wonderful 20 years as the Elmer L Andersen Chair of Corporate Responsibility at the University of Minnesota in 2009. As I retired from a permanent appointment, I completed 41 years of teaching in higher education. Some part-time teaching through 2012 has added another 3 years. It is now time to move on.

When I left the University of Delaware to join the faculty of a PhD granting institution in philosophy and in management, I finally had the opportunity to mentor doctoral students, one of the real joys of my life. My own research in this field has benefited greatly from my work with them. Denis Arnold has gone on to be President of the Society for Business Ethics and Editor-in-Chief of *Business Ethics Quarterly*. Jared Harris, University of Virginia; Scott Reynolds, University of Washington; and Jeffrey Smith, University of Redlands are supporting Denis as members of the BEQ editorial board.

I am proud to be one of the founders of the Society for Business Ethics (SBE). SBE is everything a scholarly organization should be and more. The organization is small enough for the annual meetings to be intellectually stimulating and yet enjoyable. The members of SBE cooperate with one another to advance research in business ethics. It is what John Rawls would call a social union. I have many close personal friends in this organization and I have benefited from my conversations with them over the years and have enjoyed their company. Fear of leaving someone out prevents me from naming them all, but you know who you are.

I want to give readers of this book some idea of what to expect. Many readers will associate me with the application of Kant's ethical theory to business ethics. They may be familiar with *Business Ethics: A Kantian Perspective* and with several articles (some co-authored with former students) that apply Kantian ethics to a particular business ethics issue. However, this is **not** a book on Kantian business ethics. Only one of the 12 chapters is devoted to that theme. Chapter 4 in this volume reflects my latest thinking on the application of Kant's ethical theory to business ethics. Business ethics is a rich field with many important issues to be discussed. As I have watched the issues in business ethics that get attention change over the years, I wanted to write about some things that now seem to be getting attention in the first quarter of the twenty-first century and that I have not written much about in the past. These include ethical issues at the macro-level of the economy and more discussion of international issues. The chapters on these topics are being published for the first time. In some cases, I am revising earlier articles that remain relevant in the early twenty-first century but where my opinions have changed—often in response to the criticism of colleagues. What I am attempting to do is to give the reader a snapshot of what I believe the driving issues in business ethics are in the early part of this century.

I also want to say something about the style in which some chapters are written. It is much more informal than found in standard scholarly works. In several chapters, I try to provide some historical context to the chapters and explain why my thinking has evolved as it has. In some cases, my thinking has been strongly influenced by experience in research and in the classroom. This is particularly true of the chapter on teaching. I hope readers will not be put off by these instances of informality but will see them as providing some personal reflections on the part of one of the founders of SBE on the evolution of research and teaching in business ethics.

Two chapters are reprinted in their entirety. I wish to thank Emilio D'Orazio and *Politeia* for permission to reprint "Economics: Friend or Foe of Ethics" that was published in *Politeia* (2008) 89 13–26. I also wish to thank George Brenkert, Tom L Beauchamp and Oxford University Press for permission to reprint "Organizational Integrity and Moral Climates" that appeared in *Oxford Handbook of Business Ethics* (2009) 701–724. Two chapters are greatly revised versions of earlier published articles. The early version of "Fair Markets" appeared in *Journal of Business Ethics* (1988) 7 89–98. The early version of "Money Morality and Motor Cars Revisited" appeared in *Business Ethics and the Environment*, edited by W Michael Hoffman, Robert Frederick and Edward S Petry Jr (1990) Quorum Books, 89–97. I wish to thank W. Michael Hoffman and the Center for Business Ethics at Bentley College for permission to reprint those portions of "Money, Morality and Motor Cars" that I retained in "Money, Morality and Motor Cars Revisited." I am also grateful to Springer publishers for their policy of allowing their authors to reprint articles or portions of articles that they have published in Springer publications. This policy applied to "Fair Markets" and to some material in "The Limitations of Pragmatism as a Theory of Business" which originally appeared in a paper entitled "Business Ethics, Postmodernism, and Solidarity" in *Applied Ethics in a Troubled World*, Eds. Edgar Marscher and Otto Neumaier, Kluwer Academic Publishers. pp. 179–193 Chap. 9 is a joint collaboration with my long-time friend and colleague Ronald Duska. That chapter and all the remaining chapters have not been published elsewhere, although some paragraphs from "A Reply to My Critics" were published in *Kantian Business Ethics: Critical Perspectives* edited by Denis and Jared Harris Edward Elgar Publishing (2012). This material will be found in Chap. 4. Again I wish to thank Denis Arnold, Jared Harris and Edward Elgar Publishing for permission to reprint those paragraphs. A few paragraphs from my review of *Stakeholder Theory: The State of the Art* from the January 2012 issue of *Business Ethics Quarterly* are incorporated into Chap. 5. I wish to thank *Business Ethics Quarterly* for permission to use that material. A version of Chap. 7 was presented at a 2001 meeting of Social Issues in Management at The Academy of Management and still later at the

University of California-Riverside. An early version of Chap. 10 was read at the 2006 Transatlantic Business Ethics Conference at the Wharton School. I am indebted for the many helpful comments I received on those occasions.

Finally I want to thank the two anonymous reviewers who provided helpful comments and made this a better book. I want to thank Neil Olivier, Senior Editor, Philosophy of Law and Ethics, Springer Science and Business Media B.V. and Professors Wim Dubbink and Mollie Painter-Moreland, general editors of the Business in Ethics Series of which this book is a part, for their guidance and their support. Special thanks go to Diana Nijenhuijzen and Sunil Padman from Springer who helped me get this manuscript into the right format for publication. Also I wish to thank my wife Maureen for her support and encouragement during this long process.

Norman E. Bowie

Contents

Part I
Economic Issues in Business Ethics

Chapter 1
Fair Markets Revisited

It is not uncommon to have businesspersons appeal to the principle, "If it is not illegal, it's ethical". The strategy behind the appeal is to limit the moral responsibilities of management. The *only* moral obligation of management is to obey the law. I shall refer to this position as the minimalist position regarding business ethics.

Criticisms of this principle are fairly common. Some have provided examples of corporate activities which, although legal, are allegedly immoral, e.g. firing a person employed at will for no reason. Many of the activities during the 2008–2009 financial crises were of this type. See the Academy Award winning documentary, *Inside Job*, for a vivid set of examples. In addition, still others, e.g., Christopher Stone, have argued that the law simply cannot constrain certain harmful corporate activities.[1] For example, if corporation X does something immoral which is later made illegal because the act was immoral, the law is powerless to punish X for that act.

I will not elaborate upon these well-known arguments. Rather I will argue that the sentence, "If it's not illegal, it's ethical" is hardly a minimalist strategy at all. The premises of my argument are as follows:

1. The law, as embodied in statutes, the common law tradition, and the judgments of juries, appeals to fundamental ethical notions.
2. These ethical notions are not given precise legal definition and, hence, cannot be reduced to legal terms.
3. Therefore, the law frequently requires corporate conduct to adhere to broad open-ended standard of morality.

If these premises are true, it means that business activity, in being held accountable to the law, will be held accountable to morality as well. If the obligation of business is to follow the law and if the law demands adherence to morality-where

---

This chapter is an updated version of Sections I–V of my "Fair Markets" in *Journal of Business Ethics* 7 (1988) 89–97. This chapter contains a number of new arguments for the position argued in that paper. Material from the original article is reprinted by permission of Springer.

[1] Stone, Christopher D. (1973). *Where the Law Ends.* New York: Harper & Row Publishers.

N.E. Bowie, *Business Ethics in the 21st Century*, Issues in Business Ethics 39, DOI 10.1007/978-94-007-6223-7_1, © Springer Science+Business Media Dordrecht 2013

what is moral is not reducible to what is legal-then the injunction that all business should do is obey the law is likely to be badly misunderstood. The reason is that that injunction neither substantially limits the moral obligations of business nor provides much guidance to the manager who is trying to determine what her company should or should not do.

Of course, this point would be of limited interest if there were a consensus in both the business community and in the law as to what the legal demands of morality are. But there is no consensus. Moreover, to make matters worse from the standpoint of the manager, the classical account of the function of the corporation (maximize shareholder wealth) will often not provide an acceptable moral defense in the courts. In other words, although there is no consensus on what the legal requirements of morality are, there is a growing consensus that the traditional business views are inadequate. When I wrote this last sentence in 1988, my point was mostly directed at the fact that the business schools were finding room for business ethics and the resulting critique of profit maximization as the sole purpose of business. As I write the revised version of this essay in 2011, the skepticism about the ethical views of business is directed by the public with special emphasis on the large banks and other financial institutions that the public holds responsible for the 2008–2009 financial crisis. Although the courts are more conservative now, I still believe it is the case that the manager of a corporation faces the disconcerting possibility of appearing before a court, when neither she nor her company had done anything previously illegal nor contrary to stockholder interest, to be found morally and hence legally blameworthy. I am speaking here of civil cases.

In the remainder of this chapter, I will provide evidence and argument for the thesis outlined above. I will focus on the notion of fairness to make my points. Other ethical concepts could be used as well. Finally since a complete analysis of fairness is not found either in the legal literature or in society as a whole, I will try to show that it is a presumption in the law that unfair transactions are either coercive or involve inequality of bargaining power. If this analysis of fairness is adopted the moral and thus the legal obligations of business will be expanded.

Morality as a Ground of Legal Decisions

The first claim to be established is that the law as embodied in statute, the common law, and jury judgments uses fundamental ethical notions.

At the most general level, the Uniform Commercial Code which has been adopted in every state provides that good faith is assumed in every transaction governed by the code.[2] The requirements of good faith cannot even be waived by a voluntary agreement among the parties.

---

[2] Quoted from *Business and Its Legal Environment*, Thomas W. Dunfee, Janice R. Bellace, and Arnold Rosoff (eds.), 1983. Englewood Cliffs: Prentice-Hall, 209.

A number of business relationships are fiduciary in nature. Any business person takes on a fiduciary duty to her principal (e.g. employer) when she acts on the principal's behalf with regard to third parties. Corporate directors and officers have a fiduciary relationship with the stockholders. And what are the moral requirements of that relationship. Hear Justice Cardozo.[3]

> Joint adventurers, like carpenters, owe to one another, while the enterprise continues the duty of the finest loyalty. …A trustee is held to something stricter than the morals of the marketplace. Not honesty alone, but the punctilio of an honor, the most sensitive, is then the standard of behavior.

As for labor law, Section 7 of the Wagner Act (National Labor Relations Act) specifically forbids an unfair labor practice. One of the unfair labor practices outlawed by the act is "…to refuse to bargain collectively with the representatives of his employees."[4] But what counts as refusal to bargain. In 1947 Congress enacted Section 8d which appealed to explicitly moral concepts. "For purposes of this section, to bargain collectively is the performance of the mutual obligation of the employer and the representatives of the employees to meet at reasonable times and confer in good faith with respect to wages, hours, and other terms and conditions of employment."[5]

At this point, those who argue that if it's legal, it's OK (morally permissible) might agree that statutes make use of moral concepts. Legislatures create laws that make moral obligations legal obligations as in the examples above. However, until the statute is duly passed, business has no legal obligation and thus also no moral obligation with respect to the issue at hand.

But that is not strictly true. Often a law is written that requires a legal obligation to play fair but leaves to the courts or future legislative action what is to count as fair. A manager facing this kind of statute needs to act before what counts as legally fair is determined. It seems to me that the most prudent business decision is to act from the public understanding of what constitutes fairness because it is that standard to which future legislators and future court decisions will appeal. In other words the business person cannot wait for the law; the good business decision is to assume that the law will ultimately embrace common morality standards of what constitutes fairness. Thus, even in the cases cited above, the strategy of "If it's legal, it is OK" (morally permissible) won't work. The law requires adherence to fairness but most likely relies on common morality standards of fairness to tell the business person what to do. I will have more to say about this issue after providing some cases in common law that are decided on ethical grounds.

If one moves from statutes to the common law, the requirement that the law requires the ethical is seen in a number of classic cases. Consider the evolution of laws protecting the consumer. In traditional tort law a claim against another was based on "privity." To sue someone for damages you had to be in a direct relation

---

[3] *Mienhard v. Salmon* (1928) 164 N.E. 545 at 223.

[4] http://www.nolo.com/legal-encyclopedia/content/nlra-act.html, Downloaded September 18, 2012.

[5] Ibid.

with the party you are suing. Consider the automobile manufacturer who uses dealers to distribute the product. If privity were strictly enforced, you could only sue the dealer, not the manufacturer.

In a classic case a Mr. Henningsen purchased a Plymouth from Bloomfield Motors. Later Mrs. Henningsen was injured when the car suddenly ran off the road, presumably as a result of a defective steering mechanism. The defendants, Chrysler Corporation and Bloomfield Motors, denied responsibility under privity. Chrysler had not sold Mr. Henningsen the car and neither Chrysler nor Bloomfield Motors had sold the car to Mrs. Henningsen. In *Henningsen v. Bloomfield Motors Inc.*,[6] the New Jersey Supreme Court disagreed that privity protected Chrysler and Bloomfield motors and they based their decision on grounds of morality.

> The Defense of Lack of Privity Against Mrs Henningsen
> Both defendants contend that since there was no privity of contract between them and Mrs Henningsen, she cannot recover for breach of any warranty made by either of them. On the facts, as they were developed, we agree that she was not a party to the purchase agreement. Her right to maintain the action, therefore, depends upon whether she occupies such legal status thereunder as to permit her to take advantage of a breach of defendant's implied warranties... We are convinced that the cause of justice, in this area of the law can be served only by recognizing that she is such a person who, in the reasonable contemplation of the parties to the warranty, might be expected to become a user of the automobile.[7]

Manufacturers have also used warranties in the effort to limit legal liability. In the same Henningsen case, the defendants tried to argue that there were no warranties expressed or implied other than the one providing for the replacement of defective parts. Again the court appeals to canons of justice in deciding for the plaintiffs.

> The Effects of the Disclaimer and Limitation of Liability Clauses on the Implied Warranty of Merchantability
> ...[W]hat effect should be given to the express warranty in question which seeks to limit the manufacturer's liability to replacement of defective parts, and which disclaims all other warranties, express or implied?...
> The warranty before us is a standardized form designed for mass use. He [the buyer] takes it or leaves it and he must take it to buy an automobile. No bargaining is engaged in with respect to it. In fact, the dealer through whom it comes to the buyer is without authority to alter it; his function is ministerial-simply to deliver it.
> The gross inequality of bargaining position occupied by the consumer in the automobile industry is thus apparent. There is no competition among the car makers in the area of express warranty....
> ...*In the context* of this warranty, only the abandonment of all sense of justice would permit us to hold that as a matter of law, the phrase, "its obligations under this warranty being limited to making good at its factory any part or parts thereof" signifies to an ordinary reasonable person that he is relinquishing any personal injury claim that might flow from the use of a defective automobile.
> ...The verdict in favor of the plaintiffs and against Chrysler Corporation establishes that the jury found the disclaimer was not fairly obtained....[8]

---

[6] *Henningsen v Bloomfield Motors* (1960) Supreme Court of New Jersey 161 A2d 61.
[7] Ibid.
[8] Ibid.

The impact of this case was to bring consumer protection law closer to the public's understanding of what fairness and justice require. Indeed at this point in the twenty-first century the arguments of the Chrysler Corporation and Bloomfield Motors seem outrageous.

Still another court decision that supports my point is in the area of patent infringement. In Beaumont, Texas, the DuPont Company was constructing a new plant for making methanol. An unknown third party hired the defendants Rolfe and Gary Christopher to fly over the facility and take photographs. This flyover was discovered and DuPont sued. In response the Christophers said they had done nothing legally wrong (The "if it is legal, it is morally ok." Defense).

In delivering his decision, Judge Goldberg admitted that the Christophers had neither trespassed, breached a confidential relationship, nor engaged in other illegal conduct. Judge Goldberg then invoked the rule from the Restatement of Torts which provides, "One who discloses or uses another's trade secret, without a privilege to do so, is liable to the other if (a) he discovered the secret by improper means."[9]

Judge Goldberg continued

> The question remaining, therefore, is whether aerial photography of plant construction is an improper means of obtaining another's trade secret. We conclude that it is and that the Texas courts would so hold. The Supreme Court of that state has declared that "the undoubted tendency of the law has been to recognize and enforce higher standards of commercial morality in the business world."

A standard defense in a violation of trade secrets case is to show that the defendant did not protect the trade secret in question. Justice Goldberg used moral concepts to totally reject that defense.

> To require DuPont to put a roof over the unfinished plant to guard its secret would impose an enormous expense to prevent nothing more than a school boy's trick. We introduce here no new or radical ethic since our ethos has never given moral sanction to piracy. The market place must not deviate far from our mores. We should not require a person or corporation to take unreasonable precautions to prevent another from doing that which he ought not do in the first place. Reasonable precautions against predatory eyes we may require but an impenetrable fortress is an unreasonable requirement and we are not disposed to burden industrial inventors with such a duty in order to protect the fruits of their efforts. "Improper" will always be a word of many nuances, determined by time, place, and circumstances. We therefore need not proclaim a catalogue of commercial improprieties. Clearly, however, one of the commandments does say, "Thou shall not appropriate a trade secret deviously under circumstances in which countervailing defenses are not reasonable available."

Several observations can be made from Judge Goldberg's decision. First he admitted that the Christophers had broken no specific law. He then appealed to a general law against the improper securing of trade secrets. He then appealed to ordinary standards of morality to show that the flyover was improper. Again what drove the legal decision was the mores of ordinary morality.

One more piece of evidence comes from the highly controversial Delaware decision regarding defenses again hostile takeovers.[10]

---

[9] *E.I DuPont de Nemours & Co. Inc., v Christopher* (1970) Justice Goldberg 431 F2d 1012.

[10] *Unocal v Mesa Petroleum Co.*

Unocal Corporation fought off a bid by T Boone Pickens' Mesa Petroleum Company by offering to buy shares of all stockholders except those held by Mesa. In other words, the Board of Directors created two distinct classes of Unocal stockholders and treated them differently. In point of law such disparate treatment is only permitted for a valid corporate purpose; it cannot be used by the directors to keep themselves in power. Moreover, the moral principle of "treat equals equally" would *prima facie* condemn such a two-tier classification of stockholders.

Much to the dismay of many in the business and financial community at that time, the Delaware Supreme Court supported Unocal. And it did so on the ground that Unocal's defense was legitimate and proper given the nature of the Mesa threat. In other words Mesa's behavior was sufficiently questionable on grounds of fairness that this extraordinary defense passed legal muster.

That the offer was unfair has to be extracted from the Court's comments on the case. Central to the issue of fairness was Mesa's two tiered stock offer. For the first 64 million shares of Unocal stock, Mesa offered $54 a share. For the remaining shares Mesa would offer securities that were allegedly worth $54 a share. In fact, the backing on the remaining shares was such that both the market and the court termed the securities "junk bonds."

In passing moral judgment the court said.

> It is now well recognized that such offers are a classic coercive measure designed to stampede shareholders into tendering at the first tier, even if the price is inadequate out of fear of what they will receive at the back end of the transaction.[11]

Given the nature of the threat, the Unocal response was legitimate. "Thus, while the exchange offer is a form of selective treatment, given the nature of the threat posed here, the response is neither unlawful nor unreasonable."[12]

An interesting sidelight is the fact that the court used a standard technique in ethical reasoning to further condemn Pickens' takeover attempt. Mesa had sued on the grounds of a discriminatory exchange. Yet the court noted that Mesa had a history-"a national reputation" as a greenmailer and since greenmail itself was a discriminatory exchange, the court found Mera's allegation of discriminatory exchange to be "ironic." Philosophers would use such terms as "inconsistent" or "in violation of the ethical principle of universality." Immanuel Kant would have been proud of the court.

A Rejoinder and Reply

Some may accept the conclusion that the law embodies moral terms such as "improper," "coercive," and "good faith." They would also concede that in the first instance these terms have not been legally defined and that when the first decision comes down the appeal is often made to common morality or the morality of the "reasonable person." However, once the legal system has adopted a definition of these moral terms, we then

---

[11] *Unocal v Mesa Petroleum Co.* (1985) 493 A2d at 956.
[12] Ibid.

have a legal definition of the moral terms. So Bowie's point is well taken at the beginning but really isn't all that important in the long run.

I reject that move. First, any business person who confronts a law that says it should not behave in a coercive manner and that it should act in good faith needs to know what those terms mean. In the absence of a legal decision, the prudent advice is to follow common morality or the morality of the reasonable person. In those cases where there is no legal option the prudent strategy is to do what morality requires.

Once a business person or firm has a set of legal decisions, the firm does have some guidance as to what the law requires about issues of morality. Is it a wise business strategy in those cases for the firm simply to consult the lawyers? I argue that it is not because in most instances the definitions of terms like "good faith" and "improper" are evolving as societal attitudes change.

Moreover, nearly all the decisions discussed in Section 1 appeal to a broad theory of morality to justify the decision. In Henningsen the warranty is rejected as unjust In Unocal, the court admitted that it might seem that Unocal's refusal to accept Mesa's offer was a violation of Unocal's fiduciary obligation to stockholders and a violation of the principle that all stockholders should be treated equally. But in these particular circumstances the court argued that the defensive strategies were fair.

What is significant about Du Pont v Christopher is that the court used philosophical views about ethics to expand the nature of law. The notion of "improper" is in part defined by the moral principle, "Thou shall not appropriate a trade secret deviously under circumstances in which countervailing defenses are not available."

Even where an attempt to provide a legal definition is given, that is hardly the end of the matter. Consider the Wagner Act which attempts to define an unfair labor practice not to bargain in good faith. What does "bargain in good faith" mean? One of the more frustrating aspects of collective bargaining is the fact that each side initially makes demands that it knows the other side will not accept. There is then a long process of give-and-take which, after much posturing, results in a compromise reasonably close to what both sides would have anticipated. I speak as a former union president here.

In the 1960s General Electric decided that the whole process was time-consuming and inefficient. General Electric then did a study and prepared a contract offer which it believed was fair. In public announcements General Electric said it intended to do right voluntarily. However, the position was to be firm-basically take it or leave it.

In a celebrated U.S. Court of Appeals Second Circuit case, National Labor Relations Board v General Electric Company,[13] GE was found guilty of bargaining in bad faith, first, because its take-it or leave-it strategy made the union powerless and useless, and second because management argued that it was the defender of the employee's interest. The GE strategy was a violation of the process, even if the specific contract being offered was fair. In this case the Court decided what was fair in this context. The actions of GE unfairly compromised the position of the union as a bargaining agent. The GE strategy was to try to eliminate the possibility of bargaining at all. As an aside, Kant would approve of the Court's decision, because

---

[13] *National Labor Relations Board v General Electric Company* (1969) Judge Irving Kauffman, 418 F2d 736.

if GE's tactic were to be universalized, there would be no point to having a union whose chief task was to collectively bargain.

The use of concepts of philosophical ethics to ground legal decisions comes as no surprise to philosophers working in fields such as jurisprudence. Ronald Dworkin has given the most explicit and detailed argument for putting morality as a basis for law.[14] What interests Dworkin is the "hard" cases in which statutes and precedents may be vague, unclear, or in apparent conflict. How are such hard cases to be decided? Dworkin points out that the judge must get behind the statutes and precedents to the principles and policies that underlie them. Any theory regarding the applicable principles and policies will depend on a proper understanding of our legal institutions. However, a proper understanding of our political institutions is ultimately rights based. I think you see this kind of reasoning in the GE case discussed above.

For Dworkin, it is this last step in the hierarchy that is peculiarly moral. Such a hierarchy is required if opinions in hard cases are to be justified and not simply amount to a matter of judicial discretion. Dworkin appeals to the actual practices of judges to support his claim.

Hence we can see that a court can use philosophical or broad societal moral notions to make a decision or even on occasion actually uses such notions to declare what was previously legal to be illegal. Those moral notions are taken over and applied by law but not defined by law.

What is the implication of all this for managers? It should be clear that the principle, "If it's legal, it's moral" cannot be used to limit what is morally required of a business. Given the analysis provided here, we see that what is legal is often a function of what is moral. This is particularly true in just the instances where management wants to use the "If it's legal, it's, moral" principle. After all what the manager wants to say when he or she is criticized for acting in an ethically controversial way is that he or she did nothing illegal. But what is determined to be legal in these cases is what morality would have required. In other words, a business must often show that it acted morally if it is to make its legal case, and it can often be found legally culpable if it did not act morally.

Advice for Managers

But how is a manager to know what business activities the courts will consider moral and which activities the courts will consider immoral? At this point the business ethicist might have a contribution to make. Let us return to the decisions and statutes discussed thus far. In summary fashion here are the results:

1. All business transactions must be made in good faith.
2. Corporate directors have a duty of loyalty to stockholders.
3. Management and labor are forbidden to engage in unfair labor practices.
4. The obligations of manufacturers rest upon the demands of social justice.

---

[14] Dworkin, Ronald. (1977). *Taking Rights Seriously.* Cambridge, MA: Harvard University Press.

5. Trade secrets may not be obtained in an improper manner.
6. Defense measures, including differential offers to stockholders, are legally appropriate responses to hostile takeovers when the takeover offer is based on a coercive two tiered buyout where those tendering their stock early get cash and those tendering later get junk bonds.

The key terms here are "good faith," "loyalty," "unfair," "justice," "proper," and "coercive." What do these terms mean?

Characteristics of Fairness

The business manager might look to society at large for the answer and sometimes the courts will invoke societal norms. But an appeal to societal norms is incomplete or inadequate when either there is no clear societal norm or when there is considerable disagreement as to what the norm is and should be. These kinds of disagreements are to be expected in a highly pluralistic society like our own. Indeed these conflicts over ethical norms help explain why even business firms that are recognized by the business community itself as ethical firms are nonetheless sometimes targets of ethical criticism. And of course the Christophers in the DuPont case and Boone Pickens in the Unocal case would not agree that they acted unfairly.

Perhaps we should return to the court decisions to see if there is one moral notion that captures the variety of decisions. The moral terms mentioned above could then be defined in terms of that notion. My suggestion is that the underlying concept is "fairness." Intuitively here are some of the considerations that lie behind that statement. What counts as an improper obtaining of trade secrets is attempts that are unfair. The law recognizes the competitive nature of enterprise but tries to set limits on what is acceptable competition and what isn't. If a corporation doesn't make a reasonable attempt to protect its trade secrets, then they cannot complain when their trade secrets are used by another. In building its plant, however, DuPont was defenseless since it could not protect its trade secrets from that kind of espionage. Just as there are rules which protect the punter, and now the quarterback, in football, so there are rules to protect companies when those companies cannot protect themselves. Hence the principle enunciated by the court in the DuPont case, "Thou shall not appropriate a trade secret deviously under circumstances in which countervailing defenses are not reasonably available," is really a principle of fairness.

Similarly, in the Henningsen case, both the warranty and the appeal to privity were seen as unfair. The customer's position was too vulnerable. All the advantages lay with the automobile manufacturer and distributer. So even though the court in Henningsen uses the term "justice" the underlying notion is "fairness"- a result that would not surprise John Rawls who defines "justice" as "fairness."

Although the General Electric labor relations case is based on a situation where the intent is very different, I submit that the judicial reasoning was based on similar considerations. To allow GE to dictate the terms eliminated the opportunity for a fair fight. And finally in the defense against a hostile takeover case, the defense was fair because it was made in response to a coercive threat. A coercive threat is not fair. On the other hand, if the threat had not been coercive, the defense probably would not have passed legal muster because it would not have been fair.

However, critics might argue that I have simply pushed the issue out one more step. At this point I am telling the manager that he or she must behave fairly and that it is not enough to simply look to norms of fairness in common morality. So what is the manager to do? Let us return to some of the court decisions and consider some others as well in order to determine if we can detect some common essence to notions of fairness at least with the courts.

In Unocal v Mesa Petroleum, the issue is one of coercion. Coercion is unfair. There are other statutes and court cases that speak against the morality of coercion in the marketplace. For example, many states have followed New York in passing laws that permit a cooling off period for consumers who buy from door-to-door salespeople. These laws have been greatly expanded especially in the banking industry. All are based on the presumption that there is something coercive about offers that are made under very tight time pressures. By allowing consumers to void the contract within 24 h, the element of coercion is mitigated- at least for those who know the law.

In Henningsen, the issue is the inequality in bargaining power between the consumer and the seller. Again there are other statutes and court cases that speak against the morality of taking advantage of great inequalities in bargaining power. The Uniform Commercial Code invalidates unconscionable contracts or clauses. "If a court as a matter of law finds the contract or any clause of the contract to have been unconscionable at the time it was made the court may refuse to enforce the contract" [15] What makes a contract or clause within a contract unfair?

One of the more common judgments made on grounds of unconscionability is in the area of sales contracts. The case of Jones v. Starr Credit Corporation serves as a good example. The plaintiffs bought a freezer worth $300. They bought it on the installment plan whereby they paid $900 for the freezer and an additional $334.80 of financing charges. In finding for the plaintiffs, the court said:

> There was a time when the shield of caveat emptor would protect the most unscrupulous in the marketplace—a time when the law, in granting parties unbridled latitude to make their own contracts allowed exploitive and callous practices which shocked the conscience of the legislative bodies and the courts.
>   The efforts to eliminate these practices has [sic] continued to pose a difficult problem. On the one hand it is necessary to recognize the importance of preserving the integrity of agreements and the fundamental right of parties to deal, trade, bargain and contract. On the other hand, there is concern for the uneducated and often illiterate individual who is the victim of gross inequality of bargaining power, usually the poorest member of the community.[16]

We see in this case that the court explicitly appealed to gross inequality of bargaining power as the basis for the decision. In the case, unlike the GE case discussed

---

[15] http://www.law.cornell.edu/ucc/ucc.table.html, Downloaded September 18, 2012.
[16] *Jones v Star Credit Corporation*, 1969 Supreme Court of New York 298 NYS 2d 264.

earlier, the gross inequality of bargaining power in this case refers to inequality of knowledge rather that inequality of economic power.

By the way it is this inequality of knowledge that makes insider trading unfair. Hence there are laws against insider trading because insider trading is unfair, even though such laws are extraordinarily difficult to enforce and some have argued that insider trading is efficient on economic grounds. In *SEC v. Texas Gulf Sulphur*, the court explained its position on Rule 19b-5 of the Securities Exchange Act of 1934.

> …The core of Rule 10b-5 is the implementation of the Congressional purpose that all investors should have equal access to the rewards of participation in securities transactions. It was the intent of Congress that all members of the investing public should be subject to identical market risks. … The insiders here were not trading on equal footing with the outside investors. They alone were in a position to evaluate the probability and magnitude of what seemed from the outset to be a major strike; they alone could invest safely, secure in the expectation that the price of TGS stock would rise substantially in the event such a major strike should materialize, but would decline little, if at all, in the event of failure, for the public, ignorant at the outset of the favorable probabilities would likewise be unaware of the unproductive exploration, and the additional exploration costs would not significantly affect TGS market prices. Such inequities based upon unequal access to knowledge shouldn't be shrugged off as inevitable in our way of life, or in view of the Congressional concern in the area, remain uncorrected.[17]

Perhaps a transaction should be defined as unfair whenever it is coercive or when there is great inequality of bargaining power or great inequality of knowledge among the parties. If this line of thinking is correct, we have some specific advice for managers. If your action is likely to be considered coercive or if you are engaged in a business activity where there is great inequality of bargaining power, the courts may determine that you are behaving unfairly and because you are behaving unfairly you are behaving illegally.

This way of characterizing unfairness has some plausibility. There are some important parallels between labor law and product liability law. Until the 1930s, employment agreements were modeled on individual contracts that were the common feature of the marketplace. As the size of business enterprises expanded, the individualist model where each individual employee bargained with the individual employer was widely perceived to be irrelevant. Society believed the bargaining relationship between a large steel company and an individual steel worker was excessively unequal. The steel company had too much power. Hence the typical individual employer/employee labor contract was unfair. As a result Congress passed the Wagner Act that gave employees the right to bargain collectively. Presumably, collective bargaining equalized the equation. The power of the large individual corporation was pitted against the collective power of the labor union. During the 1940s some argued that the balance of power had swung too far in favor of labor. Both the Taft Hartley Act and the Landrum Griffin Act contained provisions designed to curb what was seen as the excessive power of unions. (Given this history, a story needs to be told as to how labor has lost power in the United States and how the United States has become the most anti-union country in the G-20.)

---

[17] *S.E.C. v Texas Gulf Sulphur Co.* (1968) United States Court of Appeals Second Circuit, 401 F2d, 833.

On the basis of this analysis, I can now give some general advice to managers.

1. American business activity is legally bound to compete fairly.
2. Three necessary conditions of fairness recognized by law are reasonable equality of bargaining power, reasonable equality of knowledge and non-coerciveness.

Managers cannot rely on the law alone to tell them what is right. They must ask whether their action violates morality by being coercive, an abuse of inequality of bargaining power or an abuse of inequality of knowledge (information asymmetry). Failure to consider morality in this way may leave the company open to charges of illegal activity because the action of the manager was unethical.

Objections and Replies

Since the earlier version of this paper was published in 1988 and my examples are mostly from the mid-twentieth century, perhaps my analysis is less persuasive now that the courts are more conservative. Specifically we have more judges who are strict constructionists about the law and thus these judges are less likely to appeal to moral notions in their decisions. What counts as fair is what the statute or precedent says is fair.

There are a number of possible responses to this objection. First, I must concede that it is partially true. I think there is less likelihood now that judges will decide legal cases on moral grounds. That does not mean that the issue of fairness-even for the most conservative judges has gone away. Let's take a look at some examples.

On October 18, The New York Times, reported that Supreme Court Justice Samuel Alito was troubled by a case where following the law would clearly be unfair.[18] Mr Cory R Maples was on death row in Alabama. The deadline for an appeal had past. The reason no appeal had been made was the result of a series of errors. The article describes those errors as follows:

> A court clerk in Alabama sent two copies of a crucial court order in his case to his lawyer in New York who had left the firm. The firm's mail room returned the envelopes unopened and marked "return to sender." The court clerk did nothing more, and the deadline for an appeal passed.

Now Justice Alito faced this case at least twice before and the tenor of the article is that Alito is trying to come up with principles that will enable him to balance his concern with justice with his concern that the courts would be overwhelmed with cases where error by courts or lawyers were alleged. In one 7–2 case involving Jose Padilla, a Honduran who had lived in the United States for 40 years, the court did decide on the basis of justice. Padilla was arrested for possession of more than a thousand pounds of marijuana. He lawyer told him that if he pleaded guilty and served his sentence, he would not be deported. That was false. In this case, the court found for Mr. Padilla.

---

[18] Liptak, Adam. (2011). "When Fairness and the Law Collide, One Jurist is Troubled," *The New York Times National*, October 18, A 18.

I am not claiming that Justice Alito, a conservative justice, will always try to correct injustices. But I find it interesting that he is trying to come up with principles that will guide justices when they want to see justice done. Then on January 18, 2012, the United States Supreme Court ruled 7–2 in favor of Maples. Justice Alito was included in the majority. In writing for the majority, Justice Ruth Bader Ginsburg wrote, "In these circumstances, no just system would lay the default at Maples's death-cell door."[19]

Since the publication of the original version of this paper, a number of companies have been sued under the Alien Tort Act for violations of human rights. These cases again introduce ethics into the law. In one case, Sosa v. Alvarez-Marchain, the United States had arranged for the abduction of a Mexican national suspected of murdering a Drug Enforcement Officer in Mexico. The Supreme Court (2004) determined that the United States government could not be sued for criminal action but it held open the possibility that Alvarez-Marchain could use international norms of ethics for a civil suit. That still leaves open questions regarding the legal liability of corporations. The Supreme Court had agreed to hear Kiobel v Royal Dutch Petroleum during the 2011–2012 term as to whether corporations could be sued under the act for violations of human rights. Individuals had successfully sued corporations but the United States Court of Appeals for the Second Circuit in New York had ruled that corporations could not be sued under the Act. A similar decision was reached by the United States Court of Appeals for the District of Columbia circuit. On March 5, 2012 the Court ruled for reargument. Reargument is set for October 1, 2012. Should the Supreme Court reverse these decisions, American corporations would be subject in certain circumstances to be sued for violations of human rights. If so courts will be appealing to international moral norms as a basis for their decisions.[20] Here may be another way for what is ethical to determine the legal.

Conclusion

Managers need to manage ethics for prudential reasons as well as moral ones. In this chapter, I have looked at the principle, "If it's legal, it's moral." By looking at statutes, court cases, and reports of the deliberations of justices, I have shown that managers cannot adopt the, "If it's legal, it's moral" principle. Often it is the moral that determines what is legal-the very opposite of the proposed principle.

For managers who are convinced by my arguments, I have tried to provide some practical guidance. I have argued that when the law takes morality into account, the special concern seems to be with fairness in commercial activity. Upon further analysis I have argued that there seem to be three features of unfairness that attract the attention of the law-coercion, gross inequality of bargaining power, and information asymmetry.

---

[19] Quoted in Liptak, Adam. (2012). "Justices Rule for Inmate After Mailroom Mix-Up," *The New York Times*, January 19, A 11.

[20] http://www.jdsupra.com/legalnews/the-alien-tort-statute-at-a-crossroads-27623/, Downloaded September 29, 2012.

Some managers may argue that this advice is not sufficient. What counts as coercion, gross inequality of bargaining power, or abuse of information asymmetry? I admit that these are legitimate questions. To some extent managers could look to societal norms to answer these questions. In the earlier version of this paper, I accepted a definition of coercion by Gregory Dees.[21] However, I also argued that if Dees' definition were accepted the ethical responsibilities of business would expand greatly. Philosophical discussions of the definition of coercion have grown more complex over the past 25 years and this is not the place to argue for one of the competing definitions in the philosophical literature.

As a practical matter, what my analysis shows is that the manager cannot simply send ethical issues to the legal department. If a manager can be held legally responsible for unethical decisions, then the manager needs to approach issues where unfairness especially in terms of coercion, gross inequality of bargaining power , or information asymmetry are present with caution. Consider again GE's take it or leave it offer. Since GE might have thought that the offer was a fair one in substance, they neglected to consider the fairness of the process of collective bargaining. What this chapter does is argue that managers cannot avoid the hard task of ethical analysis. Pushing ethical questions to the legal department is a bad business strategy. My new proposed principle is "If it's unethical, it may not be legal." Thus the manager must try to figure out what is unethical.

---

[21] Dees, Gregory. (1986). "The Ethics of Greenmail" in James E Post (ed.), *Research in Corporate Social Performance and Policy,* Vol. 8. Greenwich: JAI Press, Inc., 165.

Chapter 2
What's Wrong with Efficiency and Always Low Prices

Introduction

In this chapter I want to challenge the fundamental assumption of economics as it is currently understood and taught. The key assumption as I understand it is that a society should use the tools of economics to maximize the production of scarce goods and resources. A society that does that will be maximally efficient and given that resources are scarce a society ought to be as efficient in its economy as it can be. In the more formal language of economics a society should be Pareto optimal. A society is Pareto optimal when you cannot make someone better off without making someone worse off.

I can also put my thesis in ordinary language. In this chapter, I wish to challenge the notion that in economic terms we should always do the most efficient action-the action that will squeeze the most resources out of the economic system or that will result in lower prices to consumers thus enabling consumers to buy more goods and services.

As I see how these assumptions are playing out, I believe that a society ought not be as efficient as it can be. Economics should provide the tools for all individuals to have a better life. Often we ought to make someone worse off economically in order to make someone else better off. I also want to argue contrary to those who want to be neutral about what people choose economically that some choices or economic ends are objectively better than others. Although comments like this will surely infuriate most economists, I will try to show that consumers behave inefficiently and for good reason. To twist a phrase, "Economists maximize, does anybody else."

My challenge to traditional economics takes place within a larger discussion about economics waged by philosophers, political scientists and some economists over the past 30 years or more. However, I am raising an even more radical critique of traditional economics as I will show below.

Before building my case a number of caveats are in order. First I am not waging a full scale attack on efficiency. Often, perhaps usually, efficiency is something we should seek to achieve. For example, we should continue to improve the efficiency of our automobiles, heating systems, and electrical appliances so that they are more

N.E. Bowie, *Business Ethics in the 21st Century*, Issues in Business Ethics 39,
DOI 10.1007/978-94-007-6223-7_2, © Springer Science+Business Media Dordrecht 2013

energy efficient. Fossil fuels are getting scarce and they will run out. We should be as efficient as possible in their use. So I wish to make clear at the outset that my critique of efficiency is a limited one.

In the 1990s several philosophers were concerned with the commodification of certain things that had not been commodified before. For many feminists the classic case of an illegitimate commodification is prostitution, where sexual intimacy which is normally freely given, becomes a service that can be purchased for money. However, the concern of these philosophers extended well beyond sexual intimacy. They noted that many goods that were not commodities before had recently become commodities. Moreover they noted that prominent thinkers were arguing for the commodification of things that would have been totally off the table a decade of so earlier.

For an excellent example of this work, see Margaret Jane Radin's *Contested Commodities*.[1] Radin challenges the idea that people should be allowed to sell body parts like one of their kidneys, for instance. The selling of kidneys is allegedly widespread in parts of Asia, especially India and also in some Central and South American countries. In addition. Radin also challenges the practice of surrogate motherhood. Gary Becker and Richard Posner have proposed that there be a market in babies, namely that babies should be bought and sold.[2] They argue that a market in babies would provide babies to those who most want them which would be good in and of itself. Such a market scheme would also dramatically reduce the number of abortions because now mothers would have a reason to bring the fetus to term since a baby has economic value. In other words a market in babies would increase efficiency. Radin's book is an extended attack on all these practices and ideas. Her fundamental arguments are based on issues of justice but the details of her account are beyond the scope of this chapter.

My argument has a relation to this discussion since I would challenge the value of efficiency that the proposed market in babies would bring about. However, my challenge to efficiency goes beyond the fact that babies should not be treated as commodities. I agree that there is too much commodification. But I want to argue that even with legitimate or accepted commodities, there is too much emphasis on getting commodities cheaply. There is too much emphasis on efficiency. Thus my critique is more radical than Radin's.

Other critics have argued that human beings are not simply rational economic actors. Behavioral economists have challenged the rational actor assumption and some have even won the Nobel Prize in Economics for their research.[3] The challenges

---

[1] Radin, Margaret Jane. (1996). *Contested Commodities*. Cambridge: Harvard University Press.

[2] See Posner, Richard A. (1992). *Economic Analysis of Law*, 4th ed. Boston: Little Brown and Elizabeth M. Landes and Richard A. Posner. (1978). "The Economics of the Baby Shortage," *Journal of Legal Studies*, Posner later pointed out that he did not advocate a market in babies. See his "Mischaracterized View" *Judicature* 321 (1986).

[3] Herbert Simon may have been the father of behavioral economics. He won the Nobel Prize in 1978 for his work on decision making in organizations. In 2002 David Kahneman also won the Nobel Prize in Economics. Other prominent behavioral economists Include Robert Shiller, Richard Thaler and Amos Tversky.

by economists to the "rational actor" thesis are based on empirical work about how human beings behave. The central argument of these economists is that human beings do not behave as rational actors. I have been greatly influenced by the work of these economists and their research has significantly changed the nature of the discipline. But this empirical work is not the concern of this Chapter.

Elizabeth Anderson has provided a normative critique of the rational actor model- a critique that has been influential among philosophers.[4] Anderson and Radin would both agree that there are plural goods such that different plural goods cannot be commensurately exchanged. For example, Anderson believes that neither women's labor nor a clean environment should be treated as commodities. However, Anderson wants to go beyond the claim that certain goods should not be treated as commodities. Anderson's goal is "...to formulate a new theory of rationality and value..."[5] She believes that rationality involves "a matter of intelligibly expressing our varied concerns to others."[6] There is much to admire in Anderson's work but my goal here is not to add to that particular discussion.

Other critics have argued that human beings have what you might call dual personalities. Sometimes what they want as consumers is different from what they want as citizens. Mark Sagoff has made this important distinction in the discussion of environmental ethics.[7] One of his concerns is how to make people act and buy green. In his discussion, he recognizes that human beings have dual roles as consumers and as citizens. The consumer in us seems reluctant to go green, but the citizen in us often endorses a green agenda. The task is to find ways to give the citizen more priority. Again I think Sagoff is correct in making this distinction and a part of this essay can be seen as an endorsement of giving more priority to our role as citizens. But I wish to go further. I want to argue that even as consumers we ought to be less concerned with always getting the most out of "scarce" resources, or of always getting things at the lowest price.

With these caveats in mind, it is time to say what it is about the demand for efficiency that I find suspect.

The Problem

To make this discussion less theoretical, let us consider the Wal-Mart phenomenon. Wal-Mart's philosophy epitomizes the kind of philosophy that I wish to challenge. Wal-Mart's best known advertising slogan is "Low Prices Always." Wal-Mart is one

---

[4] Anderson, Elizabeth. (1993). *Value in Ethics and Economics*. Cambridge, MA: Harvard University Press, The journal *Ethics* had a special section of its V. 106 #3 April 1996 issue devoted to Anderson's book. See pages 508–554.

[5] Ibid., xii.

[6] Ibid., xiii.

[7] Sagoff, Mark. (1988). *The Economy of the Earth*. Cambridge: Cambridge University Press, 7–8.

of the most successful companies in the world.[8] Wal-mart's website reports $419 billion in sales in fiscal 2011. Wal-Mart has 9,700 retail stores in 28 countries. It is the world's largest private employer with over two million employees. It is the largest retailer in the world. Additional statistics on Wal-Mart are provided by Online Marketing Trends.[9] Wal-Mart has 3,600,000 fans on Facebook. Americans spend $36 million per hour at Wal-Mart. 90 % of Americans live within 15 miles of a Wal-Mart store. Worldwide, Wal-Mart's profits were $40,000 per minute. 200 million people a week make purchases at Wal-Mart.

Obviously Wal-Mart's commitment to "Low Prices Always" is not without its costs. An important point for the argument in this Chapter is that not every community wants a Wal-Mart. Wal-Mart may bring lower prices and with that a presumed increase in efficiency because people in a community with a Wal-Mart will have more money to spend that they did before. So why would any community turn Wal-Mart down?

One possible reason for this willingness to accept inefficiency is that lower prices at the retail level lower the wages of all persons working in retail trade where Wal-Mart is a legitimate competitor. For example, in California, supermarkets have claimed that in order to be competitive with Wal-Mart superstores they have had to lower the salaries and benefits of workers. In the first decade of the twenty-first century unions at Safeway furiously engaged in a long and bitter strike. 70,000 workers were involved. However, the strikes were to no avail. Wages at grocery stores in California and elsewhere when faced with Wal-Mart competition have fallen.

Note that we have an issue of efficiency here. I have assumed in the discussion above that all things considered having Wal-Mart with its low prices will provide more purchasing power for the citizens in proximity to the Wal-Mart (enable people to enjoy more goods that they have been able to achieve in the past). Yet the citizens in a few of these commodities do not want the efficiency that Wal-Mart brings. They are willing to have less in order to keep Wal-Mart out. Are these citizens simply being irrational as traditional economic theory would maintain? I think not. Indeed I think the citizens in these communities have an insight that I wish to expand upon.

Some Observations from Home and Abroad

I was first led to this discussion by my international travels, especially in Japan, during the first decade of the twenty-first century. Japan is a service oriented economy par excellence. At the hotel, I could not help but notice the official greeters and the people standing by ready to offer tea. I also noticed that there was no line to check in.

[8] http://www.onlinemarketing-trends.com/2011/02/size-of-walmart-statistics-and-trends.html, Downloaded February 12, 2012.

[9] http://www.onlinemarketing-trends.com/2011/02/size-of-walmart-statistics-and-trends.html, Downloaded February 12, 2012.

Indeed from an American perspective the hotel had too many people waiting for people to check in and certainly no need for all those greeters. There is no doubt in my mind that any American MBA would recommend that the number of people at check in could be reduced-indeed reduced dramatically. By the way the MBA graduate would also note all the flowers, especially the artful ikebana. No need for that extravagance. Also let the people checking in pour their own tea if the hotel really thinks it needs tea. All these extra services and especially extra people takes away from profit. That profit could be put to work elsewhere in a more efficient way.

Normally my only experience with airports in Japan is arriving by then Northwest at Tokyo's Narita Airport. However, once I had the opportunity to fly domestically from Tokyo to a regional airport in northwest Japan. Again there was an abundance of people to help us board the plane and an abundance of people to greet us on arrival. Although the flight was a short one-well under 2 h, a meal was served in coach. Since my ticket was paid for by my hosts, I can only estimate that the flight cost about $300. A similar flight in the United States might be had for little more than $100 although of course with no meals and fewer people (and in many cases a fee for checked luggage). I assume that if JAL wanted to be more profitable (efficient) it would do better to cut the service and the meals and lower the ticket price to what a similar flight would cost in the United States. But I think it is fair to say that neither the hotel nor JAL would think of following any of this advice.

Although Japan is at one end of the extreme, there is general agreement that you get more service and attention on foreign airlines than on domestic airlines. My wife and I took an Air France coach class flight from Venice to Paris in the late evening-well after nine o'clock. And yes a fine French meal with wine was part of the deal. Wouldn't it be more efficient to do away with late meals and charge for the wine?

If you get a sandwich in London-even at the smallest and most undistinguished sandwich shops-it always comes with a little salad. Often there is no little salad as part of the sandwich order in the United States-unless of course you pay for it. My experiences are not unique. Just ask any frequent traveler abroad. I know many people who will do anything to avoid flying on an American carrier when they go abroad. There is general agreement that the service on American carriers is near the bottom of the major international carriers. But American carriers usually are cheaper.

Now let's shift our attention to the United States. Ever notice how all the transaction costs of an exchange are being shifted to the consumer. You can start with the airlines. You book on line, print your own ticket, and check your own bags. When then Northwest made the switch from people to machines, I think the figure I was quoted was that each machine saved the airline $47,000. The movement then went to grocery and retail stores. You either used the self-check outs or stand in long lines to deal with a live person. In grocery stores there is evidence that these self-check outs do not work very well. There is lots of room for honest error and dishonest theft. Nonetheless, my favorite check-out person at Giant-a large grocery store in Easton Maryland-told me that even with the theft and honest error, these self-check-outs were still cheaper than real people serving as check out clerks. Management will even accept theft in order to save money.

What most of these examples illustrate is classical economics in action. Always substitute a cheaper factor of production for a more expensive one. In fact the economically literate are told to continue to substitute a cheaper factor of production for a more expensive one until the marginal productivity of each is equal. Technological improvements in machinery have enabled the retail trade and a big chunk of the service industry to substitute these devices for labor and get the consumer to absorb the transaction costs in the bargain. I am sure we all have examples where people have been cut to increase profits. The result has been a decrease in service and/or a shift so that what once was service to the customer becomes self-service. All this leads me to ask as a consumer, "What has all this efficiency stuff gotten me?"

Of course philosophers have weird thoughts and the direction I am heading would indicate to those trained in economics that I simply do not understand the free market. I will discuss the obvious objections to my analysis soon enough. However, in my reading and television watching, I discovered other people, including some pretty distinguished ones, asking the same question even if they did not frame it the same way that I did.

What Some Others Are Saying

I thought the assassination of John F Kennedy would be the worst thing that happened in my lifetime. Then came the terrorist attack of September 11, 2001. Many have pointed to this situation and said that if people had done their jobs or communicated better, the attack might have been avoided. One bit of second guessing that is relevant to this Chapter concerns a claim made by John Farmer in *The Ground Truth: The Untold Story of America Under Attack on 9/11*.[10] Farmer claimed that massive budget cuts to North American Aerospace Defense Commad (NORAD) reduced alert sites from about two dozen to seven. That limited their ability to respond to 9/11 attacks.

Suppose that Farmer is right about this and the reduced alert sites were one of the factors in the disastrous attack. My critics will point out that this example does not undercut efficiency. It simply shows that what people thought was efficient wasn't. Fair enough but my concession here allows me to make another point. The first problem with the worship of efficiency is that there is a natural tendency to focus on short term efficiency. Most economists I am familiar with do not discuss the timeline on efficiency. They tend to look at any given transaction and ask is this transaction the most efficient of current available alternatives? But I submit that that is the wrong question. At a minimum we need to contextualize efficiency and ask what is most efficient in this context. With national defense we need to ask at a minimum what is most efficient in the long run.

---

[10] Farmer, John. (2009). *The Ground Truth: The Untold Story of America Under Attack on 9/1*. New York: Riverhead Books.

This point was driven home to me by an interview on April 8, 2011 on the Bill Mahr show that Mahr had with Capt. Chesley B. "Sully" Sullenberger who landed his crippled US Airways jet on the Hudson River.[11] Captain Sullenberger referenced the fatal crash in Buffalo New York of commuter flight Colgan Air 3407 that killed all 50 aboard. The cause of the accident was attributed to pilot error. Sullenberger explained the circumstances around this "pilot error"-circumstances created by cost cutting (increased efficiency) by the airline industry in general and the commuter airline industry in particular. The pay for captains and first officers in the commuter airline industry is terrible. The first officer of the ill-fated flight was paid so little that she was forced to live with her parents. One her way to her Colgan Air assignment she could not afford to sleep in a hotel and instead slept in airport lounges for two nights before the crash. The Captain of the ill fated flight had never trained on the simulator for the condition he experienced. As for the airline industry as a whole, Sully pointed out that the "cost" of low airfares was low salary for pilots and the dissolving of pensions so that the best people were avoiding the industry. Sully admitted that there had been a back log of pilots who were trained before 9/11 but that the day was fast approaching when there would be a pilot shortage. In the mean-time Sully admitted that he could not recommend becoming a pilot to any young person out there. As a father of a son in the industry, I concur.

The defender of efficiency will again argue that long run efficiency was sacrificed for short term efficiency. But as before where is the discussion in the economics litera-ture about short vs. long run efficiency? The typical comment by economists is to quote John Maynard Keynes and say that in the long run we are all dead. But the point to notice here is that the emphasis on short-run efficiency is threatening an entire industry. And note that people in the airline industry are NOT treating this as a short term issue. They are arguing that absent government mandates, this is the future of the airline industry. But if that is so we are now approaching the point I want to make. An emphasis on efficiency as the airline industry and much of the public define it is not sustainable. Eventually the industry will not be able to find pilots to fly the aircraft.

In 2011 I finally got around to reading Tom Friedman's *The World is Flat*. Friedman recognizes that we occupy different roles with respect to the economy. As consumers, we like low prices always or the philosophy of Wal-Mart. But as employ-ees or citizens we do not. Why? Because Wal-Mart pays much lower wages and provides less in the way of benefits than their competitors-Costco for example. The unavailability of health care or its un-affordability for Wal-Mart workers means that a large number of Wal-Mart employees end up on Medicaid with the taxpayers pay-ing the bill. The tax-payer is subsidizing Wal-Mart's policy of "Low Prices Always" and of course contributing to Wal-Mart's profit. As Friedman puts it,

"Yes, the consumer in me wants Wal-Mart prices, with all the fat gone. But the employee in me wants a little fat left on the bone, the way Costco does it, so they can offer health care to almost all its employees, rather than just less than half of them."[12]

---

[11] Real Time With *Bill Maher*: April 8, 2011.

[12] Friedman, Thomas L. (2006). *The World is Flat, Updated and Expanded*. New York: Farrar, Straus and Giroux, 257.

Even some economists seem to think that efficiency (or more accurately put- growth through efficiency) can be overemphasized. A Stanford economist and another Nobel Prize in Economics winner[13] (2001) Michael Spence put it this way, "I think there's been an overemphasis on growth... Research establishes pretty clearly that typical notions of happiness-that more is better-really don't correspond to the way people think and feel."[14]

In the process of writing this article, I discovered someone who had the same frustrations as I did. Writing in the Sunday *New York Times* October 30, 2011, Craig Lambert asked, "Why are lawyers who make $300,000 a year scanning their own groceries?[15] His answer which differs from mine is that machines are taking over. The result he points out is that although we refer to the United States as a service economy, the service part is disappearing. We are getting less service and doing more ourselves-self-service. Lambert refers the work that we take on ourselves-work that used to be done by others- as "shadow work." This shadow work is driving up the unemployment rate. His long list of examples is similar to my own. Lambert cites pumping your own gas, self-service kiosks for check in at airports, and taking on the tasks that travel agents used to perform. Lambert also points out that you can no longer find people in department stores to help you find things and that secretaries and other support staff are a thing of the past. We have taken on this shadow work as part of our duties. All of this strikes me as on target. However, I believe that technological invention that allows shadow work is an enabler in the drive for efficiency. The real culprit in this story is the homage that is paid to efficiency.

The Issue or Issues

We are culturally attuned to treat efficiency as if it had intrinsic value. But efficiency is an instrumental value and a prima facie one at that. If I want to save on energy costs, I should be more efficient in my use of electricity. Efficiency in using electricity enables me to achieve my goal of saving on energy costs. But suppose I value personal contact when I engage in a market transaction. In a case like that I may be willing to incur more cost for the service just because I prefer dealing with a person rather than with a machine.

Some of the friction and inefficiencies are the result of culture. As Thomas Friedman says, "Some of these inefficiencies are institutions, habits, cultures, and traditions that people cherish precisely because they reflect non market values like social cohesion, religious faith, and national pride."[16]

---

[13] Although Spence was not honored for work related to the topic under discussion here. He shared the award with others for work on the economics of asymmetric information.

[14] *Newsweek* June 18, 20, 2011.

[15] Lambert, Craig. (2011). "Our Unpaid, Extra Shadow Work," *The New York Times,* October 30, "Sunday Review", 12.

[16] Friedman, op.cit., 237.

This quotation reflects my sentiments as well. For me I like personal contact in most of my transactions. When I make a call, I want to be connected to a live person and I resent the disembodied voice that first wants to know if I want to "converse" in English and then takes up valuable time giving me a menu of options only one of which-if that many-is the one I want. So one important issue is this: sometimes consumers want to choose inefficiency because they value something else more.

What I really want to do is speak to a live person. I realize that this preference may simply be a function of age. After all teenagers enjoy texting , rather than inter-acting in person. Perhaps we do not need personal interaction, but if we do, that is one job that cannot be outsourced as Thomas Friedman pointed out.[17]

It may seem as if my attitude on the value of personal interaction would have much in common with those who oppose commodification. To some extent that is right. But not exactly. In dealing with people in economic transactions who are paid for serving me, the transaction is an economic one. It is just that I want the transaction mediated by a person rather than a non person. I would argue that the value of personal interac-tion requires me to give up some of the product or service because it is more costly to have personal interaction. That is somewhat different than saying that personal inter-action should never be a commodity. So my first issue with efficiency is that I am willing to give up some economic gain in order to incur a transaction cost that I value. For me the prominent example is that I am willing to incur an additional transaction cost in order to be served by a person. In that respect I am like those citizens in some places who would rather have the higher expenses associated with small town busi-nesses than a new shopping mall anchored by Wal-Mart outside of town.

However, my main concern with the focus on efficiency is that it is ultimately self-defeating. Many of the examples I have mentioned involve the substitution of machinery for people or the imposition of transaction costs on customers. So self-checkouts replace grocery store clerks decreasing employment. So does the elimination of meals on air-crafts and longer lines at hotels etc. As we continue to find ways to eliminate people, there will be fewer and fewer people to buy the goods and services produced which in turn will lead to the further elimination of jobs (people). Simply put the focus on efficiency is reducing employment. The United States is no longer creating enough jobs and what is true in the United States is true in many other parts of the world as well.

I am not the only person concerned with this issue. My concerns here are an example of what is often called "The Paradox of Thrift." John Maynard Keynes provided the rationale for the paradox as follows: "Every such attempt to save money by reducing consumption will so affect incomes that the attempt necessarily defeats itself." [18] The paradox only exists when certain conditions in the economy obtain, so no one should think that Keynes is arguing that we should always be consuming. Indeed in periods of high inflation, people should consume less. I also realize that the concept has come under scrutiny and is widely criticized by right wing economists. However, I find their objections to the concept so long as the concept

---

[17] Ibid., 306.

[18] Keynes, John Maynard. (1936). *The General Theory of Employment, Interest, and Money*. New York: Harcourt, Brace and World Inc., 84.

is properly limited to be unconvincing. When cutting costs is applied to wages even when there is no business reason to do so, then something like the paradox takes shape. In 2010 Motts an apple juice producer and a subsidiary of the Dr Pepper Snapple Group tried to cut wages at a unionized apple juice plant in Western New York. Both Motts and the parent company were highly profitable so there was no business reason to cut wages except for the fact that the high unemployment rate in that part of the country meant that Motts and Dr Pepper Snapple could get away with it. Writing in *Newsweek,* Daniel Gross put it this way.

> Lowballing is most dangerous when it comes to wages. … If you lowball your own workers, they'll spend less, or shift to cheaper goods, or start lowballing their service providers. In 1914 Henry Ford instituted the $5 a day for employees at his booming auto plants. … because he believed it was good for his business. Ford reasoned that paying his assembly line workers more would allow them to buy cars.[19]

I think Ford had a point. In times like this, the search for efficiency can be a drag on employment.

My last concern with efficiency has to do with the distribution effects of the gains from efficiency. When a hotel cuts the number of check-in persons or when an airline substitutes self check in machines for people, who gains from the savings? In theory the gains could go to any of the stakeholders, cheaper products for the consumers, increased dividends for stockholders, increased salaries for executives, or even theoretically increased salaries for the remaining workers. One needs to study the particulars of each industry to make that determination. Certainly the flying public has benefited from lower prices in the airline industry. However, the gains in many instances have gone to the executives whose compensation has risen markedly vis-à-vis all the other stakeholders, especially the employees. Put another way the gains from increased efficiency are going disproportionately to the most wealthy. The benefits of efficiency have contributed to the rising inequality in the United States. Less efficiency would lead to a smaller Gross Domestic Product but less efficiency might lead to less inequality as well.

What's to Be Done

One thing to be done is for those who think as I do is to act as we talk. We should patronize those businesses that provide personal services even if it costs more to do so. Given a critical mass, the market, in some cases at least, will respond. There is at least one bank that advertises that you will always speak to a live person. Southwest Airlines has done a number of customer friendly things-among a number of smart business things it has done- that other airlines do not do and has gained market share as a result. But Southwest still has lots of those self-check ins and they encourage interaction on line rather than be phone. There is a limit as to how far markets will or even can accommodate people who want personal contact.

---

[19] Gross, Daniel. (2010). "Rock-Bottom Prices," *Newsweek*, September 20, 40, 47.

Another thing that can be done is to legally require certain kinds of personal service. If you travel in New Jersey you cannot pump your own gas. Self-service gasoline stations are illegal in New Jersey. New Jersey has made a public policy decision to opt for less efficiency and more jobs- at least at gasoline stations. How often and in what circumstances government entities should behave in this fashion is a matter for discussion. At this point in time the gasoline attendant requirement in New Jersey is an anomaly. But is there something here that should be emulated?

And if coercion sounds draconian, how about tax breaks or other incentives to encourage businesses in the service industry to hire employees? The Obama administration had recommended tax breaks for employers who hire additional people. In a deflationary world where technology and outsourcing increase unemployment, encouraging job growth especially in the service industries might be just what is needed.

Objections and Replies

I am sure that many reading up to this point will think that I simply do not understand elementary economics. Those with training in economics will make the following arguments: After all, mandating job creation in one place will raise costs and therefore there will be more jobs lost than the mandate creates. If individuals pay more for personal service, they simply have a different utility function than most people, but they do economize. If there is not a critical mass for a product or service so that the market will not provide it, so be it. Besides that does not happen very often.

Let's discuss my idiosyncratic desire to have personal contact wherever possible in economic transactions. When I deliberately incur a higher cost in order to satisfy my desire for personal contact, traditional economists argue that I really am being efficient for me Given my desires, incurring the cost of personal contact is efficient for me; since many people do not have that desire what is efficient for them is different. We just have different utility functions, but we both maximize (behave efficiently) along those utility functions. That makes everyone a utility maximizer in his or her own way-something that was assumed for a long time in classical economics.

But we know that people are not utility maximizers because they behave irrationality. I, however, want to make a different point and it is a moral point. We ought to want personal contact in our transactions because (1) dumping all the transaction costs on the consumer is not fair and (2) we ought to take into consideration whether our actions in the market place are job sustaining or job killing. Choosing to go to the self-serve checkout in the grocery store when one could use a human clerk is choosing the job killing option and is morally suspect. I know this is a strong claim, but it is no stronger than Peter Singer and others who claim that we ought to consider how animals were raised before we sit down to eat meat. Singer wanted to make the routine eating of meat into a moral issue. I want to make the routine choosing of self-service when one has another option into a moral issue.

Now let us look at attempts to maintain employment as New Jersey does with the gasoline pumping attendants. I know the objection. First jobs always disappear in a dynamic capitalist system. Look at all the jobs that have been created in the high tech industries, industries whose products did not exist 20 or 30 years ago. I concede all that. I have one simple question: Is our economic system creating enough full time jobs to employ those that want them? The answer to that question seems to be, "No." And all the economic forecasts I hear is that unemployment in the United States will exceed the so-called desirable 5 or 6 % for many more years. I do understand that at the micro level, technological advance makes some jobs obsolete and that with the technological advance new jobs are created. However, at the macro level we are not creating enough jobs and that is not only true of the United States but true of many other countries as well. By the way in the great depression we created jobs as a matter of public policy. That is what the Works Progress Administration (WPA) was for and a lot of useful work got done.

The next objection is that if we force a company or industry like New Jersey filling stations to hire people they do not need, we are not allocating labor in the most efficient way. We may increase employment in the filling stations but that increase will be more than be offset by a decrease in employment elsewhere. By the way this is similar to the argument against the minimum wage. An increase in the minimum wage will help a few people but decrease aggregate employment. Only problem with this argument is that it is at best controversial. Adding a small amount to a product's cost because of a slight increase in labor is unlikely to affect demand for that product. If you want to get technical whether an increase in cost will affect demand depends in part on the elasticity of demand. Elasticity of demand is a measure of how sensitive a product or service is to an increase in price. Most products produced by minimum wage workers have low elasticity of demand and therefore there is little response in demand to a small increase in price. Small gradual increases in the minimum wage will not put McDonald's out of business. Requiring human beings to pump gas will not raise the unemployment rate in New Jersey.

As we consider knocking efficiency off its pedestal, we need to look at the distribution effects of less efficiency. By being less efficient, we are making some worse off. So let us look at where the major job losses are. Most of the losses that have been discussed in this paper are in predominantly low skilled jobs or medium skilled jobs that have been or can be replaced by less costly machines. Think of the clerks at Wal-Mart. Suppose there were a law that required that for every self-check out there must be two clerks. In other words the number of clerks in any Wal-Mart would out number the self-check out machines 2–1. That would increase Wal-Mart's expenses. Either they would have to increase prices or reduce profits. To the extent that they reduce profits, the investing class would take the hit. And what is wrong with that? If Wal-Mart increases prices then customers will pay more. However, the price increases to customers will be very small, while the payoff to those who were underemployed or who are not employed will be huge. It is a public policy trade-off that I am willing to make. In general given the large amount of inequality in the United States I am willing to penalize the most wealthy to assist the least wealthy or I am willing to penalize the wealthy in order to bring the unemployment rate down. Willingness to trade efficiency for equity is hardly a new idea. See for example

Arthur Okun's *Equality and Efficiency: The Big Tradeoff*.[20] Economists have recognized that trading efficiency for equality is a public policy decision and that from a public policy perspective a gain in equality at the expense of efficiency is sometimes worth it on political or moral grounds. I would argue that at this point in American history, some tradeoff in favor of more equality certainly is worth it.

If unemployment keeps rising and if the middle class continues to shrink, what is the impact on the rich? There has to be people to buy the goods and services that our corporations provide. Note that the poor and middle class spend almost all their incomes. They do not or cannot save much. Thus an extra dollar for the poor or middle class helps keeps the economic engine running. We do not lack the funds for increased investment. There are trillions of dollars on the sidelines waiting to be invested. Bank deposits have grown so large that some banks are charging some customers some of the cost of Federal Deposit Insurance. Not only are interest rates impossibly low, but now banks are thinking of, and some are, charging you for the privilege of saving. This is unprecedented.

Also high unemployment and large and growing inequality threaten social stability. Occupy Wall Street may just be the first act if things do not improve. A second act is likely to be more unsettling and violent than the first act. We can look abroad to the Mid-East and Europe if you want to see what happens when a society cannot provide enough jobs for the young, for example, Egypt, or where public policy slashes salaries and benefits while the costs of goods and services goes up and unemployment increases as a result, as for example in Greece.

And if you find the coercive policy I am considering too radical, consider tax incentives and other options. Richard Thaler and Cass Sunstein have written an important book, *Nudge: Improving Decisions About Health, Wealth, and Happiness*,[21] which encourages policy makers to present options in the way that would most likely lead consumers to make the right choices from a policy perspective. As they point out, the arrangement of food in a cafeteria influences what children will choose to eat and whether you are asked to opt-in or opt-out of a pay deduction in order to save for retirement influences whether and how much individuals will put away for their retirement. To the extent that policy makers can structure choices so that people will choose the options that result in greater employment, we should do so. Influenced choice is always better than coerced choice.

Conclusion

In this essay I am urging that we think outside the box. We live in a land of abundance rather than scarcity. We have lots of goods and services for sale and we could easily produce more. If the demand were present there is plenty of money on the

---

[20] Okun, Arthur M. (1975). *Equality and Efficiency: The Big Tradeoff*. Washington, DC: The Brookings Institution.

[21] Thaler, Richard H. and Cass R. Sunstein. (2008). *Nudge: Improving Decisions About Health, Wealth, and Happiness*. New Haven: Yale University Press.

sidelines ready to invest. However, our economy has focused on efficiency through cost cutting and the elimination of labor. Eliminating labor has allowed some industries to increase the workload of customers. There is the cost of the product and the transaction cost of checking out and bagging your own purchases. We need to reduce unemployment and inequality. As individuals and as a society we need to think of cost, not only in terms of the price of the product or service purchased, but also the cost of transferring transaction costs to the customer and the cost of greater inequality to social stability and economic growth. Let's take a break from "Low Prices, Always."

Chapter 3
Economics, Friend or Foe of Ethics

Economics as Foe

Business ethics has not had an easy time of it. Its position in the business school is precarious at best-even at institutions with business ethics faculty who are considered leaders in the field. The conventional wisdom is that the chief opposition to business ethics is found in the finance departments-that finance faculty are the most hostile to business ethics. Of course there are some exceptions to this generalization but the claim is substantially correct. Finance departments are dominated by economists, whereas many management departments have a good mix of psychologists and other social scientists among the economists.

There are many reasons why traditional equilibrium economists would be opposed to ethics. These economists argue that given certain assumptions, a free market capitalist system is Pareto-optimal. That is, no one can be made better off, without some being made worse off. Allegedly that is the only value judgment that these economists make. A Pareto optimal society has maximized utility.

However, the claim that for the most part traditional economics is value free is simply false. Let's begin by looking at the assumptions. For a capitalist economy to be in Pareto equilibrium, there must be no transaction costs, there must be perfect information, economic actors must be perfectly rational, labor must be completely mobile, there must be no monopolies, and each economic actor is a utility maximizer.

The Chapter was originally given as a talk at the Fourth Annual Politeia Forum on Business Ethics and Corporate Social Responsibility in a Global Economy, Milan Italy September 13, 2007. That talk was then published in "*notizie di politeia*", XXIV, 89, (2008), pp 13–26. Reprinted by permission of Emilio D'Orazio, editor.

N.E. Bowie, *Business Ethics in the 21st Century*, Issues in Business Ethics 39, DOI 10.1007/978-94-007-6223-7_3, © Springer Science+Business Media Dordrecht 2013

Foe: Adherence to Psychological Egoism

Note that the doctrine that everyone is a utility maximizer is usually stated in a way that makes it equivalent to psychological egoism. Psychological egoism is the doctrine that everyone is motivated to look after his or her own perceived best interest. There are a number of well-known difficulties with psychological egoism. First, it appears to be false. There seem to be many counterexamples- cases where people act for the benefit of others. Second, an attempt to include concern with others as yet another example of one's own perceived best interest makes the theory vacuous. It then becomes equivalent to saying that whatever one does, one does what is one's perceived best interest. But what most of us want to know about others is will they keep their promises for example, even when it is not in their perceived best interest as conventionally understood. To be told that they will if it is in their perceived best interest does not tell us much. We want to know who will keep a promise because it is a promise. Third, if psychological egoism is true, ethics is pointless. Because taking the moral point of view requires that one do the right thing even when it is not in one's perceived best interest as conventionally understood. If psychological egoism were true taking the moral point of view would be impossible. Thus a commitment to classical equilibrium economics with all the surrounding assumptions makes economics a foe of ethics. Economics obliterates ethics.[1] However, this is a very old story and the world of economics has moved significantly beyond classical equilibrium theory.

Foe: Assumptions of Agency Theory

Although the criticisms of the utility maximization assumption are hardly new, there has not been a significant change in the assumption in the management field. We can begin with agency theory. Agency theorists act as if all people are psychological egoists. They assume that agents will act on their own behalf rather than on behalf of their principals for whom they are agents. A central issue for agency theorists is how to monitor or create incentives so that the agent acts, not on his or her own behalf, but rather on behalf of the principal's. With respect to corporate managers including the CEO, the issue was aligning the incentives of the organization so that managers would work for the benefit of the shareholders, rather than be self-serving. Business history presents many cases where CEO's have promoted their own interests at the expense of the shareholders. This seemed especially prevalent at the beginning of the twenty-first century.

There has been a tendency for agency theorists and others who work with incentive systems to ignore the dark side- the possibility that those responding to incentive

---

[1] For a full account of this argument see my "Challenging the Egoistic Paradigm" (1991) in the first issue of *Business Ethics Quarterly* 1, 1–21.

systems will always behave in an ethical manner. That assumption seems unrealistic and agency theorists should be the first rather than the last to consider this. Ethicists, including this one, have often criticized agency theorists for adopting a cynical view of human nature, -for acting as if all people were psychological egoists. After all agency theory assumes that human beings are self-serving, that each will pursue his or her own interest at the expense of the principal's. One might argue that self-regarding behavior at the expense of a principal on the part of an agent is itself unethical. All that remains is the next step where violation of the agency relationship turns into something more serious from the moral point of view. In other words agency theorists have not been cynical enough. They recognized that employees could be self-serving, but they usually have not gone the next step and assumed that when the incentives were wrong agents could act in ways that are illegal or violate the basic norms of morality.

There is empirical support for the view that agents do cross the line from permitted self-serving behavior to self-serving behavior that is illegal or unethical. One of the devices for aligning the objectives of top level managers with the stockholders that became increasing popular was the use of stock options. However, in path-breaking research Jared Harris and Philip Bromiley in "Incentives to Cheat: The Influence of Executive Compensation and Firm Performance on Financial Misrepresentation,"[2] wanted to see what effect certain compensation schemes, especially the granting of stock options, had on the likelihood that a firm would have an accounting restatement as a result of misrepresentation. They also wanted to see what effect poor performance—either as compared to peers in the industry or as compared to past benchmarks of the firm itself—had on similar accounting restatements. In other words, to what extent do these factors serve as pressures to cheat? Using a matched sample data set they found similar companies where one had experienced an accounting restatement due to an accounting irregularity and one that had not. The U.S. General Accounting Office provided the data on the accounting irregularities. What might explain the difference between two similar companies? They showed conclusively that the granting of a large amount of stock options significantly increased the likelihood of accounting misrepresentation, whereas the comparatively smaller bonuses did not have that effect. In addition, they demonstrated that poor performance relative to other firms in the industry also increased the likelihood of accounting misrepresentation.

What lesson can we take away from this? Economists and their allies in agency theory have not thought through the full implications of their position. I suspect this failure results from the fact that they do not take ethics seriously in their theoretical discussions. However, like average people, they assume in their daily life that most people will not engage in self-serving behavior that is illegal or blatantly unethical? But surely this assumption is as naïve as the assumption that people are always

---

[2] Harris, Jared D., and Philip Bromiley. (2007). "Incentives to Cheat: The Influence of Executive Compensation and Firm Performance on Financial Misrepresentation," *Organization Science*, 18(3), 350–367.

self-serving. In any human transaction or relationship, we need to distinguish between two questions:

1. Will the person I am dealing with, sometimes put my interests over his interests?
2. Will a person who always behaves in a way that is self-serving, do so when such behavior is blatantly unethical or illegal?

Traditional agency theorists have assumed that the answer to the first question is yes and the answer to the second question is no. But that is too simplistic. Human behavior is more complicated than that. The first step in deciding whether economics is a friend or foe of ethics is to recognize that scholars in both economics and ethics must deal with the utility assumption or maximization assumption in a more sophisticated way. Rethinking this assumption is not as revolutionary as one might think. The other assumptions surrounding equilibrium analysis have already been modified and economic theory is more robust as a result.

Dropping the "No Transaction Costs" Assumption: Transaction Cost Economics

One significant change is the dropping of the assumptions of equilibrium analysis. With the rise of behavioral economics, people began to introduce the insights of psychology into economic theorizing. One of the first assumptions to fall was the assumption that people are perfectly rational in their choices. The behavioral economists showed that people were in fact not rational in their choices. Perfect rationality was replaced by bounded rationality. People have limited knowledge and limited cognitive abilities that bound their ability to act rationally. As the behaviorists have gained influence the extent to which our rationality is bounded continues to enlarge. People make elementary mistakes in reasoning that can be easily understood when pointed out but yet remain stubbornly difficult to correct.

Other economists have dropped the assumption that there are no transaction costs and have developed a new subset of economics called transaction cost economics.[3] From the transaction cost perspective, the first and perhaps most important attribute for assessing a transaction and identifying the appropriate governance structure is the degree to which individuals involved in the transaction must invest dedicated assets. Dedicated assets are transaction specific and have high asset specificity. Suppose a large retailer seeks a supplier to provide a product with specifications that are unique to that retailer. To provide the product, the supplier must invest in the resources that will enable it to meet the unique specifications of the retailer. Those resources would

---

[3] The classic statements of transaction cost economics can be found in Williamson, Oliver E. (1975). *Markets and Hierarchies*. New York: The Free Press, and Williamson, Oliver E. (1985). *The Economic Institutions of Capitalism*. New York: The Free Press.

be dedicated assets and have high asset specificity. On the other hand, suppose a supplier provides products for a number of retailers all of whom have the same specifications. In these circumstances, the resources of the supplier can be used for any of the retailers; the resources are not specific to one retailer. In such cases we say that the resources have low asset specificity; they are not dedicated to one retailer.

The existence of assets that are highly specific can create moral problems. In the literature, transaction cost economists, showed how suppliers with resources that were characterized by high asset specificity could be subject to what is called "the hold-up" problem. The supplier invests in the resources to make the specific product only to face demands by the retailer to lower the prices. Since the supplier's resources are dedicated to that retailer, he has little choice but to lower the price. It is alleged that many of Wal-Mart's suppliers were subject to the hold-up problem.

A significant problem with transaction cost economics from the ethical point of view is that transaction costs economists have not given up the utility maximizing assumption. The founder of transaction costs economics, Oliver Williamson, is explicit in keeping this assumption and has even referred to the behavior of economic actors as "profit seeking with guile."[4] Later I will argue that if Williamson dropped this assumption, ethicists could use some of the insights of transaction cost economics to shed light on some problems in business ethics.

Turning Economics from Foe to Friend

Despite the fact that transaction cost economics has maintained a strong variation of the utility maximization assumption, some of the concepts of transaction cost economics can be helpful to ethicists as they seek to explain ethical behavior or lack thereof in the real world. Four examples will be discussed in some detail. First I will show how the distinction between high and low asset specificity can explain why codes of ethics by themselves are useless as a sign of ethical behavior, why an ethical climate is difficult to copy, and why multinational corporations will insist on universal standards throughout their organizations world wide-at least with respect to their core values. Finally I will show how the explanatory power of economics and the management theory based on it can be increased by introducing fairness as a constraint of the utility maximization assumption.

Codes of Ethics

When people in the public arena speak of organizational ethics, one of the first questions is, "Does the organization have a code of ethics?" In the scholarly business ethics literature, there is a large literature on codes of ethics. People think that codes

---

[4] Actually Williamson's view on opportunism is more nuanced. See *The Economic Institutions of Capitalism* Appendix to Chapter 2.

of ethics are important for maintaining organizational ethics. I disagree. Codes of ethics are not a good indicator of an organization's commitment to ethics. In addition, a code of ethics is only useful if the other factors that contribute to organizational ethics are present. To see why this is so, we need to return to our discussion of transaction cost economics and specifically consider the distinction between high and low asset specificity.

I want to use the insights of transaction cost economics and the distinction between high and low asset specificity to establish my claim that codes of ethics have a rather minor role to play in organizational moral integrity. Codes of ethics have low asset specificity. They are easily copied. Enron had one of the best codes of ethics, yet the ethical climate at Enron was terrible even before the collapse. Thus a good code of ethics is not a good indicator as to whether an organization has high ethical standards or low ethical standards. For this reason, I do not consider codes of ethics to be an important factor in organizational ethics.

The Importance of a Good "Ethical Climate"[5]

Unlike codes of ethics that have low asset specificity, I believe organizations with an ethical climate have an asset with high asset specificity and that such organizations thereby have a tremendous competitive advantage. An ethical climate involves ethical commitments that have the following characteristics: they are values based and the values are embodied in the character of the organizational members and in the organization's routines and incentive structures. Experience teaches us that ethical climates are difficult to copy.

What is the evidence of that? Both the scholarly literature and the business experience speak to the fact that it is very difficult to change a corporate culture and an ethical climate, where it exists, is part of the corporate culture. One good example here is the contrast between Ashland Oil Company and Exxon-Mobil. When Ashland Oil was involved in an oil spill at its facility in Floreffe, Pennsylvania in 1988, the CEO John Hall and other corporate officers quickly went to the site of the spill, admitted fault and directed the clean-up. This action was wise from both an ethical and a business perspective. Ashland oil had its fines reduced and suffered less litigation as a result of their behavior. They also gained respect as an ethically responsible company. Within 2 years Exxon, as it was known then, had the Exxon Valdez oil spill. Exxon had learned nothing from the Ashland Oil incident and thus was subjected to much litigation and a serious blow to its reputation. Corporate culture and specifically an ethical climate have high asset specificity and are not easily copied. Thus it should not come as a surprise that Exxon really did not learn anything from the Ashland Oil spill. Organizational learning or organizational sense making is intimately tied to and to a large extent constrained by its culture. Exxon Oil had a

---

[5] The classic work on moral or ethical climate is Victor, Bart and John B Cullen. (1988). "The Organizational Bases of Ethical Work Climates," *Administrative Science Quarterly*, 33, 101–125.

very different culture from Ashland Oil and Exxon's sensitivity to ethical issues (its ethical culture if you will) was different from Ashland Oil's You can observe the same phenomenon with respect to climate change. Both BP and Shell recognized that climate change was taking place and both were proactive in devising strategies, including a public relations strategy, for dealing with it. Exxon Mobil only recently has recognized the importance of climate change and its strategy, unlike BP's and Shell's, is limited to technological fixes. BP wants to be an energy company; its slogan Beyond Petroleum speaks to that. Exxon Mobil sees itself as an oil company.[6]

Thus to achieve organizational integrity, an ethical climate is key and a code of ethics is only useful and effective as part of an ethical climate. One can see this when considering one of the more "famous" ethical codes-Johnson and Johnson's Credo. The Credo is evaluated periodically to see if it still reflects the values and vision of the company and if it is still useful as a tool for helping resolve ethical issues or dilemmas the company might face. Thus there is a symbiotic relationship between the ethical climate at Johnson and Johnson and the Johnson and Johnson credo.

Multinationals and Universal Standards

While teaching Executive MBA's in Minnesota as well as teaching Polish executive MBA's at the Warsaw School of Economics, I discovered that multinational corporations sought to instill their core values across all their subsidiaries. Thus, for example, the 3M Corporation had a universal policy against bribery. 3M employees were not allowed to pay bribes anywhere-even in countries where bribery was commonplace. I was tempted to believe that this statement of commitment to policy might be just ethical window dressing. As we know from the argument above, a code of ethics divorced from an ethical culture may not mean much. However, my Polish students who worked for multinationals-US, German, and French, complained that these companies insisted on doing things the way they were done in their home countries. These Polish students could not understand why these multinationals did not attempt to adapt more to their host countries. In other words, why don't multinationals adopt more of a "When in Rome do as the Romans do" policy?

I want to limit the discussion here to the core ethical values of a multi-national corporation (MNC). One reason that a MNC might give for making their core ethical values universal across all their operations is because it is the right thing to do. But I think there is another argument for doing that. This argument is limited to those MNC's that believe that their core ethical values are an essential part of their brand. In other words, being a socially responsible corporation is part of the Johnson and Johnson brand. Johnson and Johnson believes that its reputation as a

---

[6]Needless to say this paragraph was written before BP's Deepwater Horizon explosion and oil spill in the Gulf of Mexico in 2010. We now realize that much of BP's Beyond Petroleum campaign was not backed up with action.

socially responsible corporation gives it a competitive advantage. Companies like Johnson and Johnson could give the following argument for applying their core ethical values universally.

The Argument for Universal Ethical Values[7]

1. Certain ethical values are believed by the management of a MNC to provide the MNC with a competitive advantage.
2. Those ethical values which provide a durable competitive advantage abroad will tend to be knowledge based, be embodied in individual employees or firm routines and be characterized by high asset specificity.
3. Highly specific assets associated with high return should not be diluted.
4. If ethical values are such assets they should not be diluted.
5. If ethical values vary among subsidiaries, these assets will be diluted due to the phenomenon of cognitive dissonance.
6. Therefore a MNC should have common ethical values in all its subsidiaries.

Let's examine the argument in detail. The first premise limits the argument to those corporations that believe that their ethical values give them a competitive advantage. Premise two describes the nature of ethical values or perhaps more accurately of an ethical culture in the multinational corporation (MNC) that embodies those ethical values. Using the terminology of transaction cost economics, premise 2 asserts that the nature of an ethical climate is such that it has high asset specificity and thus cannot be easily copied. Given premises 1 and 2, we have MNC's that believe that their ethical values are a competitive advantage and if the transaction cost economics story is right, these MNC's have a competitive advantage that is hard to copy. For one doing corporate strategy, this is an ideal situation. A MNC like Johnson and Johnson has an asset that gives it a competitive advantage and it is an asset that it is very difficult for its competitors to copy. Given that, it is easy to see why premise 3 is true. A MNC that has an asset that gives it a competitive advantage and cannot be copied has an asset that it does not want to dilute. Premise 4 simply identifies the asset in this argument as ethical values.

Suppose a MNC considers adopting the "when in Rome do as the Romans do" philosophy with respect to ethical values. In other words if bribery is widely practiced in a country where it does business, the company policy would be that it is ok to bribe in those countries. However, employees could not bribe in countries where bribery was forbidden and not practiced. Since employees on track to be senior executives of a MNC do multiple postings abroad, in such an environment they would suffer from the psychological phenomenon of cognitive dissonance. Cognitive dissonance is a state of discomfort or tension that results when people hold or are asked

---

[7] This argument was developed in 1999, "Some Arguments for Universal Standards," with Paul Vaaler in *International Business Ethics: Challenges and Approaches*, ed., Georges Enderle, University of Notre Dame Press, 160–173.

to hold incompatible beliefs. In our example of the MNC that adopts the "when in Rome do as the Romans do" strategy with respect to bribery, up and coming managers are told that company policy with respect to bribery is that it is ok to bribe and it is not ok to bribe according to the circumstances. Strictly speaking there is no logical contradiction here since whether the employee should bribe or not bribe depends on the circumstances. However, as a matter of psychology there is a tension, because if people think that bribery is wrong (or right), they would tend to think that it is right or wrong universally. Most people cannot contextualize their core ethical values.

Adding the knowledge regarding cognitive dissonance to the knowledge about the nature of the competitive advantage of ethical values, gives us the conclusion that a MNC of that type should impose its ethical values universally in all its subsidiaries. The first piece of good news here is that transaction cost economics gives us an argument why a MNC like Johnson and Johnson should not bribe.

But there is a second piece of good news. Suppose that premise 1 of the argument is true in fact. By that I mean it is not only the case that certain multinationals believe that their core ethical values give them a competitive advantage, but it is also true that their core ethical values give them a competitive advantage. In other words, the beliefs of those MNC's are true beliefs. We could then rewrite premise 1 as follows:

1. Certain ethical values of a MNC provide the MNC with a competitive advantage.

What should the response be of a MNC that adopts the "when in Rome do as the Romans do strategy"? Such a MNC could hold to the strategy. However, other things being equal, economists would say that such stubbornness would have to end in failure. If the MNC's that do not have the "when in Rome do as the Romans do" strategy, really do have a competitive advantage, then eventually those companies will win out in the competitive struggle. A company that has a "When in Rome do as the Romans do" strategy will eventually, other things being equal, go bankrupt. In that case, the wise strategy is to try to develop an ethical culture with ethical values that are adopted universally. In other words the appropriate strategy is to make a universal commitment to certain ethical values a part of the MNC's brand. This strategy is rational even though it is hard to achieve. It is hard to achieve because an ethical culture with universal ethical values is hard to copy. Nonetheless, the company strategy should be to try. And this is good news for the raising of international standards of business ethics. Here is the formal argument for that claim.

An Argument for Truly Universal Standards of Business Ethics

1. Certain ethical values are either necessary for the MNC's economic success or provide it with a competitive advantage.
2. Thus, other things being equal, MNC's will be driven by market forces to adopt those ethical values which are necessary for economic success or provide competitive advantage.

3. Thus other things being equal, market forces will favor the development of at least a common core of ethical standards. Thus all MNC's will ultimately tend to adopt nearly identical standards whatever their beliefs of the competitive advantage of ethical commitments.

Up to this point I have not specified what ethical values are necessary to give a MNC a good reputation and provide it with a competitive advantage. I suggest two, a commitment not to bribe, and a commitment not to discriminate on racial or sexual grounds. I will state this in the form of hypotheses.

H1: If MNC's that do not bribe have a competitive advantage, then there will be a tendency for all MNC's to accept norms against bribery.
H2: If MNC's that do not discriminate on the basis of sex or race have a competition advantage, then there will be a tendency for all MNC's to accept norms against discrimination.

Thus the additional good news here is that there is reason to believe that bribery and discrimination based on sex and race will diminish in international business practice. And the good news gets better still. That seems to be happening. In other words, the two hypotheses are turning out to be true. Multinationals, with or without the cooperation of governments, are adopting industry-wide codes against bribery. And discrimination against woman seems to be on the decline throughout Asia. I have certainly seen a change in Japan over the 15 year span that I have visited that country.

There is much more to be done here. Further hypotheses regarding ethical values that will become universal in international business practice can be provided, argued for and perhaps even tested. My own two hypotheses should be subjected to rigorous testing as well. Thus there are great opportunities here for further research.

A Complication

Of course, it is still too early to tell if the trends toward less bribery and less discrimination on the basis of sex will continue. In addition there are some disturbing countertrends as well. You will notice that I have not said much about discrimination on the basis of religion. Religious belief, especially the alleged beliefs of many subscribers to the Muslim faith, raises problems for this analysis. There is widespread sex discrimination in many Muslim countries, especially those in the Middle East. The argument about the competitive superiority of a no sex discrimination policy does not seem to work in a country like Saudi Arabia. Will countries like Saudi Arabia be forced to change as a result of competitive market pressures? I am less than hopeful here. The reason the argument does not work well in a country like Saudi Arabia is because its chief product-oil- is not a part of a competitive market but is under the control of a cartel. In addition the demand for oil is very strong. There are simply no competitive pressures from the market that would lead countries like Saudi Arabia to change their norms regarding the treatment of women.

In addition there seems to be an increasing tendency for Muslims to see themselves in an ideological battle with the West. Any criticism of Muslim norms only makes many Muslims dig in their heals and become more conservative. The rise of Muslim conservative thinking is evident in Muslim cultures throughout the world. Herbert Simon is credited with the notion of bounded rationality.[8] Bounded rationality reflects the fact that human beings have limited cognitive abilities that constrain human problem-solving. In a world of bounded rationality, religious beliefs that conflict with good economic thinking trump economic arguments-especially among those who believe that the world will eventually convert to their beliefs one way or the other. The energy crisis and the rise of religious fundamentalism, especially Islamic fundamentalism, provide challenges to the hypothesis that non discrimination based on sex or religion will become a universal value.

However, even here there is reason for cautious optimism. Economics is cosmopolitan in ways similar to the cosmopolitan thinking of the Enlightenment. Immanuel Kant focused on what human beings had in common and built his ethical philosophy on respect for human beings as autonomous, rational, responsible persons.[9] All human beings shared these essential features that entitled them to respect as ends in themselves. Being members of a different tribe, or a different religion were unimportant from the moral point of view. It was the essential sameness of humans and not their differences that were important for Kant's ethics.

For the most part, economists also avoid making differences in tribe, religion, sex, etc. important. The important point for an economist is whether two human beings can enter into a mutually beneficial voluntary exchange. If a Muslim and a Jew can make such a transaction, it makes sense to do it. The fact that one party to the transaction is Muslim and one is a Jew is irrelevant to the beneficial nature of the transaction. Thus again we see that economics is a friend of ethics. Both economics and ethics reject the thinking that puts us against them or the thinking that focuses on our differences rather than our similarities.

I am well aware that this kind of thinking goes contrary to the postmodern thinking of many intellectuals. These intellectuals glorify otherness and condemn the Enlightenment for focusing on sameness rather than on difference. Some of these postmodern thinkers have much in common with pragmatists.[10] However, if we take a pragmatist perspective, it seems obvious to me that the focus on otherness-especially a focus that sharply contrasts us from them-is responsible for much of the evil in the contemporary world. Shiites slaughtering Sunnis and Sunnis slaughtering Shiites because each has a different slant on Islam is crazy. It is crazy from an economic perspective and it is crazy from a moral perspective as well.

---

[8] Discussions of bounded rationality can be found in Simon, Herbert. (1956). "Rational Choice and the Structure of the Environment," *Psychological Review,* 63, 129–138 and Simon, Herbert. (1955). "A Behavioral Model of Rational Choice," *Quarterly Journal of Economics,* 69, 99–118. His economic papers are in *Models of Bounded Rationality,* 3 vols. Cambridge, MA: MIT Press, 1982.

[9] For more on Kant's philosophy as it applies to business, see Chap. 4.

[10] For more on this topic, see Chap. 5.

Recognizing how much human beings are alike is the key to peace and prosperity-a fact recognized by many ethicists and by many economists.

Fairness as an Explanatory Variable in Economics and Management Theory

In the early part of this paper, I argued that one of the assumptions that made economics a foe of ethics was the assumption that everyone was a psychological egoist or that everyone always acted on his or her perceived best interest. That assumption makes ethics impossible because ethics requires that we sometimes act against our own perceived best interest. Suppose we relax that assumption and see what happens if people behave-at least sometimes-not on the basis of self-interest, but on the basis of a norm of fairness.

The possibility of using a norm of fairness owes much to the rise of behavioral economics. The notion that people behave rationally has been challenged by such economists Daniel Kahneman, Herbert Simon, and Richard Thaler. In 2002, Kahneman, along with the experimentalist, Vernon Smith received the Nobel Prize in economics. For these economists the rationality assumption of equilibrium analysis is thus relaxed. A less well known concept from behavioral economics is the notion of "bounded willpower." Bounded willpower reflects the fact that human beings make choices that are not in their self-interest. The assumption of equilibrium analysis that people are utility maximizers is thus relaxed. Once economists had a notion of bounded willpower, there was an opening for looking at the role of fairness in economics-an opening that has been brilliantly taken by the economist Robert Frank.[11] Actually experiments on an ultimatum bargaining game provided the laboratory basis for Frank's work.[12] Frank cites numerous economic phenomena that cannot be explained on what he calls the self-interest model. Among these phenomena are the facts that people tip in restaurants to which they will not return, that restaurants and barber shops do not charge more for meals or haircuts on weekends, that people who will consume a beer on the beach will pay more for the beer at a hotel than at a grocery, and that compensation is not simply a function of productivity but also of status. By that Frank means that low ranked workers receive more than productivity would justify and high ranked workers receive less. This phenomenon is explained, Frank argues, by fairness. Fairness explains the fact that low ranked workers are paid more to offset their lower status. Frank also points out that pay is higher in more profitable firms than less profitable ones. In an openly competitive market that should not be the case. But again fairness requires that firms with higher profits share some of those profits with the employees in the form of pay.[13]

---

[11] Frank, Robert H. (1988). *Passions Within Reason*. New York: W.W. Norton & Co.

[12] Guth, Werner, Rolf Schmittberger, and Bernd Schwarze. (1982). "An Experimental Analysis of the Ultimatum Bargaining Game," *Journal of Economic Behavior and Organization, 3*, 367–388.

[13] A fuller account of these examples can be found in Frank, op.cit., Chapter 9.

Frank even introduces a definition of fairness in economics transactions, based in part on the experimental evidence. He says, "A fair transaction is one in which the surplus is divided (approximately) equally. The transaction becomes increasingly unfair as the division increasingly deviates from equality."[14]

These insights are helpful to those working in business ethics. Many professors in the business school wonder what ethics has to add to management training. Consider a Coca-Cola case concerning a newly invented Coke soft drink dispenser that can adjust the price of a Coke to temperature. Thus Coca-Cola could charge more for a coke on a hot day than on a cold day. To the standard marketing or finance student, this invention should be welcomed. A firm can usually increase profits if it can successfully differentiate markets. This new soft drink dispenser allows Coke to differentiate the hot day and cold day markets. However, this invention was never realized in the market, contrary to what one would expect.

The first public reference to Coca-Cola's invention was made in an offhand comment to the Brazilian press by CEO Ivester. That quotation was picked up by the *New York Times*. A huge public outcry followed. Charging more for a coke on a hot day was perceived as unfair and the public let Coca-Cola know their feelings. The chief competitor Pepsi piled on saying they would never use such a soft drink dispenser. An invention that would increase profits never saw the light of day. Why? It was perceived to be unfair.

Many of my students were outraged at this turn of events. They accurately point out that differential pricing is often accepted and makes sense. What my students forgot were lessons about bounded rationality and bounded willpower and that perceptions of fairness matter in marketing.

The impact of notions of fairness in economic transactions is not culture bound. It is not limited to citizens of the United States. For example, I had the opportunity to teach a section on ethics to a number of Chinese students in Minnesota's joint program with a university China. I had given the following assignment to my Chinese students: Write up an example of an ethical issue in business in China. A number of students chose the same issue. They pointed out that during the SARS epidemic in 2003, a rumor circulated the vinegar would prevent SARS. The students pointed out that the price of vinegar rose precipitously and the students thought this was unfair.

Assume I am right in the claim that there are norms of fairness regarding pricing in all cultures. Of course, what price rises are considered unfair might vary from culture to culture. An interesting piece of research would be to discover the factors that lead some differential pricing decisions to be considered fair and others unfair. As a start it seems that large price increases in responding to so-called acts of God are considered unfair. Thus charging more for candles, water, or gasoline after a hurricane is considered unfair and in the US such price increases are punished as price gouging. Are there other factors that are relevant? For example, how important is the fact that a person has no choice but to purchase an item in question? It is important to realize that if one did not relax the assumption that everyone only acts on their perceived best interest, this research could not get off the ground.

---

[14] Ibid., 165.

Conclusion

The discipline of economics has undergone some significant changes-changes that have the potential of turning economics from a foe to a friend of ethics. Some of the concepts in the newer economic fields like transaction cost economics can be adopted by ethicists to make more sophisticated ethical analyses-even if adherents in those fields of economics themselves still have assumptions that make the field a foe rather than a friend. I have used the distinction between high and low asset specificity to provide a deeper analysis of certain ethical business phenomena. In addition, relaxing the self interest assumption in economics itself allows both economists and ethicists to introduce a bona fide ethical concept like fairness into economic models. I have given some examples here but there is much opportunity for additional research into the role that fairness plays in economic life. If economics and ethics can be friends rather than foes there is a wonderful opportunity for collaborative research in economics and ethics.

Part II
Philosophical Issues in Business

Chapter 4
Kantian Themes

Why Kant

I would contend that my most important work in business ethics has been the application of Kant's moral philosophy to ethical issues in business. Some may ask, why would I choose Kant? After all Kant, as the leading figure of the Enlightenment, has been out of favor with many even though there has been a devoted band of scholars who have championed Kant's ethics through the last quarter of the twentieth century and the twenty-first century thus far. The contemporary movement to Kant is highlighted by the publication of John Rawls' *A Theory of Justice*. I was enamored with Kant as an undergraduate and wrote my Senior Honors Thesis on Kant's philosophy of man. I went to the University of Rochester to study with Lewis White Beck, one of the leading Kant scholars at that time. My second scholarly publication in 1971 was "Aspects of Kant's Philosophy of Law."[1] When I began to do scholarly work in business ethics in the mid 1970s, it was natural for me to focus on Kant as I grappled with issues in business ethics.

However, explaining why I focused on Kant does nothing to address the larger and more important question of why those working in business ethics should take Kant seriously. First, I think all the great ethical thinkers have something to contribute to business ethics. If they did not, why should anyone take the great ethical theorists seriously? They are great ethical thinkers because they have something to say to us about how to live a moral life. So what does Kant have to contribute to business

---

Several paragraphs from my "A Reply to my Critics," *Kantian Business Ethics: Critical Perspectives*, Denis Arnold and Jared Harris eds. Edward Elgar Publishing 2012, 202–228 are included in this chapter. Endnotes appear in the appropriate places to let the reader know that the following material is taken from that article. Reprinted by permission of Edward Elgar Publishing.

[1] Bowie, Norman E. (1971). "Aspects of Kant's Philosophy of Law," *The Philosophical Forum*, 11(4), 469–478.

ethics? First, business executives often think and act as utilitarians. Indeed business decisions based on cost-benefit analysis, risk management, and the like are fundamentally utilitarian. However, sometimes, it is just the use of these decision techniques that get business executives into ethical trouble. What seems "rational" from a cost benefit perspective, sometimes seems unjust or unfair to those whose interests are sacrificed in the utilitarian calculus.

Thus, second, corporate stakeholders such as employees, customers, and the local community, for example, sometimes think that their interests, rights, and values are not respected and Kant's ethical theory gives them a language or narrative for making their point.

Third, Kant's transcendental methodology gives a means for justifying even some of the most basic ethical rules or intuitions. Some business school faculty think it is enough to tell students that they should not do anything they would not want to see written up on the front page of the *Wall Street Journal*. That is sound advice but is simplistic. Such advice shows a person might be embarrassed by something he did if it appeared on the front page but what we want is an explanation of why he would be embarrassed or why he should be embarrassed if he is not. Kant can provide a justification for ethical norms against lying, stealing, free-riding and the like. Kant's derivation of the various formulations of the categorical imperative gives one way of providing a rational foundation for many of the judgments that business ethicists make about business ethics issues.

Fourth, Kant's moral philosophy usually gives sound advice in ethically tricky situations. Kant's emphasis on the dignity of persons-a dignity that deserves respect is the foundation for many of the enlightened human resource practices and his emphasis on the value of autonomy is a foundation for the norms of participative management. His insistence that ethical norms be universalized explains why it is wrong for companies to deliberately withhold or severely delay payments to suppliers. In a Kantian business community there would be no "hold-up" problem because no one could universalize a norm that permits one to take advantage of great inequality in bargaining power.

Fifth, Kant's ethical theory can make business ethics inspirational. If a business is seen as a cooperative enterprise that adds value to all the corporate stakeholders and thus enriches their lives, business is no longer simply about money grubbing. Business is a means for persons to join together in a cooperative enterprise to make the world better by providing the goods and services that people need. As we shall see Kant's ethical theory can even provide the basis for a philosophy of corporate social responsibility.

For these reasons I think Kant has much to offer business ethics and in this Chapter I want to show how my thinking about Kantian ethics and the thinking of a new generation of Kantian business ethicists can broaden and enrich our understanding of business ethics. Before moving to that task, I should give tribute to the contemporary scholars on Kant's ethics whose original insights have inspired me. I think it important to mention these people because far too often I heard criticisms of Kant that after reading the work of the scholars below seem shallow and misguided.

John Rawls, himself a Kantian, mentored a number of influential students who have provided great critical insights into Kant's ethics. They include Christine Korsgaard, Thomas Hill Jr. Barbara Herman, and Onora O'Neill. I was greatly indebted to their work that was published in the 1990s when I wrote *Business Ethics*: *A Kantian Perspective*. Since the publication of that work Korsgaard and Herman have published additional books, which have perceptions on ethics and ethical theory that are unique to them, that nonetheless draw heavily on Kant's ethics.[2] Once again I find their insights useful in my own work. Moreover, since the publication of my book, I have read a great deal of the work of Allen Wood.[3] Since Wood rejects significant aspects of the Kantian scholars mentioned above who were all trained by John Rawls, my understanding of Kantian ethical theory is deeper. I also profited from reading Paul Guyer's 2006 book, *Kant*.[4] It is clear there is a flourishing community of Kant scholars within traditional ethical theory.

Manfred Keuhn has written a delightful and lengthy new biography of Kant that will change our assumptions about the life of the somber philosopher from Konigsburg.[5] Actually for an extended period of time Kant was quite the party animal and something of a prize dinner party guest. He also frequently dined with royalty. Some important women were enamored with him. He also was deeply involved in academic politics and could get into trouble with the authorities. Keuhn's book makes Kant a more well- rounded and social animal-more of a full human being than the picture you get from older biographies and especially from caricatures of his moral philosophy.

Organization of This Chapter

The cornerstone of my application of Kant's philosophy to business ethics is my 1999 book. I begin the Chapter by considering some of the criticisms of that book and also I indicate how my thinking in that book has changed in part due to the criticisms the book received and in part due to further reflection including reflection from reading scholarly contributions that have appeared since 1998.

Finally I will take account of those who have applied Kantian theory to topics in business ethics that I have not addressed. I will often function as a cheerleader and occasionally as a critic in this endeavor. I conclude with some suggestions for the further application of Kantian ethical theory to problems in business ethics.

---

[2] Specifically I have in mind, Korsgaard, Christine. (2009). *Self-Constitution: Agency, Identity, and Integrity*. Oxford: Oxford University Press, and Herman, Barbara. (2007). *Moral Literacy*. Cambridge: Harvard University Press.

[3] Wood, Allen W. (2008). *Kantian Ethics*. Cambridge: Cambridge University Press.

[4] Guyer, Paul. (2006). *Kant*. London: Routledge.

[5] Manfred Kuehn. (2001). *Kant: A Biography*. Cambridge: Cambridge University Press.

Rethinking and Defending *Business Ethics: A Kantian Perspective*

In undertaking this rethinking and defense, I will follow the original chapter outlines and consider criticisms and my response to these criticisms for each chapter. I will also indicate where I have changed my mind on certain topics. Where appropriate I will apply the latest in Kantian scholarship to my thoughts on the various topics.

Chapter 1 Immoral Business Practices

In this chapter, I wanted to show how the first formulation of the categorical imperative (the universal law formulation) could serve as a test for maxims proposed for action. I adopted Kant's distinction between maxims that were formally inconsistent and ones that were practically inconsistent. I then argued that certain maxims in business would be inconsistent in one of these two senses. I pointed out that all cases of free riding would be subject to being formally inconsistent. Showing that all cases of free riding would be inconsistent enabled me to show how robust Kant's theory could be when analyzing business practice. I also gave several examples where the attempt to follow inconsistent maxims in the real world of business led to the undermining or collapse of a business practice. I consider one of the main achievements of that chapter to be my argument that business practices that undermine trust are pragmatically inconsistent. The argument was presented formally on page 31 and I am unaware of anyone challenging it. I would argue that understanding and using the notion of pragmatic inconsistency would increase the robustness of Kant's ethical theory particularly as it is used in applied ethics

I also believe that I avoided some of the common mistakes of interpretation in my application of Kant. For example, I never treated my analysis as a deduction from the universal law but always explicitly stated that the universal law was a test for maxims. I did not in that chapter try to answer the common objections that are raised against Kant's philosophy. In particular I did not try to answer the objection that it is hard to formulate the appropriate maxim and that it seems rather easy to formulate maxims that result in false positives and false negatives. The maxim "It is morally permissible to tell a lie" would result in a formal contradiction in a way that it looks as if it is always wrong to tell a lie. On the other hand if one tries to narrow the maxim to include legitimate exceptions such as "it is ok to lie to a murderer at the door", then you run the danger of morally permitting actions that ought not to be permitted. Kant was always very cognizant of the human ability to think up excuses or rationalizations for unethical actions.[6]

---

[6] For example, see Wood, op.cit., 250–251.

This kind of discussion about the ability to formulate the appropriate maxims is used by particularists in moral theory to deny that a principle based approach to ethics is a useful one. The particularists point out that principles must of necessity be indeterminate guides to moral action. The particularity of a situation matters and must be taken into account. In addition it is argued that we do not think about ethical decision making the way a principle based account would require. We do not generalize from particular cases to a moral principle.[7] There are particularist business ethics scholars as well, for example, the late Robert Solomon, Joe Desjardins, and Geoff Moore.

Kant scholars such as those mentioned earlier in this chapter have responded effectively to these particularist critics. This is not the occasion for providing the details of their account. However, in business ethics, the definitive response to the particularists has been provided by Jeffery Smith and Wim Dubbink.[8] Although I cannot provide the full details of their account, let me give the reader an overview of their overall argument. Smith and Dubbink accept the distinction that Kantian ethicists draw between justifying a principle and applying a principle. Kant's discussion in the *Groundwork for the Metaphysics of Morals* is primarily about the justification of principles and what counts as appropriate moral motivation. The justification of principles is abstracted from any particular facts about agents and of necessity cannot be applied directly to particular actions. Indeed, as Smith and Dubbink point out, Kant himself understood that applying principles in concrete situations is difficult, that agents often stumble in applying them, and that agents have some latitude in applying them.[9]

Smith and Dubbink point out the principle based ethics like Kant's have been criticized on grounds of what they call, the indeterminacy objection and the generalism objection. The indeterminacy objection basically says that moral principles cannot contain enough information to directly resolve particular ethical issues. The generalism objection claims that those who adopt a principle based ethics do not understand how agents actually reason about moral problems.

But we have already seen that Kant at least does not claim that moral principles can contain enough information to be applied directly. So the indeterminacy argument has little force since most principle based ethicists do not have the view of moral principles that the particularists claim they hold. As for the generalism objection, Smith and Dubbink show decisively the role that principles play in ethical decision making and thus show how reasoning from principles does take place and appropriately so in ethical decision-making. They agree with Barbara Herman that principles are necessary to direct our attention to the morally salient features of a particular case. They also provide a "kind of practical training" in shaping our

---

[7] Some of the best known particularists include Johnathan Dancy, John McDowell, David Wiggins, and Margaret Little.

[8] Smith, Jeffery and Wim Dubbink. (2011). "Understanding the Role of Moral Principles in Business Ethics: A Kantian Perspective," *Business Ethics Quarterly,* 21(2), 205–231.

[9] These points are all made in Kant, Immanuel. (1798, 1991). *Metaphysics of Morals.* Cambridge: Cambridge University Press.

perceptions and interpretation of circumstances that call for ethical scrutiny. Violations of certain ethical principles seem to require explanation if they are to be justified. A person who does no harm to another does not need to explain why she acted in that way. A person who does harm another does need to explain why. Thus principles provide reasons for actions.

I totally accept the Smith/Dubbink criticisms of the particularist position as well as their account of the role of principles in moral decision making. And I agree that their account is Kantian. I encourage business ethicists to read the complete article for a full account of their argument that I have merely sketched out. If I were to revise Chapter 1, I would emphasize that my examples are merely illustrative. They show how the use of the categorical imperative can enable us to provide reasons for actions and enable us to pick out morally salient circumstances in business life. I am not in Chapter 1, simply applying the categorical imperative to get correct answers about business ethics.

Chapter 2 Treating the Humanity of Stakeholders as Ends Rather than as Means Merely

This chapter uses the second formulation of the categorical imperative-the respect for the humanity in a person principle- to evaluate a number of human resource practices in business. It is obvious that on Kantian morality the use of coercion or deceit is a violation of the humanity in a person and that coercive or deceptive practices treat the humanity of a person as a means merely. A major philosophical question that I finessed was "What counts as coercion?" The issue arose specifically when I had been asked whether layoffs were coercive. If one takes the perspective of individual labor contracts, it appears that layoffs are not coercive. A person taking a job knows either explicitly or implicitly that he or she can be laid off. Many employment contracts have an explicit reference to "employment at will." Union contracts, where they exist, specify the procedures for layoffs as do civil service contracts. Even tenured university faculty can be laid off in times of genuine financial emergency. However I never was comfortable with that analysis. Having a job is required if one is to have more than a minimal existence. A homeless person sleeping in a car or under a bridge is living a minimal existence. And in this culture having a job is, if not a necessary condition for self-respect, is usually an essential condition for self-respect. I now realize there are two ways to handle my discomfort. One is to make a case for the notion of institutional coercion. I raised that possibility in Chapter 2 but I never developed it. I also pointed to some of the legal cases where the court determined there was coercion and argued by analogy to coercion in labor contracts. That argument deserves further consideration.

A second way, to which I am now inclined, is to argue that every person has a right either to a job or to a safety net and retraining in time of unemployment-so long as he or she is willing to work. Moreover, I maintain with some organizational theorists like Jeffrey Pfeffer that businesses are too quick to lay people off.[10] Pfeffer provides business reasons for not being so quick; I would add moral reasons based on the fact that a business has a relationship with employees that is more than simply economic. We used to talk about a business being a family. We certainly have given up that idea, but we still hear terms like "loyalty", "teamwork", and a "new social contract" applied to contemporary businesses. All these terms imply that it is wrong to dump people on the street when it is not necessary.

Some have tried to argue that as a Kantian, I must be committed to a no layoff policy.[11] I do not see why that is the case. The application of the humanity in a person formulation of the categorical imperative is not deductive. I see nothing wrong with saying that business should try to avoid layoffs but that if layoffs are necessary, some government agency or perhaps charitable institutions have a duty to provide a safety net

In Chapter 2 of *Business Ethics: A Kantian Perspective,* I also took the Kantian line that the humanity in a person as an end formulation of the categorical imperative requires positive duties as well as the negative duties of avoiding deception and coercion. I argued that the humanity in a person formulation required a company to provide meaningful work for its employees. I listed six criteria for meaningful work but said very little in defense of them. I followed up some years later with a paper, "A Kantian Theory of Meaningful Work."[12] My discussion of meaningful work has stimulated a lot of critical comment. Perhaps this is a good place to provide some additional commentary on the subject including some response to some of the objections.

Let me explain why I am interested in this subject. If we divide the 24 h clock up, for 5 days a week we spend 8 h a day sleeping, 8 h a day working and 8 h on other.[13] Some spend an additional hour or more commuting to work and another hour or more commuting home from work. Many now hold two jobs so they work more than 8 h a day. Americans work more hours and take less vacation time than the citizens of any other country. Despite the number of hours spent at work and going to work, dissatisfaction with work is at a record high. This is reflected in academic studies and in our ordinary language. Not only do we have TGIF (Thank God it's Friday) but also Blue Monday and Hump Day (Wednesday-half way to Friday).

The language of TGIF is more common than language about vocation or calling. Kant believed that we were morally required to develop our talents. Education and then work provides the means for doing that. If we do have such an obligation and if work is one-and for most a common and important- way to develop and

---

[10] For example see Pfeffer, Jeffrey. (1998). *The Human Equation.* Boston: Harvard Business School Press.

[11] Patricia Werhane has made that criticism for example.

[12] Bowie, Norman E. (1998). "A Kantian Theory of Meaningful Work," *Journal of Business Ethics,* 17, 1083–1092.

[13] Most of this discussion of meaningful work is taken from Bowie, Norman E. (2012). "A Reply to My Critics" in Denis Arnold and Jared Harris (eds.), *Kantian Business Ethics: Critical Perspectives.* Cheltenham: Edward Elgar Publishing.

practice our talents, then it seems to me that an organization-including a business organization- should be supportive of that end rather than contribute to people hating their jobs. Although I agree that I have not always expressed myself well on this point, I think the goal of changing people's attitude toward their jobs from dissatisfaction-even hatred-toward something meaningful is the correct goal. And I think Kant would approve.

Joanne Ciulla is surely correct when she argues that it is one thing to say that a company has an obligation to provide meaningful work and quite another to overcome the obstacles to actually providing it.[14] I do confess that I have been overly optimistic in this respect. Ciulla is right in saying that my Kantian theory of meaningful work rests on both negative and positive freedom. Ciulla thinks that the emphasis should be put on negative freedom-freedom from coercion-because historically the issue between employers and employees is about power and employers tend to want to impose their will on their employees. Indeed Ciulla argues that taking a job requires giving up freedom in some respects.

One might respond by saying that a Kantian could accept freely limiting one's freedom in one area in order to have more freedom in another. Thus the pay one receives from working could provide freedom to obtain a number of one's important goals even at the cost of giving up freedom in the workplace. Free choices do constrain. Now as Ciulla points out there seems to be a correlation between higher paying jobs and the amount of freedom one has-both negative and positive. That is an important observation and provides a reason why I think we should pay more attention to issues of freedom for lower paid workers. It is harder to provide meaningful work in retail sales or the assembly line than at a university or law firm-although even there freedom is not unlimited.

Ciulla also points out that people need to work in order to make a living and that for many-especially the unskilled in times of high unemployment- the "choice" is a stark one. Indeed that is why it is important that children are encouraged to become educated to the full extent of their abilities. A good Kantian would praise a society that educates its young so that the choice of employment would not be as stark as it sometimes is. I also agree with Ciulla that unions provide a means for enhancing employee freedom. I say that as a former union president at the University of Delaware and as one who would argue that the United States is now the most anti-union country in the G-20.

Ciulla also speaks eloquently about the dangers of having a corporation determine what will count as employee self-realization or in enhancing their negative freedom. She is probably right when she says that I am too optimistic about avoiding these dangers in contemporary corporate life. Besides who is to decide what is to count as self-realization-especially if self realization by the employees undermines the self-realization of employers and stockholders? These are valid points. But let's think of small and medium size enterprises, especially ones on the edge of technological development. Or think of companies with a strong corporate culture like Google or Apple.

[14] Ciulla, Joanne B. (2012). "Worthy Work and Bowie's Kantian Theory of Meaningful Work" in Denis Arnold and Jared Harris (eds.), *Kantian Business Ethics: Critical Perspectives*. Cheltenham: Edward Elgar Publishing, 202–228.

These companies provide examples of organizations that give meaning to one's life. Employees want to work there; there is no disconnect between the employer and the employee. In my Kantian ideal it is that harmony of interests in pursuit of a common goal that provides meaning and there is no conflict between how an employer defines self-realization and how the employee defines it. This goal may not be realistic for many companies but I see no ethical problem in endorsing it as a goal. And this goal may conflict, as Ciulla points out, with self-realization in other areas of one's life- with one's responsibilities to family for example. And Ciulla is also right in reminding me that achieving meaningful work in a global society is even more difficult. However, I would point out that over time the global market place will provide work that is more meaningful for more of the world's populations. Living standards are on the rise in Asia and South America. If the late C.K. Prahalad is correct there is even hope for those at the bottom of the pyramid.[15]

Finally Ciulla argues that there is no one definition of meaningful work, that different people have different notions of meaningful work and that there is no way a corporation can provide meaningful work to everyone. Hard to argue with that. Also I would agree that some people find meaning in places other than work. Those facts do not convince me that I do not have a theory of meaningful work. Cuilla would characterize my account as a theory of worthy work. In an earlier draft of her paper Ciulla says the following:

> The most meaningful jobs are those in which people express themselves, help others, or create products that in some way improve life. Work makes life better if it makes a contribution; alleviates suffering; or eliminates difficult, dangerous or tedious toil; or makes the people healthier and happier; or aesthetically or intellectually enriches people; or improves the environment or the society in which we live.

I could not agree more and if it makes sense to call this worthy work rather than meaningful work, let's do it. If work meets those descriptions, TGIF will be a day of celebration rather than a day of relief.

Another of my critics, Joseph Desjardins focuses on work itself. He distinguishes the conventional view where work is an instrumental good that must be tolerated in order to achieve other ends from the human fulfillment view that treats work as "a key activity through which people can develop their full potential as human beings."[16] I clearly reject the instrumental view and would like to associate a Kantian ethic with the human fulfillment view. But can I? Taking the perspective of political theory, Desjardins points out that my actual position is a middle position between the conventional instrumental view and the self-fulfillment view. That is because as a traditional liberal I have a thin theory of the good- one based on protecting the process or form of rationally chosen ends. But I have no substantive theory of the good and Desjardins thinks the liberal view is too impoverished.

---

[15] Prahalad, C.K. (2005). *The Future at the Bottom of the Pyramid: Eradicating Poverty Through Profits*. Upper Saddle River: Pearson Education Inc.

[16] DesJardins, Joseph. (2012). "Meaningful Work" in Denis Arnold and Jared Harris (eds.), *Kantian Business Ethics: Critical Perspectives*. Cheltenham: Edward Elgar Publishing.

On the basis of my published work, Desjardins is correct in characterizing my account in this way. In light of Desjardins' comments, what would I say now? First Desjardins has provided a number of goods that I could adopt and still maintain that these goods still fall under a thin theory of the good. He cites a number of intellectual virtues such as "diligence, concentration, attentiveness, thoughtfulness, and self-awareness." I might also accept psychological goods such as "self-esteem, self-confidence and self-respect." Meaningful work would be work that supports these intellectual virtues and psychological goods. I hereby amend my account to include these items.

Desjardins has an even more intriguing idea. In describing my account, he points out that I might have tried to develop a thicker theory of the good. Perhaps a thicker theory of the good could be derived from Kant's imperfect duties to develop one's talents and aid the needy. Desjardins correctly points out that I did not do that. But in the future? Great idea I thought! However, he argues that I cannot go in that direction. He says, "I think Bowie has no option but to retreat from these ends because, as a Kantian, he lacks the philosophical resources to develop either in a substantive way."[17] However, the only argument Desjardins provides is that if I move in that direction I will run afoul of my "avoid paternalism" condition. But why? It is not paternalistic to insist that one do one's duty especially when the duty is a requirement of rationality as Kant believes. Or alternatively, if paternalism is a problem it seems to be as much a problem for those who defend the thin theory of the good as for those who defend a more robust theory.

So let's take a look at Desjardins' more robust self-fulfillment theory. He points out that work plays a major role in self-identity. It helps determine who we are and I agree that work is certainly meaningful in that sense. As Desjardins says, "Meaningful work would be work at which individuals express their identities and which allows individuals to flourish in all their diversity."[18] I agree and in passing this characterization seems perfectly compatible with a thin theory of the good. Different individuals might achieve somewhat different identities in work situations. There are important differences between being a professor and being a farmer. Teaching and research will contribute to being a different person from a farmer who raises food for us to eat. Both careers are legitimate and both can be meaningful in Desjardins' sense. He also points out that meaningful work should help us improve ourselves over time. Right on but I do not see anything substantive here unless a substantive theory of what counts as improvement is provided. That brings us to the imperfect duty to aid others or to be concerned with the happiness of others. What would count as meaningful work in that context? Desjardins said, "Meaningful work is work that creates products and services that are truly good, that contribute to human well-being and human flourishing."[19] I agree and would point out that there is much in common between his robust self-fulfillment account and Ciulla's account of worthy work. On reflection, I endorse this

---

[17] Ibid., 141.

[18] Ibid., 144.

[19] Ibid., 145.

self-fulfillment view. I would only point out that it too might be characterized as a middle position since so many of the characteristics are compatible with multiple theories of the good. Desjardins is really defending an Aristotelian theory of meaningful work. As I indicate later in this chapter, contemporary Kantian scholars are building bridges between Kantian ethics and Aristotelian ethics. I would like to continue the conversation to see if a Kantian and an Aristotelian convergence might develop around a self-fulfillment theory of meaningful work.

Chapter 3 The Firm as a Moral Community

In this chapter I have attempted to move the level of analysis from the individual to the firm although I did not specifically put it this way. In the first two chapters, I had provided arguments and examples of what ethics might require of business people in general (Chap. 1) and of managers, especially human resource managers, in particular (Chap. 2) In this chapter I wanted to see what an organization governed by Kantian principles might look like. I have actually gone beyond Kant and tried to characterize an organization with integrity more generally. That essay is included as Chap. 11 in this volume.

One of the first difficulties is to determine what the third formulation of the categorical imperative actually is. This problem is not unique to the third formulation since the universal law formulation is stated in two or three different ways. Kant scholars distinguish between the Universal Law formulation and the Formula of the Law of Nature.[20] There is general agreement that the third formulation has something to do with a realm of ends although Wood included a Formula of Autonomy and a formula of the Realm of Ends as versions of the third formulation.[21] My own way of stating the formula is slightly different from the way it is stated by other Kant scholars. I defined the third formulation as follows: "…you should act as if you were a member of an ideal kingdom of ends in which you were sovereign and subject at the same time."[22] I think my way of stating the third formulation captures much of what Wood includes in the Formula of Autonomy and the Formula of the Realm of Ends. However, not much hinges on this issue.

Since the realm of ends is an ideal, some might argue that the norms that apply in the ideal realm of ends do not apply or even cannot apply to the imperfect world of business organizations. However, I think that would be a mistake. Kant believed that the third formulation captured the first formulation (the form) and the second formulation (the material)[23] Since the first and second formulations of

---

[20] See for example Wood, op.cit., 66.

[21] Ibid., 66–67.

[22] Bowie, Norman E. (1999). *Business Ethics: A Kantian Perspective*. New York: Blackwell, 87.

[23] Kant, Immanuel. (1785, 1990). *Foundations of the Metaphysics of Morals*. New York: Macmillan Publishing Co.

the categorical imperative can serve as tests of maxims in the imperfect world, I see no reasons why the third formulation cannot serve the same function as a test of maxims or practices that seek to create organizational integrity. Since the third formulation has a distinctly Rawlsian flavor and since Rawls was concerned with institutional perfect justice rather than imperfect justice, my strategy here might be out of favor with Rawlsians. However, many Rawls scholars have taken Rawls into areas he did not intend or even countenance and to good affect. The person who has done the most work in that regard is Nien-hê Hsieh.[24] Finally, as noted earlier Allen Wood has taken vigorous exception to the Rawlsian constructivist interpretation of Kant by the students of Rawls. However, I think my use of Rawls in this chapter is fairly uncontroversial and does not embroil me in the above dispute-which seems particularly bitter between Wood and Korsgaard.

This chapter has not received much critical comment. My principles of the moral firm needed some fleshing out-something I did with "Organizational Integrity and Moral Climates" included in this volume. In a separate article, I made a case for worker participation and I strongly criticized top down management and Taylorism adding to the arguments I made in the book on these topics.[25]

My strategy throughout the book was to try to find companies that had implemented Kantian ideals. I thought that if Kant were to be relevant to business people, there should be instances where Kantian ideals had been put into practice. One of the troubling events since publication of the book was the fact that most of the companies cited as good Kantian companies had fallen by the way side. Hewlett-Packard, Merck, and even Johnson and Johnson had lost their Kantian halos.[26]

Recently my discouragement has lifted a bit as I have discovered a number of companies that seem to practice business as Kantian ethics would require. First I call your attention to *Profit at the Bottom of the Ladder: Creating Value by Investing in Your Workforce*.[27] This book provides information on companies that have profited by adopting the good human resource practices and community investment practices that I had identified as consistent with Kantian ethics in this chapter. Significantly in the age of globalization, the book contains stories on a number of non U.S. examples. However, one shining example from the United States is Costco. If you want your hope for Kantian business ethics restored put this book on the top of your reading list. An international example is Jorma Ollila former CEO Nokia and Chair of its Board and Former Chair of Board Royal Dutch Shell. What he describes as Nordic capitalism looks very much what I describe in the book as

[24] Hsieh, Nien-hê. (2009). "Does Global Business Have a Responsibility to Promote Just Institutions?" *Business Ethics Quarterly*, 19(2), 251–273.

[25] Bowie, Norman E. (2005). "Kantian Ethical Thought" in John W. Budd and James G Scoville (eds.), *The Ethics of Human Resources and Industrial Relations*. Champaign: Labor and Employment Relations Association.

[26] For more on this fall from grace and its implications for business ethics, see Chap. 11 "Organizational Integrity and Moral Climates" in this volume.

[27] Heyman Jodi. (2010). *Profit at the Bottom of the Ladder: Creating Value by Investing in Your Workforce*. Boston: Harvard Business Press.

Kantian capitalism. He argues that there is more to business than shareholder profits, that the human role is important, that business should be concerned with social solidarity.[28] It is interesting to note that the notion of social solidarity ties in with the philosophy of Rawls and even Rorty as well as Kant.

Even when a business or business person manages according to Kantian ideals, the name "Kant" is usually never mentioned. However, recently I discovered an exception- Tom Chappell Co-founder and former CEO of Tom's of Maine. Chappell explicitly stated that he guided the company by common theories of Edwards(Jonathan) and Kant.[29] On page 20 Chappell makes explicit reference to the categorical imperative.[30] Later he argues that bonuses at Tom's of Maine are awarded "in ways that conform to the guidelines expressed in Kant's principle of moral universalism,"[31] He also points out that Tom's of Maine will have fair compensation policies based on performance that benefit all stakeholders.

Chapter 4 Acting from Duty: How Pure a Motive?

In this Chapter I struggled with the issue of the purity of the good will. If the only thing good in itself is a good will and I also argue that in many cases good ethics is good business, then an action we would normally call good but done because it was good business is not a truly moral action. There have been a number of attempts by scholars to get around this problem. One standard way is to point out that there can be multiple motives for an action. Thus a company could perform a socially beneficial act both because it is the right thing to do and because it is good business. So long as the company would do this act even if the good business motive were not present, the act would pass the Kantian test, it is argued, and be done out of duty and thus worthy of moral esteem.[32] Recent work by Allen Wood and Barbara Herman lead me to think that this problem is partly a false problem created by a common misconception of Kant. If they are correct there is no need to worry about multiple motives.

Wood argues that there is nothing wrong with doing the right thing from a self-interested or prudential motive. The important point in moral choice is when one should go against self-interest or prudence and do the right thing. To act out of duty

---

[28] The Financial Times article articulating his philosophy can be found at http://royaldutchshellplc. com/2009/03/23/jorma-ollila-champion-of-nordic-capitalism/

[29] Chappell, Tom. (2009). *Goodness in Business*. Waltham: Bentley College Center for Business Ethics.

[30] Ibid., 9–10.

[31] Ibid., 23.

[32] For a scholarly discussion around this point, see Henson, Richard. (1979). "What Kant Might Have Said: Moral Worth and the Over-determination of Dutiful Action," *Philosophical Review*, 88, 39–54 and Herman, Barbara. (1993). *The Practice of Moral Judgment*. Cambridge: Harvard University Press, Chapter 1.

in those cases is when the agent deserves moral esteem.[33] Thus a business person who does the right thing because it is good business does something morally good but does not deserve any special moral credit for that. Right and that is exactly in accord with our moral intuitions. The public is happy to have business do the right thing when it is good business to do so. However, to earn special moral credit with the public the business must sacrifice profit in order to do the right thing. It is interesting to note how Kantian the general public is in this regard. However, it is also true that if a business is to stay in business this latter event cannot happen too often so for most businesses the trick is to find the business strategy that lets the business do the right thing and be profitable. The public often does not understand that. There is nothing inconsistent with Kantianism in holding this position.

One could argue that the issue about the purity of the will, moral esteem, and good action is the main focus of Barbara Herman's *Moral Literacy*. One cannot adequately summarize this book length argument here. Herman's strategy is to deny the sharp separation between desire and reason and then to argue that desires can respond to reason. As she says early on in the book,

> But if we are no longer restricted to a rigid oppositional model-if the system of desires is itself reason responsive-the content of desires need not remain unaffected by our developing moral and rational capacities, and the exclusion of all desire from moral action will not follow so easily.[34]

I believe the remainder of the book is a careful exposition of the quoted passage although in providing that exposition, Herman provides a Kantian theory of character, moral development and a Kantian theory of virtues. This book is a must read for serious scholars of Kant's ethical theory.

I am sympathetic to Wood's and Herman's interpretations. Perhaps the critics of the "good ethics, good business" argument have misunderstood Kant. As a result of this kind of scholarship I am less concerned about criticisms that you cannot argue that you are a Kantian and argue the "good ethics is good business" line.

However, my own way of avoiding this criticism works independently of these advances on Kantian scholarship. The problem is not that the critics of "good ethics is good business" have misunderstood Kant; rather the problem is that these critics have not understood that in a public corporation making a profit is itself a moral obligation.

Specifically my way out of this dilemma was to point out that in a publicly held corporation, managers are agents of the stockholders and are contractually obligated to seek a profit. Since a contract is a type of promise, seeking profit is itself a morally required action. It is only because people do not see profit seeking as a moral act that a split is seen between doing the right thing and making a profit. Thus there is no separation thesis between doing the right thing and profit-seeking. Indeed since profit seeking is contractual and thus a kind of promise, it is, in Kant's language a perfect duty. Interestingly I am not aware of any critical comment on this

[33] The argument for this position is carefully worked out in Wood, Allen W, op.cit., Chap. 2.
[34] Herman, Barbara. (2008). *Moral Literacy*. Cambridge: Harvard University Press, 13.

move, although it is unique in the literature and certainly could be the subject of critical comment.

Put in a more formal way than I did in the book, the argument would run as follows:

1. In a publicly held firm the managers have entered into a contract with the stockholders;
2. A contract is a type of promise
3. The terms of the contract are that the managers should attempt to maximize profits for the stockholders (Milton Friedman) or should have a major concern for profit (stakeholder theory or sustainability capitalism)
4. For Kant, keeping a promise is a perfect duty
5. Therefore managers have a moral obligation-indeed a perfect duty- to at least seek profit.

Thus doing good when it leads to profit is a moral duty, all else being equal.

However, my solution to the purity of the will problem does create another issue. I, like many others, have argued that corporations have duties to aid society or to help solve social problems. These are, in Kant's words, imperfect duties. Imperfect duties are real duties, but they are not duties that you need to fulfill on all occasions. Some argue that corporations do not have such duties. I will not consider that argument here. See my discussion of the work of Dubbink and Smith who argue against that position below. However, if the duty to seek a profit is a perfect duty and the duty to solve social problems or aid society is an imperfect duty, does that mean whenever there is a conflict between profitability and aiding society, the company should always aim for profitability?

That is an excellent question. If the duty to seek profit is a duty to maximize profit the problem is more serious. It seems that in such a case, the manager should always seek profit whenever there is a conflict. But if the duty to seek a profit is treated less stringently, then sometimes some profits can be sacrificed. Actually more and more states are understanding the contract between management and the stockholders that way. These states have enacted laws that give explicit permission for management to consider other factors besides profits. Also many stockholders themselves would allow management to make these tradeoffs in the short run so long as they contributed to profits in the long run.

All of this supports my overall position that the job of a manager is to find a win-win where aiding society or helping to solve social problems is achieved while making a profit. Indeed some for profit companies are founded for the sole purpose of solving social problems. This whole field is called social entrepreneurship. Ethical management requires that ways be found to practice business in ways that are both ethical and financially successful.

Suppose we agree that in short-run situations and in win-win situations, there is an imperfect duty for corporations to aid society or help solve social problems. What is the status of the duty to help society or solve social problems? It is a genuine duty that falls on corporations, but there is considerable latitude on how often and in what way, a corporation exercises this imperfect duty. Moreover, I would now add that the corporation should focus on social problems where it has some expertise. Drug companies rather than oil companies should focus on getting low cost drugs to undeveloped countries. Oil companies have their own social problems to consider. If social responsibility is a duty it is accompanied by the duty to act within one's spheres of competence. In business language the duty should be strategic-tied to the overall strategy and mission of the firm.

Chapter 5 The Cosmopolitan Perspective

The last chapter of *Business Ethics: A Kantian Perspective* pointed out how cosmopolitan Kant was and how cosmopolitan Kant's ethical theory is. In this age of globalization, it seemed to me that Kant's enlightenment optimism was just what was needed as a philosophical grounding for ethical global capitalism. My first task in that chapter was to argue that capitalism rested on a set of moral imperatives- a market morality if you will. As capitalism spread throughout the world, the common morality would become more evident. We would see evidence of a universal morality in the marketplace. Specifically I predicted that there would be economic reasons why discrimination and bribery should decline, that trust and honesty among market participants in different cultures would increase. I cited empirical evidence that these trends had already begun. Later with my colleague Paul Vaaler, we developed a transaction cost economics argument in support of these trends.[35]

I also argued that ethical global capitalism could foster world peace, universal rights, and democracy. This view was widely held by enlightenment thinkers, especially Kant, but also Hume, Mill, and of course Adam Smith. This was also the time when Fukuyama's work on the end of history and trust was all the rage.[36] Two years after the book was published, 9/11 upended all these optimistic assumptions. The final chapter of the book was criticized as overly optimistic and unrealistic. More importantly it was criticized for having an essentially Western orientation and that as a result its claims about a universal morality of the market were suspect. Critics claimed that it also assumed a Western interpretation of human rights and democracy.

Am I guilty as charged? Political theorists have cited Kant with approval when they pointed out that democracies do not go to war with one another. I recall a number of discussions with colleagues at the University of Minnesota in the 1980s around this very point. That generalization seems to hold true.

[35] Vaaler, Paul M. and Norman E. Bowie. (2010). "Transaction Cost Economics, Knowledge Transfer and Universal Business Norms in Multinational Enterprises," *International Journal of Strategic Change Management*, 2(4), 269–297.
[36] Fukuyama, Francis. (1992). *The End of History and the Last Man*. New York: The Free Press Macmillan, and Fukuyama, Francis. (1995). *Trust*. New York: The Free Press, Macmillan.

Recently I was able to read completely Thomas Friedman's important book *The World is Flat*. Chapter 14 is titled "The Dell Theory of Conflict Prevention," which is named after a view of Dell CEO Michael Dell. And what is that theory? Countries that are both part of a major global supply chain will not fight one another.[37]

If that generalization holds true, we can predict that the United States and China are less likely to go to war. China is no democracy so we cannot depend on that factor. But the economics still works in our favor. Economically we simply cannot afford it, as Friedman points out. Apparently this view is held by the CEO's of a number of major international corporations. And this argument is not limited to the US and China. See for example Craig Addison's "A Silicon Shield Protects Taiwan from China."[38] More than a decade after that article was written the shield holds. Of course just as 9/11 upset my optimistic assumptions about the reign of cosmopolitanism, so could a conflict erupt that results from a nation not a part of a major global supply chain waging a war of aggression on a country that is a member of a major global supply chain. An attack by Pakistan who is not a participant in the flat world against India which very much is a participant is one possibility. And then there are truly rogue states like North Korea. But as the world becomes flatter and the economies of the world become more intertwined, then a quotation from Kant that I used in Chapter 5 still rings true- at least with respect to the expense of war.

> In the end, war itself will be seen as not only so artificial, an outcome so uncertain for both sides, in aftereffects so painful in the form of an ever-growing war debt (a new invention) that cannot be met, that it will be regarded as a most dubious undertaking. The impact of any revolution on all states on our continent, so clearly knit together through commerce will be so obvious that other states, driven by their own danger but without any legal basis, will offer themselves as arbiters, and thus they will prepare the way for a distant international government for which there is not precedent in world history.[39]

Since 9/11 raises such questions about the future of globalization and the ability of countries and people to get along, it is worth confronting the elephant in the room-Muslim extremism. Not all Muslims are terrorists and not all terrorists are Muslims. However, a disproportionate number of terrorists are Muslims. Moreover, the condemnation of Muslim terrorists by other Muslims who should be vocal in saying that terrorism is a perversion of the Muslim faith has not been particularly vocal or widespread. Is the Muslim religion an impediment to global economic cooperation and mutual tolerance? Quite honestly I thought it was until I read Friedman's book.

Friedman made some important distinctions among Muslim countries that fit my application of Kant to the global scene quite well. Friedman pointed out that

---

[37] Friedman, Thomas L. (2006). *The World is Flat*. New York: Farrar, Straus, and Giroux, 522.

[38] Addison, Craig. (2000). "A Silicon Shield Protects Taiwan from China," *International Herald Tribune*, September 29, 2000.

[39] Kant, Immanuel. (1784, 1963). "What is Enlightenment" in *On History*. Indianapolis: Bobbs Merrill, 23.

the country with the second largest Muslim population in the world is India (And Saudi Arabia is not number 2). As of 2005, not one of India's 150 million Muslims had been associated with al- Qaeda. To my knowledge that remains true in 2012. What is remarkable about that fact is that there have been serious tensions between Hindus and Muslims in India. What is the explanation? Friedman cites the secular, free-market, democratic features of India.[40] Muslim anger and thus the propensity to join terrorist organizations is focused in authoritarian societies. As Friedman also points out, many of these Muslim countries ruled in an authoritarian way have oil as their chief resource-something you dig out of the ground but do not make and then trade.[41] Many have written of the curse of oil while others have challenged the notion that having oil as your main resource is a curse.[42] It will be interesting to see what happens as these authoritarian regimes come under increasing pressure as we saw in 2011. As of this writing Mubarrak was ousted from Egypt, Kaddafi was ousted with NATO support from Libya and Syria teeters on civil war. Perhaps the version of the Muslim faith that is compatible with a global economy will prevail after all. In any case, Kant would not be surprised by the distinctions that Friedman pointed out.

It has been more than 15 years since I began the research which led to *Business Ethics: A Kantian Perspective*. Much has changed during those 15 years. There has been an explosion of scholarship on Kant's ethics. Political events have created a time of turmoil in the first decade of the twenty-first century that exceeds any turmoil during the last decade of the twentieth century. Despite this the main arguments and conclusions of the book stand. Indeed the new scholarship on Kantian ethics and the turmoil in the world only strengthen the arguments-especially the normative arguments and conclusions of the book.

Recently I have been delighted to learn that Wim Dubbink will write a full length book on business ethics based on a Kantian approach-*Commercial Life and the Retrieval of Morality: A Philosophical Introduction to Business Ethics*. In the preface he points out that the Kantian approach to business ethics has been out of favor because the critics of the Kantian approach have very outdated views of what Kantian scholarship is all about. I could not agree more.

Perhaps I will get an opportunity to publish a revised edition of the book and if I do, I know his insights will enrich that revised edition. But if I do not, let these remarks serve as my final thoughts on what I tried to accomplish when I wrote *Business Ethics a Kantian Perspective*.

---

[40] Friedman, op.cit, 559.

[41] Ibid., 564.

[42] The former position is taken by Kashi, Ed. (2008). *Curse of the Black Gold: Fifty Years of Oil in the Niger Delta*. Brooklyn: PowerHouse Books and Mahmous A. El Gamal and Amy Myers Jaffe. (2010). *Oil Dollars, Debt and Crises The Global Curse of Black Gold*. New York: Cambridge University Press, while the latter position is taken by Luong, Pauline Jones and Erika Weinthal. (2010). *Oil is not a Curse: Ownership Structure and Institutions in Soviet Successor States*. New York: Cambridge University Press.

The New Generation of Scholars Applying Kant to Business Ethics

One of the more exciting developments in Kantian business ethics is the fact that a number of other scholars in addition to Wim Dubbink and Jeffery Smith have taken up the Kantian project. These scholars have produced a number of important papers and I am aware of a lot of research that is in the pipeline. Certainly an essay on contemporary Kantian business ethics needs to consider this work. Before considering some specific contributions by Kantian business ethicists, let me take note of some recent developments in Kant scholarship that have implications for business ethics in the twenty-first century.

Aristotle-Not Kant

Except for the post-modernists and the pragmatists who get a chapter of their own in this book, the biggest critics of the Kantian approach to business ethics come from the Aristotelians, including some of my friends, Ronald Duska, Joseph Desjardins, and the late Robert Solomon. One way to respond to my friends and their like minded colleagues is to show how their picture of Kant rests on misinterpretations of the Kantian text-misinterpretations that are now out of date. Another approach that I will develop briefly here is to show how several of the most distinguished scholars of Kantian ethics are arguing that Aristotle and Kant have much more in common than one might think. In other words it is not Aristotle vs. Kant or Aristotle or Kant but Aristotle and Kant. It is significant that three of the major Kantian ethics scholars Allen Wood, Barbara Herman and Christine Korsgaard have taken this line. Since Wood and Korsgaard/Herman have quite different interpretations of Kantian ethics, I find it interesting that all three of these Kant scholars are looking for ways to join Aristotle and Kant or at least to see some possibilities for connections. Marcia Baron has gone even further. In her 2003 Presidential address to the Central Division of the American Philosophical Association entitled "Manipulativeness,"[43] she says that she shows her Kantian colors but takes an Aristotelian approach. I will not comment further on Baron's address but I will say a bit about the work that Wood, Korsgaard and Herman are doing to bridge the gap between Aristotle and Kant.

As a foundation Korsgaard argues that for both Kant and Aristotle it is "the action that is either good or bad, noble or base."[44] Korsgaard goes so far as to say

---

[43] Baron, Marcia. (2003). "*Manipulativeness.*" Newark, DE: *Proceeding and Addresses of the American Philosophical Association*, 77(2), 37–54.

[44] Korsgaard, Christine M. (2009). *Self-Constitution: Agency, Identity and Integrity.* Oxford: Oxford University Press, 12.

that for both Aristotle and Kant the objects of choice are actions done for the sake of ends and that it is actions that are the bearers of moral value.[45] And Wood argues that Kant agrees with Aristotle that virtue involves desire for the right things and for pleasure and the avoidance of pain.[46] Wood points out that Kant shares many of Aristotle's views on the nature of virtue, including (1) A person is more virtuous the greater the inner strength of that person's will in resisting temptations to transgress duties, (2) virtue as acquired through practicing virtuous actions (3) that the typical temperament of virtue is joyous. In sum Wood maintains that for Kant and for Aristotle, the principle desires from which we act in being virtuous are *rational* desires.[47] In addition Korsgaard points out that she sees "no reason to doubt that Aristotle thinks that once the relevant features of the action are completely specified in its logos, it has the property of universality-that is, it would be the proper action for anyone in exactly the circumstances specified."[48] Finally, Korsgaard makes the following statement: "Kant has no more use for general rules than Aristotle does."[49] The notion that Kant's moral philosophy is a system of absolute rules as it was characterized by the late James Rachels rests on a misunderstanding of Kant. The categorical imperative is a test for proposed maxims of actions rather than a supreme principle from which rules of conduct can be derived. This point is made emphatically by Wood.[50]

Herman begins her previously mentioned book *Moral Literacy*, by arguing that Kantian ethics needs an account of moral character. Let me flesh out her view a bit more that I did earlier in this chapter. To do this, Herman wants to argue that the relation between desire and reason as motivating devices is much more complex than most interpreters have realized. Desires are not the simple things they are often pictured to be but are complex having evolved through social experience and having embedded within them a notion of the object of desired value. To this extent Herman is one with Wood in showing that the traditional picture of acting from duty is an oversimplified view. What Kantian reason adds to desire so understood is what Herman calls a deliberative field where the human agent can reflect on desire and determine whether seeking the object of desire is morally appropriate. Herman puts it this way:

"In an agent with a moral character, the motive of duty is *dispersed* in the motives that satisfy the constraints of the deliberative field."[51] As I indicated earlier, for Herman's Kant the good will acting out of duty, moral education, character and the virtues are all linked. And in any such linkage there must be a linkage between Kant and Aristotle.

---

[45] Ibid., 18.

[46] Wood, op.cit., 145.

[47] Ibid., 146.

[48] Korsgaard, op,cit., 17.

[49] Ibid., 15.

[50] Wood, op.cit, Chap. 3.

[51] Herman, *Moral Literacy* 21.

Business ethicists cannot be experts or even read all the scholarship on all the great ethicists and also properly understand the business disciplines. I have some very practical advice for my colleagues. If you take the perspective of one of the great ethicists become intimately familiar with the scholarship on that figure. Then apply that scholarship to the domain of business ethics. Avoid at all costs spending time criticizing the research of other business ethicists who have taken a great ethicist different from your own as a foundation for his or her work. I give this advice because your criticisms will seem simple-minded and off the mark to those others who know the scholarship on their chosen ethicist. Quite candidly for once in my life I followed my own advice and have limited my criticism of other philosophers to business ethics pragmatists who have consistently challenged my attempt to use Kant as a foundation for a theory of business ethics. Ironically, in preparing my rebuttal I have come to accept R Edward Freeman's contention that I am more of a pragmatist than I thought. For more on the sense in which I am and am not a pragmatist, see Chap. 5.

Kantian Accounts of Corporate Social Responsibility

Although I have discussed corporate social responsibility on a number of occasions including *Business Ethics* co-authored with Ronald Duska and in *Management Ethics* as well as in Chap. 6 of this volume, I have never specifically used Kantian ethics as the ground for the discussion. Recently there have been two contributions to the discussion of corporate social responsibility. The first is by Jeffery Smith.[52] In *Business Ethics: A Kantian Perspective*, I had argued that a business organization should be viewed as a moral community and that managers had an imperfect duty of beneficence to their corporate stakeholders. However, I did not elaborate on just what that duty consists of and how extensive it is. In his "Corporate Duties of Virtue: Making (Kantian) Sense of Corporate Social Responsibility," Smith provides an argument to show that corporations have an imperfect duty of social responsibility. He does this through a careful reading of the Kantian texts on the duty of beneficence as well as some recent Kantian scholarship on that topic. As a result of that analysis Smith argues that "the duty of beneficence is a duty regarding how moral agents should deliberate about how to live". At the corporate level, then, the duty requires that managers "integrate concern for others in their commercial dealings." Integrating this concern into corporate decision making provides a rich account of corporate social responsibility. Smith's contribution is an important expansion of the Kantian project to a topic in business ethics that has not often been viewed from the perspective of a major ethical theory. I am unaware, for example, of an Aristotelian account of

---

[52] Smith, Jeffery. (2012). "Corporate Duties of Virtue: Making (Kantian) Sense of Corporate Social Responsibility" in Denis Arnold and Jared Harris (eds.), *Kantian Business Ethics: Critical Perspectives*. Cheltenham: Edward Elgar Publishing, 59–75.

corporate social responsibility. Smith's essay is solidly grounded in the Kantian text and Kantian scholarship while providing a clear and managerially sound account of corporate social responsibility. There is no separation thesis here. I am happy to concur with his analysis and the conclusions based on it.

Another paper on this topic is "A Neo-Kantian Foundation of Social Responsibility", by Wim Dubbink and Luc van Liedekerke.[53] Many have argued that corporations have a social responsibility to improve society. However, is this responsibility a moral duty or is it voluntary-something it would be nice for corporations to do? In *Business Ethics: A Kantian Perspective*, I argued the traditional Kantian line that there is a genuine imperfect duty to help improve society but there was great latitude in how often the duty was to be acted upon and on what actions the duty to improve society might actually require. In "A Neo-Kantian Foundation of Social Responsibility" the authors ground the morality of social responsibility in political theory-specifically in free market democratic liberalism. For them, Kant's political theory and the political philosophy of his neo-Kantian followers provide the ground, while I tried to derive the obligations directly from Kant's ethical theory. Dubbink and Liedekerke begin with Kant's distinction between the duties of Right and the duties of Virtue. The former are duties imposed by law and necessary for a civil society. The latter are requirements of virtue. Are the duties of virtue morally required? Is the requirement to help others mandatory? These scholars think that at least some set of the duties of virtue are required and if that is the case, there are duties of virtue that are required and duties of virtue that are voluntary. If I understand this argument correctly, it would mean that some specific imperfect duties would always be required just as perfect duties are. However, Dubbink and Liedekerke think that the focus on the imperfect/perfect distinction is not as helpful in making their point as the distinction between duties of Right and duties of Virtue. The issue for them is whether "individuals must independently acknowledge the full set of general rules, otherwise morality would no longer be about self-governance."[54] As I understand it, they argue that some duties of virtue are always duties in the sense that they must be considered when acting. In other words, whenever the executives of a company make decisions, the duty to consider how society is affected is always present. However, in some (many?), cases any duty to improve society is trumped by other considerations. I believe this approach has much in common with the general theoretic position of Barbara Herman in *Moral Literacy*.

In addition with respect to the content of the duty to improve society, Dubbink and Liedekerke, believe that these non voluntary duties of virtue are socially determined rather than determined by individuals acting independently and in isolation. After all the kingdom of ends is a social concept. This paper fits well with the renewed interest in Kant's political philosophy and his views on duty in the *Metaphysics of Morals*. It is also grounded in the work of contemporary Kant

---

[53] Dubbink, W. and L. van Liedekerke. (2009). "A Neo-Kantian Conceptualization of CSR," *Ethical Theory and Moral Practice,* XII(2), 117–136.

[54] Ibid., 130.

scholars particularly, as mentioned, the work of Barbara Herman. Although I am completing a paper that uses the traditional perfect imperfect distinction to specify what is required of corporations to help society, I find the Dubbink/Liedekerke approach to be innovative and thought provoking.

Another debate about corporate social responsibility is whether corporations can be held to be sufficiently like persons to be held morally responsible. Dubbink and Smith consider this issue from a Kantian perspective in their paper "A Political Account of Corporate Social Responsibility."[55] In this article Dubbink and Smith revisit an issue that has longed plagued business ethicists, Does a business organization have the necessary and sufficient characteristics of personhood so that it can be held morally responsible independently of any individual or individuals in the corporation. John Ladd and Manny Velasquez were among the early scholars who claimed that a corporation did not have those characteristics. However, in a series of articles, Peter French argued that a corporate internal decision structure did provide a sufficient analogy to human personhood so that a corporation could be held morally responsible.[56]

Dubbink and Smith propose a set of weaker conditions that would still allow us to speak of corporations per se of either taking or not taking ethical decisions into account. And surprising they appeal to Kantian theory to do so. I say surprisingly because Kant's theory of ascribing moral responsibility intuitively is very strict. They argue that we humans have reason to look upon corporations as administrators of duty. "Corporations are administrators of duty to the extent that citizens come to expect that the corporation will take into account a relevant set of moral principles when it renders a judgment or decision about what course of action to take."[57] For Dubbink and Smith, corporate moral responsibility is not about making moral judgments of praise or blame or even of being held accountable for legal sanctions. They note correctly that Kant's ethics cannot say much about that because, as Kant observed, it is very hard to determine a person's true motive. With that in mind what Dubbink and Smith need to show is that corporations per se have the ability to take into account moral factors in their decision making process. It should be noted that they accept as fact that corporations have a corporate internal decision making structures along the lines that French presented. The crux of their argument then seems to be as follows:

1. Corporations are capable of rational action planning. Observation and Corporate Internal Decision Making Structures
2. Corporations can act on reasons Observation

---

[55] Dubbink, W. and J. Smith. (2011). "A Political Account of the Corporation as a Morally Responsible Actor," *Ethical Theory and Moral Practice*, XIV(2), 223–246.

[56] Ladd, John. (1970). "Morality and the Idea of Rationality in Formal Organizations," *The Monist*, 54(4), 47–60 and Velasquez, Manuel. (2003). "Debunking Moral Responsibility," *Business Ethics Quarterly*, 13, 531–562; French, Peter. (1979). "The Corporation as a Moral Person," *American Philosophical Quarterly*, 16(3), 207–215.

[57] Dubbink and Smith. "A Political Account of the Corporation as a Morally Responsible Actor," p. 233.

3. Corporations can act on moral reasons, because there is nothing special that distinguishes moral reasons from other kinds of reasons. Analogy
4. The moral reasons that a corporation must take into account are dictated by society Observation
5. 1–4 are sufficient to say that corporations are able to take ethical considerations into account in their decision making capacity.

What corporations cannot do is reflectively endorse the moral principles. Corporations are not persons to that extent. Later in the paper, Dubbink and Smith point out that it is one thing to adopt an ethical principle as a reason and quite another to justify that principle or the use of that principle in a particular case. Given their comments about endorsement, I assume they think that corporations cannot give justifications for principles. But I am not convinced here. Is it meaningful to speak of a corporation justifying a principle of finance, accounting or marketing? I think it is? Then why can't it give a justification of a moral principle as well. See premise 3 in the argument above. What I am arguing is that if the corporate internal decision-making structure is good enough to ground corporate reasons, it is good enough to provide justification for the reasons it adopts. Either a corporate decision structure works for both or it works for neither. The rub of course is that a corporation is not a conscious being so it cannot reflectively endorse. That, I suppose is why we have premise 4. But doesn't any kind of rational decision making presuppose either consciousness or something sufficiently analogous? I assume that the corporate internal decision structure is what is supposed to be sufficiently analogous. Whether the corporation internal decision structure is sufficiently analogous returns us to the original debate.

As to whether a company can also justify a moral principle if it can comply with a moral principle, Dubbink in correspondence responded as follows: You are right to argue that if a corporation can comply with a moral principle, it can also justify a moral principle-even if we would say that the actual work is done by human beings. Yet we would like to make a distinction between complying with moral principles, justifying moral principles, and grounding moral principles. Grounding is not justifying. It is more like "self-constitution" in Korsgaard's sense. That is an interesting move and the business ethics community should look forward to more elaboration on the importance of the distinction among these three concepts.

Let me return to the earlier issue of corporate personhood. Dubbink and Smith have tried to finesse the metaphysical question of corporate personhood be letting the moral principles be determined by society and thus eliminating the need for justification. In correspondence with Professor Dubbink on this issue, he stated that "We want to get away from ontology as far as possible. So what corporations are or are not is unimportant to us." However, from my perspective that simply makes the theory of corporate personhood too thin. However, my correspondence with Dubbink throws some additional light on this point. A corporation per se cannot constitute itself because corporations work through proxies (human agents). Thus, corporations are different from human agents. They are "administrators of duty." Upon further reflection, I think that Dubbink and Smith are really closer to the view of

Ladd and Velasquez than it might appear at first. Obviously there is great potential here to reopen the corporate personhood debate and the Dubbink/Smith Kantian twist is a genuine contribution to the debate.

Conclusion

I continue to believe as I said in *Business Ethics: A Kantian Perspective* that the great ethicists such as Aristotle, Kant, and John Stuart Mill have something important to contribute to applied ethics in general and to business ethics in particular. After all if ethical theory cannot be applied by people in their daily lives as they struggle with ethical issues, then we need to rethink whether in fact these ethicists really do have significant ethical theories. Of course these theories cannot be applied deductively and in the absence of a consideration of context and situation. Applied ethics is not simply a matter of reaching into the ethical theory tool box and picking the right theory to immediately fix an ethical dilemma. But an ethical theory can help especially once the ethical situation confronting a person or institution is fully examined. All these theories make important contributions but I continue to believe that Kant's ethical theory is the one that is most robust in business ethics. I am delighted that others find his work inspiring in that regard as well.

Chapter 5
Limitations of the Pragmatist Approach to Business Ethics

Background

Over the past 20 years, the most spirited conversations I have had about the appropriate foundation for business ethics are with the postmodernists and the pragmatists. It all began with my 1990 Ruffin Lecture talk at the Darden School the University of Virginia. It was there that I first introduced my initial thoughts on Kantian capitalism. I recall heated criticisms from the feminists, continental philosophers of many stripes and the pragmatists. We argued about whether we needed a foundation for business ethics, whether objectivity was possible in ethics, whether Kantian universal principles protected human rights or undermined them. People took sides and cheered on the spokespersons for their side. I came away from that conference knowing that the Enlightenment values that I resonated with and found in Kant were out of fashion and needed a vigorous defense. The lecture was published in 1998 as "A Kantian Theory of Capitalism" in a special issue of *Business Ethics Quarterly*.[1] Andrew Wicks, with whom I have had a spirited conversation on these topics over the years offered a reply.

As I indicated in Chap. 4, during this same 20 year period, a number of outstanding philosophers, many of whom were students of John Rawls interpreted, reinterpreted,

---

The material on pages 2–7 of this chapter is as slightly revised version of material that was originally published as part of the longer article "Postmodernism, Business Ethics, and Solidarity," in *Applied Ethics in a Troubled World*, E Morsher et al. (eds) 1998 Kluwer Academic Publishers, pp. 179–193. Reprinted by Permission of Springer. Some additional material is from my review of *Stakeholder Theory: The State of the Art*, R. Edward Freeman, Jeffrey S Harrison, Andrew C Wicks, Bidhan L Parmar, and Simone de Colle, *Business Ethics Quarterly* 2012, V. 22 #1 pp. 179–198. The material included in this Chapter includes the section "The Methodology of Stakeholder Theory: Criticisms and Responses", pp. 182–183 and the first seven paragraphs of the section "Should Stakeholder Theorists Adopt a Pragmatist Methodology", pp. 183–184. Reprinted by Permission of *Business Ethics Quarterly*.

[1] Bowie, Norman E. "A Kantian Theory of Capitalism," *Business Ethics Quarterly*, Special Issue #1 (This Special Issue Does Not Have a Date attached), 37–60. Andrew Wicks' reply is "How Kantian a Kantian Theory of Capitalism?" is found on 63–75.

N.E. Bowie, *Business Ethics in the 21st Century*, Issues in Business Ethics 39, DOI 10.1007/978-94-007-6223-7_5, © Springer Science+Business Media Dordrecht 2013

and defended Kantian ethics. Christine Korsgaard, Thomas Hill Jr. Barbara Herman and Onora O'Neill all wrote impressive books that greatly influenced my own thinking. In the first decade of the twenty-first century three of these four scholars have produced second books that have built an even more sophisticated view of Kantian ethics-in part by building bridges between Kant and Aristotle. In addition to these Rawlsians, Allen Wood has provided his own interpretation of Kantian ethics that shares features with the Rawlsians but also departs from them in significant respects. It is fair to say that within philosophical circles these scholars have made Kant respectable again.

Unfortunately, few of my colleagues in business ethics have had the time to read this vast treasure trove of Kantian ethics scholarship. After all they had their own theoretical perspectives to keep current with. The downside of limited time however, is the fact that many criticisms of the Kantian project in business ethics rest on outdated views of Kant's position. In this Chapter, I will not review these criticisms that are based on outdated readings of Kant's ethical theory. I do spend some time in Chap. 4 "Kantian Themes" addressing some of these issues.

In this Chapter, I will move from the defense to the offense and criticize the pragmatist approach to business ethics. That approach is represented in philosophy by Richard Rorty and in business ethics by my colleague and friend R. Edward Freeman and by many of Freeman's students but especially Andrew Wicks. Note that I will not be responding to the feminist critiques of Kant and the Enlightenment nor to those Continental philosophers who see themselves as opponents to the Anglo-American analytic tradition. Before undertaking this task however, I must say that the conversation has become a lot less heated than it was in 1990. In 2009, during a special session of the Society for Business Ethics devoted to my research, Freeman argued that in many ways I was a pragmatist and should endorse the pragmatist approach to business ethics. Quite frankly Freeman made a number of good points and perhaps I am more of a pragmatist than I realize. Freeman's comments on that occasion and my response were published in a festshrift in late 2012.[2] A Kantian with pragmatist leanings or sympathies is less bizarre than you might think. Lewis White Beck, a Kantian if there ever was one, also admired the work of C. I Lewis, a pragmatist. However, I remain convinced that pragmatism has epistemological and normative difficulties that prevent me from shifting allegiances. Some of these difficulties came to mind when I read and reviewed *Stakeholder Theory: The State of the Art* written by Freeman and several of his former students and colleagues. Let this Chapter be a review of some of the difficulties I have with pragmatism as an approach to ethics and specifically to business ethics. I have organized the Chapter as follows: First I will provide selections from my "Postmodernism, Business Ethics and Solidarity."[3] That piece was primarily a critique of Rorty's

---

[2] Arnold, Denis and Jared Harris. (2012). *Kantian Business Ethics: Critical Perspectives.* Cheltenham: Edward Elgar Publishing.

[3] Bowie, Norman E. (1998). "Postmodernism, Business Ethics, and Solidarity" in E Morcher et al. (eds.), *Applied Ethics in a Troubled World.* Dordrecht: Kluwer Academic Publishers, 179–193.

Contingency, Irony and Solidarity[4] published in 1989. I will then consider Rorty's 2005 invited address to the Society for Business Ethics later published in *Business Ethics Quarterly* with excellent comments by Richard De George, Daryl Koehn, and Patricia Werhane.[5] I conclude with considerations on the conversations and publications by R Edward Freeman and his students over the past 20 years.

Rorty's *Contingency, Irony, and Solidarity*

Many of us who were in graduate school in the 1960s remember the tightly reasoned arguments for mind-body identity theory that Richard Rorty provided. It was my pleasure to get to know Rorty personally when I served as Executive Director of the American Philosophical Association and Rorty served for part of that time as Chair of the standing committee The Status and Future of the Profession. The philosophical community had great difficulty accepting Rorty's interest in postmodernism and his acceptance of pragmatism. He left the Philosophy Department at Princeton and took a position as University Professor of Humanities at the University of Virginia. After providing a summary of Rorty's position in *Contingency, Irony, and Solidarity*, I will argue that Rorty's emphasis on literature has led him astray in his epistemology. Although strongly influenced by Dewey, Rorty forgot that Dewey insisted that artistic creation was a doing and undergoing in response to an artistic medium. The artist usually cannot just impose his or her idea on the medium, the medium constrains what the artist can accomplish. Literature imposes the least constraints of any of the arts.[6] However, in sculpture or pottery the medium places severe constraints on what the artist can accomplish. This fact has been vividly driven home to me by the fortunate fact that I have been married for over 25 years to a master ceramic sculptor and have watched her test the limits of what you can do with clay and glass.

 Contingency, Irony and Solidarity begins with a claim of radical contingency "...where we treat everything-our language, our conscience, our community-as a product of time and chance."[7] Rorty claims that Wittgenstein had adopted such a position with respect to language. Rorty believes that the acceptance of radical contingency undermines the notion of objective truth. "The truth cannot be out there-cannot exist independently of the human mind-because sentences cannot so exist or

---

[4] Rorty, Richard. (1989). *Contingency, Irony and Solidarity*. Cambridge: Cambridge University Press.

[5] Rorty, Richard. (2006). "Is Philosophy Relevant in Applied Ethics," *Business Ethics Quarterly*, 16(3), 369–380. Also in the same issue are replies to Rorty's argument. See, Richard De George, "The Relevance of Philosophy in Business Ethics," 381–389, Daryl Koehn, "A Response to Rorty," 391–399 and Patricia H. Werhane, "A Place for Philosophy in Applied Ethics," 401–408.

[6] Although literature does provide some constraints as Wim Dubbink pointed out in his review of this manuscript.

[7] Rorty, *Contingency and Irony*, 22.

be out there. The world is out there, but descriptions of the world are not."[8] Except for the emphasis on language, I frankly think that so far there is much in common with Rorty's position and Kant's position in the first Critique-an ironic turn of events. After all for Kant we can never know the world beyond our experience, the "selbst an sich". But then Rorty departs widely from Kant.

From this understanding of truth, Rorty goes on to paint a non-traditional picture of science. Science does not discover truth about the world. Rather, "great scientists invent descriptions of the world which are useful for purposes of predicting and controlling what happens."[9] Pragmatists are less interested in having science discover Truth and more interested in what science can accomplish to make life better for people through its methods to explain and predict. But Rorty is not content to leave matters here. He goes on to argue that even successfully invented descriptions that enable us to explain and predict do not get us any closer to truth.

Rorty claims there is no sense in which any of these descriptions is an accurate representation of the way the world is in itself. "…the world does not provide us with any criterion of choice between alternative metaphors, that we can only compare languages or metaphors with one another, not with something beyond language called fact".[10]

It is here that Rorty's argument seems invalid. Even if science is about inventing metaphors that enable us to explain and predict, it does not follow that the world does not provide criteria that enable us to compare metaphors. Some metaphors are successful at explaining and predicting and some are unsuccessful. What accounts for the difference? Surely nothing intrinsic to the metaphor. The difference results because some metaphors are more accurately in tune with the world or they come closer to picturing how the world is. If a scientific metaphor would have us approach the world as if the world contained contradictions, the metaphor would fail and the metaphor would fail because a world where explaining and predicting can occur is not a world where there can be contradictions. Perhaps science does not get us to truth with a capital T about the world, but unsuccessful scientific metaphors certainly tell us some things that are false about the world. Scientific metaphors which do not enable us to explain and predict do not get it right about the world.

If scientific language is metaphorical and not able to get us to objective knowledge about the world , it should come as no surprise that Rorty maintains that language about ourselves and about communities is similarly metaphorical and similarly unable to get us to truth. Ethical claims suffer the same fate. Rorty believes that it is wrong to be cruel, but he admits that on his view there can be no arguments for the belief. "For liberal ironists, there is no answer to the question "Why not be cruel?"-no noncircular theoretical backup for the belief that cruelty is horrible."[11]

There can be no argument because what counts as good reasons is historically and socially contingent on Rorty's view. It may not be too strong to say that such

[8] Ibid., 5.
[9] Ibid., 4.
[10] Ibid., 20.
[11] Ibid., xv.

radical contingency undermines the distinction between what is rational and what is irrational. For Rorty, it certainly seems to be the case that what count as rational is historically and socially contingent. Rorty abandons reason and argument in the traditional sense that reason provides objectivity, but he certainly does not end up in nihilism. Societies are bound together by common hopes and common vocabularies. But how do societies with different languages and different values communicate with and appreciate one another? Through the ability of imagination, especially the ability to imagine the humiliation that others feel when their vocabulary is not taken seriously.[12] If we are on the look out for "marginalized people" we can develop our imagination. As a result we forge a solidarity with others rather than recognize solidarity. Solidarity is made rather then seen.

I agree that solidarity is an important good and I think it is made although I also think it is seen. It is seen when we recognize another human being as a person in Kant's sense-a person who should be treated with respect and never used merely as a means. Rorty's use of imagination as a way of gaining solidarity strikes me as rather naïve. Compare Rorty to David Hume when Hume said that we care more about losing the tip of one of our fingers than we do about the starvation death of thousands in a far away land. Alas I think human history including contemporary history shows that Hume is a lot closer to the mark than Rorty. For my own part, I want to argue that solidarity is more readily created through trade and business relationships, for example. To evaluate this suggestion we will need to consider Rorty's specific remarks about business. First I want to suggest that Rorty's radical contingency results in part because he appeals to the wrong art form- to literature rather than ceramic sculpture.

Why Literature Misleads

Rorty emphasizes the creativity of interpretive metaphors but he ignores the constraints that a medium puts on the artist. As a result Rorty overemphasized the freedom that we have to interpret the world and consequently he finds more subjectivity and less objectivity than he would if he used a different art form as his metaphor. His appeal to literature might be expected from an intellectual who began his career as a linguistic philosopher and then became a professor of literature who engages primarily in literary interpretation. The writer of poems and novels works in a medium that puts few constraints on the artist. Often creative figures in literature enlarge the field by abandoning the conventional structures that constitute what makes a "good" poem or novel.

It might be useful to contrast the poet and the novelist with the sculptor and the potter. Marble and clay put many more constraints on the artist. These artistic media confine what can be said. There constraints occur at a number of levels. First, as is

---

[12] Ibid., 92.

true with any medium, certain things cannot be expressed. A novel can't sing and a sculpture can't dance. (Of course artists can try to create a novel that appears to sing or a sculpture that appears to dance.) Second certain ways of saying things are causally impossible in granite and clay. If the grain of the marble goes one way, the sculptor must work with the grain. The artist who decides to interpret her idea by "disobeying" the constraints imposed by the fault lines in the marble will not reinterpret the world. She will shatter the marble and that is a matter of objective fact. Similarly a potter cannot fire a wet clay figure. A potter who does not dry her clay sufficiently will not reinterpret pottery. She will have a figure that explodes in the kiln. An artist working in molten glass must anneal it properly or it will break. An artist who tries to speed up the process will not have a new work of art. She will have pieces of broken or shattered glass. Third, certain uses of the medium are universally not accepted. For example, a pot thrown on the wheel is either centered or not centered. No one instructs a student to throw a wobbly pot. A similar consideration arises in bronze casting. A final casting that does not look like the prototype is a failure. It is not seen as a new work of art. Fourth, most works of art are the result of the cooperative actions of the artist with the medium. A sculptor has an idea for carving a horse of a certain type with the head cocked just so and with the mane flying in the wind. The sculptor, unlike the poet who simply writes out her ideas, cannot just pick up a piece of marble and start creating the desired horse. The sculptor needs to pick out the right piece of marble, namely that marble that the artist believes can be sculpted into a horse. But selecting the right marble is not the end of the story. Once the sculpting process begins, the artist finds that she cannot carry out her ideas for the horse in the exact detail she had hoped. The marble will simply not accept all her original ideas in their detail. The sculptor is then forced by the medium to rethink her ideas. As the horse is sculpted, there is a continual transformation of the artist's ideas of what she originally wanted the horse to be. The master sculptor does not impose an idea on the marble. The master sculptor works with the marble to give birth to an idea that in a real sense is in part the marble's. Michelangelo eloquently describes this position as "liberating the figure from the marble that imprisons it."[13] As Aristotle might have said, the artist makes the potential within the marble actual. A piece of marble has the potential to be sculpted into a number of forms. But it cannot be sculpted into any form the artist wants it to take and the form that the marble takes is almost never simply a manifestation of the original idea of the sculptor. The sculpted piece is a cooperative result of the work of the artist and the potentialities of the medium.

The aesthetic theory that best captures what I have in mind is the theory of John Dewey-ironically an pragmatist hero of Rorty's. Dewey gives the medium a central place in his aesthetic theory. "The connection between a medium and the act of expression is intrinsic."[14] And the work of art that is created is the shared result of the interaction of the artist with the medium. "The painting as a picture is *itself a*

---

[13] As quoted in (1986) *History of Art*, 3rd ed. H.W. Janson (ed.). New York: Harty N Abrams Inc.
[14] Dewey, John. (1958 Originally published 1934). *Art as Experience*. New York: Capricon Books.

total effect brought about by the interaction of external and organic causes."[15] Aesthetic creation for Dewey is understood as having the same structure as any kind of experience. An experience is the result of a shared interaction between the knower who has the experience and the world that is experienced. The philosopher who ignores the world fails to understand the nature of experience. "There are therefore common patterns in various experiences, no matter how unlike they are to one another in the details of the subject matter. There are conditions to be met without which an experience cannot come to be. The outline of the common pattern is set by the fact that every experience is the result of interaction between a live creature and some aspect of the world in which he lives."[16]

What I am suggesting is that if we shift the metaphor from literature to sculpture or pottery, we can have a more robust notion of objectivity. Social institutions have a history but they cannot develop any old which way. There are constraints on what constitutes a society or an institution. As I have argued against relativism, with respect to basic norms, a society does not define morality; the existence of certain moral norms enables us to identify a society as such. If an anthropologist arrives on an island and the people on the north side of the island do not rape, pillage and kill others on the north side but they do rape, pillage and kill those on the south side of the island, you have two societies. You cannot have a society if people within it are permitted to rape, pillage and kill. So we need to look for those universals that transcend historical and social contingency.[17]

I have used this strategy of showing that ethical norms must be presupposed to explain the phenomenon in question in an analysis of capitalism itself, arguing that there are certain moral norms that must hold in a capitalist society if capitalist institutions are to thrive or even survive. And I have found Kantian moral philosophy to be useful in looking for those moral universals that must exist behind any capitalist system.[18]

Rorty's Address Before the Society for Business Ethics

In 2005 Richard Rorty was invited to address the annual meeting for the Society for Business Ethics. In that address he began with themes that were developed in *Contingency, Irony and Solidarity*. He questioned the notions of truth and objectivity in both science and ethics just as he had done in that book. He also remained focused

---

[15] Ibid., 250.

[16] Ibid., 43–44.

[17] Bowie, Norman E. (1997). "Relativism, Cultural and Moral" in Patricia H. Werhane and R. Edward Freeman (eds.), *Blackwell Encyclopedic Dictionary of Business Ethics*. Malden: Blackwell Publishing Inc, 554.

[18] Bowie, Norman E. (1994). "Economics and The Enlightenment: Then and Now" in Alan Lewis and Karl-Erik Warneryd (eds.), *Ethics and Economic Affairs*. London: Routledge, 348–366. This argument has subsequently appeared in a number of other articles.

on imagination and stated that he was more impressed with poetry than philosophy. 2006 is a long time since 1989. Rorty had been criticized for being a relativist and although as we saw above, he denied it, that denial hardly stopped the criticisms. In my opinion Rorty did little to put these critics to rest in his SBE address. Here are a few sample quotations:

> For what counts as justification, either of actions or of beliefs, is always relative to the antecedent beliefs of those whom one is seeking to convince. Anti-slavery arguments that we find completely persuasive would probably not have convinced Jefferson or Aristotle.
> Analogously the Mongol horde was perfectly justified in gang-raping the women of Baghdad, given their other beliefs.
> We are no closer to absolute justification for our moral beliefs than was Genghis Khan. We justify our actions and beliefs to each other by appealing to our own lights-to the intuitions fostered at our time and place. The Mongols did the same.[19]

All these quotations reflect the radical historical contingency that I discussed at the beginning. I cannot resist the temptation to point out that the historical evidence indicates that Jefferson as well as Madison and Monroe-especially Monroe were convinced by the anti-slavery arguments. All three had grave doubts about slavery even though they were slave owners. I would argue that on the historical record these founding fathers suffered more from a weakness of will. They did not think the pro slavery arguments were justified despite their other beliefs. It is somewhat surprising that a University Professor at the University of Virginia would get the history wrong.

One of my many criticisms of Rorty is that he confuses a psychological point with a logical point. Rorty says, "The Platonic idea that we can learn how to be morally infallible by seeking coherence among our beliefs survives in the Kantian idea that a Nazi or Mafioso, could if he reflected long enough, break out of the culture in which he was raised by detecting his own irrationality."[20]

Kant's point was a logical one not a psychological one. Kant believed that the categorical imperative provided a rational test for those who were perplexed by what they ought to do. Kant was as skeptical as Rorty regarding human nature's ability to rationalize and to fail to escape not only the bounds of his or her culture but his or her self-interest as well. What is surprising to me is how Rorty can justify his notion that there has been moral progress. He thinks we have made moral progress because we have invented new forms of human life. "Moral progress is not, on this pragmatist view, a matter of getting clearer about something that was there all the time. Rather we make ourselves into new kinds of people by inventing new forms of human life."[21]

First of all I see no way for Rorty to say that a new form of human life is progress. Are all the changes in moral attitude progress? The invention of the birth control pill arguably was progress because it liberated married people to greater enjoyment in their sexual life. But is the phenomenon of promiscuous hooking up

---

[19] Rorty, "Is Philosophy Relevant in Applied Ethics?" 371–372.
[20] Ibid., 372.
[21] Ibid., 373.

so common on college campuses progress? Second, suppose we concede that when slavery was predominant, it would be hard to convince someone in a slave holding culture that slavery was wrong. However, what about people who traffic in children today. Aren't the traffickers wrong, really wrong, regardless of what they believe?

Naturally Rorty's skepticism toward ethical theory and moral reasoning carries over to applied ethics and of course to the field of business ethics. He has much praise for Patricia Werhane's book *Moral Imagination and Management Decision Making* since as we have seen imagination is key in Rorty's view in both epistemology and ethics. He also praises Ronald Duska for "suggesting that the principal products of the business ethics community should be, on the one hand, inspiring stories of business heroes, suitably complemented by horror stories of business villains".[22] He also quotes with approval remarks by Laura Nash and Edwin Hartman that fit in with his views. Strangely from my point of view is the fact that he failed to mention the business ethicist R Edward Freeman whose views have been heavily influenced by Rorty and Freeman, in turn, has gone on to influence many students who hold a pragmatist position similar to his and who now teach at important universities.

Patricia Werhane does not accept Rorty's pragmatism and I do not believe Ronald Duska, who is much more of an Aristotelian, does either. I am much impressed by the work of those Rorty cites approvingly. However, in my opinion Rorty misses much that is important in business ethics. For example, my first question for Rorty would be, "What makes one a hero and what makes one a villain in business ethics?" I do not see that Rorty has any way of answering that question. Imagination per se is morally neutral. During the 2008 financial crisis, people used their imagination to devise all kinds of esoteric financial instruments that few people really understood. Was that use of imagination moral or immoral or perhaps amoral? How would Rorty go about answering that question?

We need to have more than imagination and stories about business heroes and villains. We need a vocabulary from ethical theory that enables us to tell those stories and that serves as a ground upon which moral imagination can work. The three colleagues who responded to Rorty's published address in BEQ all made this point in their own way.

Richard De George said, "What philosophers brought to the table that others had not was a systematic inquiry into our individual and collective moral experience in business." "Anyone who listens carefully to arguments and debates about public policy as well as about business and business practices will quickly see that the arguments typically refer either to consequences, or to rights, or to justice, or to human good and betterment. This is the language of moral discourse..."[23]

Daryl Koehn cleverly argues that Rorty's own position assumes that we are essentially rational beings. "It seems to me that Rorty also shows himself to be the kind of being for whom reason has motivating interests-if his self-respect did not

---

[22] Ibid., 377.

[23] De George, Richard T. (2006). "The Relevance of Philosophy to Business Ethics: A Response to Rorty's 'Is Philosophy Relevant to Applied Ethics?'" *Business Ethics Quarterly,* 16(3), 385, 386.

demand coherence, he would not be so concerned to maintain it in his writings."[24] Koehn also points to empirical work that shows that conceptualization may be more universal than Rorty imagines.[25]

Patricia Werhane makes a point similar to what I was trying to make with my artistic metaphors. There is something out there that constrains what we can experience. "…we cannot get at the data of our experience except through experiencing. But ordinarily, except when we are hallucinating, dreaming, or mentally ill, we do not create the whatever that we perceive."[26] Werhane also goes on to cite Adam Smith who invoked a justice (actually a sense of injustice) as something of a moral universal held by human kind.[27]

I think all these comments are on the mark and fit well with some of the points that I have made regarding Rorty's pragmatic view. Some of the arguments in Rorty's address really were not about pragmatic methodology but rather about whether philosophy or philosophers trained in ethical theory had anything special to offer business ethics. De George is surely right in saying that they do and the quotation cited above provides the kind of evidence that we need. In his response Rorty seems to agree. Most of us agree with Rorty that applied ethics including business ethics is a cooperative enterprise with many other disciplines. I note the importance of the social sciences and now the science of cognition. But historians, poets, literature, and I would add the arts all have roles to play.

Everyone agrees that history and culture influence the moral views that we have. Rorty argues that given where people stand in a history and culture, we cannot say that their views about a moral issue were wrong then. But I wonder. Let us consider the argument over segregation of the races in the United States. There are still a number of us alive who experienced that issue. Some of us were even active in bringing about change. Rorty would argue that we integrated the schools because we were better able to imagine what it was like to be a Black child in an inferior school. But that is not what happened. The change in attitude of the segregationists who did change came much later- years and years after the 1950s and 1960s. What brought about change was a Supreme Court that used data to show that "separate but equal" was not equal. What made the change happen faster were the brave African Americans and their white allies who argued that racial discrimination was wrong. Now one can understand how a person growing up in the segregated South in the 1950s would not be convinced by argument. But that is a psychological point not a logical point. The fact was that segregated schools were separate and unequal and that inequality that was based simply on the color of one's skin was wrong.

Secondly, Rorty has a set of beliefs about what constitutes as good society. He thinks that a non slave society is better than a slave society-really better. Ditto with

---

[24] Daryl, Koehn. (2006). "A Response to Rorty," *Business Ethics Quarterly,* 16(3), 393.

[25] Ibid., 395.

[26] Werhane, Patricia H. (2006). "A Place for Philosophers in Applied Ethics and the Role of Moral Reasoning in Moral Imagination: A Response to Rorty," *Business Ethics Quarterly,* 16(3), 406.

[27] Ibid.

a society that recognizes the rights of gays and lesbians.[28] The test for Rorty is what would happen if democracies were replaced by totalitarian societies. Would he think that history had changed and that the democrats were not wrong when democracy was considered to be the morally best form of government? I would suspect that if the world were totalitarian Rorty would still believe that democracy was a better form of government and I think Rorty would be right. It is worth pointing out that there is nothing inevitable about the survival of democracies. What would Rorty say if the conservative social right were able to tip the scale against marital rights for gays and lesbians? I dare say he would think that such changes were a regression away from a better society. Rorty sounds persuasive because he endorses the changes that many of us would say represent moral progress. He then closes his response to his critics by pointing out that someday it may be historically true that we no longer believe it is morally permissible to eat animals since they are not allowed to eat humans. Better treatment of animals even if we are not vegetarians is something most of us hope will come about. However, we think that our treatment of animals, the way chickens are raised for example, is wrong. Rorty ironically seems inflicted with the Enlightenment values of moral progress and optimism. He also seems "liberal" in not wanting to blame those who lived in different historical times. Perhaps he is right about not wanting to blame. After all Kant was not much into blame either. However, it is one thing to think that people in the past should not be blamed. It is quite another to think that their moral views about slavery or the domination of men, or discrimination against gays and lesbians were right. The test is to ask what would the pragmatist like Rorty say if history reversed? By the way there are some pretty good novels that describe possible worlds of totalitarianism and discrimination. And of course there are religious fundamentalists like the Taliban who would bring such changes about if they ever got the power to do so.

Rorty's direct contribution to business ethics is extremely limited. The truth is Rorty might properly be described as a democratic socialist. He was no fan of capitalism and I think he held the "Business sucks" view that R Edward Freeman thinks we should reject. Be that as it may Freeman clearly thinks the Rorty was right on some of the bigger questions of epistemology and ethics. However, in business ethics, Freeman is the central figure and it is worth pointing out that he is a convert. It is also worth pointing out that Freeman is a libertarian pragmatist. Rorty was not. No discussion of pragmatism in business ethics would be complete without discussing Freeman's views.

The Pragmatism of Ed Freeman and Some of His Students

As I indicated above, the pragmatist who has had the most influence on business ethics is R. Edward Freeman. Since his own pragmatist vision is so prominent in the field and since he has influenced so many doctoral students, it is even more important

---

[28] Rorty, op.cit., 413.

to come to grips with his version of pragmatism than it is to dissect Rorty's. Moreover, Freeman's version has a positive core about how business is to be managed on pragmatic grounds. Rorty always had a strong suspicion of capitalism in general and of business in particular. Freeman has been careful to avoid the "business sucks" story and to advance a pragmatist agenda for the successful and ethical manager.

The latest and most complete statement of Freeman's position is found in *Stakeholder Theory: The State of the Art* That book was written by Freeman and several of his students now colleagues. (Freeman was always exceedingly generous in co-authoring work with his students.) In that book the authors state explicitly that they look at stakeholder theory from the perspective of pragmatism. Let us see how Freeman and his colleagues put pragmatism to work in business ethics.

This book explicitly urges stakeholder theorists to adopt a pragmatist methodology. What would such a methodology look like?

> Pragmatists see the goal of inquiry as generating insights that help us to lead better lives.... In thinking about usefulness, the pragmatism of Wicks and Freeman encompasses two dimensions simultaneously: the epistemological (is it useful in terms of providing credible, reliable information on the subjects at issue?) and the normative (is it useful in making our lives better?).[29]

Despite its widespread intellectual and managerial acceptance, stakeholder theory has been subject to two main criticisms that have never been definitely answered in the literature. First, who is to count as a stakeholder? Second, how is it possible to manage (balance) all those stakeholder interests? For years, I have been pressing Freeman to provide his answers to these questions. Freeman promised me that *Stakeholder Theory: The State of the Art* would provide the answers. On first glance, I thought that the promise was unfulfilled. Relatively speaking, there are only a few pages in that book that address those questions.

Upon reflection, however, I realize that Freeman's answer to the questions is provided in large part by the pragmatic methodology adopted. I think Freeman would argue that if one is a pragmatist the objections lose much of their bite and may even dissolve.

Since there are a variety of business organizations and since any business finds itself in a variety of situations, who counts as a stakeholder depends on the situation. I believe that Freeman's answer to the first criticism or question, "Who counts as a stakeholder?" gets a pragmatic answer. There is no one "true" definition. Who counts as a stakeholder depends on the business and the issue it faces. Normally, of course, we can assume that employees, customers, suppliers, and the local community are stakeholders. In a publicly held corporation, the stockholders are stakeholders. But NGO's and government regulators could also be stakeholders in certain situations. The authors put it this way: "However, one way to think about the role of the definitional problem is to return to the pragmatic perspective when thinking about

---

[29] Freeman, R. Edward, Jeffrey S. Harrison, Andrew C. Wicks, Bidhan L. Parmar, Simone DeColle. (2010). *Stakeholder Theory: The State of the Art*. Cambridge: Cambridge University Press, 75.

the issues involved. Rather than seeing the definitional problem as a singular and fixed, admitting of one answer, we instead can see different definitions serving different purposes."[30]

As for the second questions, how are interests of the relevant stakeholders to be balanced, Freeman et al. say the following: (emphasis theirs)"**A stakeholder approach to business is about creating as much wealth as possible for stakeholders, without resorting to trade-offs.**"[31]

This question emerges again on pages 224–226. Here the authors simply point out that many of the biggest and most successful companies in fact practice stakeholder theory. The proof is in the pudding so to speak.

Should Stakeholder Theorists Adopt a Pragmatist Methodology?

My answer to that question is qualified. I remember my undergraduate professor defining pragmatism as a theory that says "one should believe and do whatever works." However, he quickly added that pragmatism has no theory of what works.

However, Freeman does have a theory of what works and it is closely related to Rorty's pragmatic account that Freeman quotes approvingly. What works for a business is what creates and promotes value specifically the values of freedom and solidarity.

But why those values? Why not the maximization of wealth as Friedman recommends? Can the pragmatist deny all foundationalism without ending in relativism? That is the danger although Freeman and his colleagues think they can avoid it. Freeman specifically rejects the relativism that comes with much of the anti-positivist approaches to science. "Anti-positivists elevate the human-ness of all inquiry, even that based in science, but it undercuts our ability to tackle the questions of values and meaning by making all points of view equally valid and any effort to establish a "better" or "best" narrative little more than a power grab."[32]

However, the social scientists in business schools would be suspicious of the view of science espoused in *Stakeholder Theory: The State of the Art*. The four central ideas of a pragmatist epistemology that Freeman and his colleagues endorse are (1) "the world is 'out there' but not objective", (2) "facts and sentences are intertwined", (3) all inquiry is fundamentally interpretive or narrative (4) "science is a kind of language game." "...Science is simply one more tool that can provide us with a set of narratives that can be incredibly useful as we sort out how to live well."[33] All this has a terribly subjective ring to it. What is required is some theory of objectivity even if it is not the objectivity of traditional science.

---

[30] Ibid., 211.
[31] Ibid., 28.
[32] Ibid., 74.
[33] Ibid., 73–74.

Unfortunately the book provides no account to overcome the suspicion. There are hints. One appears on page 74 that some kind of intersubjective agreement is being endorsed. This brings to mind Habermas and from American political science, the theory of "deliberative democracy." Unfortunately there is no intersubjective agreement on what it means to live well. And I see no way pragmatism can provide such a theory on its own. Freeman can appeal to freedom and solidarity. But what can a pragmatist like Freeman say when an opponent says that conformity to religious dogma rather than freedom of conscience is what it means to live well?

One of the standard functions of ethical theory is to tell us what it is to live well. A theory of living well is most explicit in Aristotle but it can also be garnered from philosophers like Kant and Rawls as well as from feminist moral theory. Freeman and his colleagues would endorse these theories as capable of providing a moral core for stakeholder theory. Indeed Freeman himself has been linked to a Kantian core, a Rawlsian core, a feminist core, and a libertarian core. If the only function of an ethical theory is to provide a normative core for stakeholder theory, then the emphasis of Chap. 7 on business ethics might make sense. I think most philosopher business ethics who have worked on ethical theory without explicit ties to stakeholder theory will feel that something is missing from the discussion and it is more than the fact that these business ethicists get hardly a mention or no mention at all. This is the only chapter in the book where there is little or no mention of several of the major players in the field under discussion. Fair enough if Freeman and his colleagues see the various ethical theories as simply providing different normative cores for stakeholder theory. If that is the case, then I think Freeman and his colleagues underestimate the value of ethical theory. What if these ethical theorists present an answer or answers to the pragmatists central question-namely a justified theory of what it means to live well? A terrorist state defending a religious orthodoxy is not simply an alternative narrative of how to live well. It is an incorrect or unjustified theory of how to live well. Ethical theory provides more than a normative core for a pragmatic view of stakeholder theory; it provides a justified account of what it means to live well and thus a justification for Freeman's values of freedom and solidarity.

In 2009 I was honored to have a session at the annual meeting of the Society for Business Ethics devoted to my research. Freeman was one of the speakers and he made a fairly persuasive case that I was (could be) a pragmatist. I do think social context and history matter. But within this contextual and historical milieu I think one must appeal to an ethical theory that can ground one's view of living well. A Kantian endorses both respect for persons and a community of moral persons bound by rules that are publicly advocated. A Freeman pragmatist focuses on freedom and solidarity. At the heart of Freeman's stakeholder theory is the principle of responsibility. At the heart of Kant's philosophy are freedom and autonomy and thus of responsibility. Are there significant differences here? I wonder. As a libertarian, Freeman certainly accepts the centrality of freedom and autonomy as the essence of his pragmatic account. I also think Freeman and his pragmatist students would endorse respect for persons and community under publicly advocated rules as well. If these values are the core of pragmatism than I guess Freeman is right. I am a pragmatist. However, I add to this pragmatist position the claim that Kantian moral philosophy provides a good justification for these pragmatic values. Indeed Kantian ethics is one way for those pragmatic values to be justified.

Freeman wants to get beyond old philosophical assumptions about language and reality and of being limited by "the trifecta of ethical theory, deontology, consequentialsim, and virtue, as the only way to frame problems." I don't disagree. As he intimates, I personally find the Kantian narrative a useful one but it is not the only one and certainly not the one and only true one. Kant's theory of what it is to be a human being worthy of respect may be limited. Some business practices that a Kantian theory might seem to endorse may not be the right ones. Certainly I do not envisage a Kantian business ethics as a rulebook for voting "yes" or "no" on specific practices. My central goal has been to tie Kantian theory to the actual business world-to show that Freeman is right when he says we should avoid the separation thesis. At his point in time with our knowledge from organizational behavior and strategy as to what constitutes good management practice, I want to argue that Kantian ethical theory is a pretty good fit.

Concluding Thought

Any argument about what is really right or good has to have an end point. Pragmatism either seems not to have an end point (whatever works) or it has an end point in terms of hope, freedom, solidarity, democracy etc. I want a foundation for these values. So I appeal to respect for persons, for example. But what if someone argues, "Why should we respect people?" That is a fair question and Kant tried to answer that question by appealing to rationality and autonomy. Kant argues that each of us believes that we have a dignity and are entitled to respect. To be a creature that has dignity and is entitled to self respect requires that one be an autonomous person. An autonomous person is free not only from responding mechanically to the laws of nature but positively free in the sense of being able to follow laws of ones own making. The formal condition for law in this sense is the categorical imperative. Being able to govern one's actions by the categorical imperative requires that one be a responsible person. Thus there is a conceptual link among autonomy, rationality, and responsibility. A creature so characterized is a creature with dignity and deserving of respect. Since each of us thinks of our self in this way, we must think of all other persons like us in this way and treat them as persons with dignity and entitled to respect. To do otherwise is to be irrational. Kant put it this way

> Rational nature exists as an end in itself. Man necessarily thinks of his own existence in this way, and thus far it is a subjective principle of human actions. Also every other rational being thinks of existence on the same rational ground which holds also for myself, thus it is at the same time an objective principle from which, as a supreme practical ground, it must be possible to derive all laws of the will.[34]

---

[34] Kant Immanuel. (1990, Originally published 1785). *Foundations of the Metaphysics of Morals.* New York: Macmillan, 36.

If this seems like a trick, another way to approach the issue is by a transcendental argument. A transcendental argument finds a premise that everyone accepts and then asks what must be true if that accepted premise is true. That is the strategy of Alan Gewirth.[35] Gewirth attacked the problem by pointing out the presuppositions of human action. Human action is purposive and each of us thinks that his purpose is good. Gewirth then asks what are the necessary conditions for human action? The necessary conditions for any human action are freedom and well-being. Without freedom and well being human beings cannot act and thus they cannot achieve their purposes. Since freedom and well being are necessary conditions for human action, humans claim that they have a right to them. If a person claims that he or she has a right to freedom and well-being then logically he or she must claim that other persons have a right to freedom and well-being as well. This is a logical point similar to the point that Kant makes in the quotation above.

Of course not everyone finds these arguments convincing but the only way to avoid the conclusion other than by being irrational is to show weaknesses in the arguments. I find those stopping points in the Kantian tradition more robust and rationally compelling than saying "whatever works" or "freedom and solidarity." If we should respect people because that is what logic requires when we want people to respect us (and we must), all a critic can say is "Why should I be rational?" But the question presupposes rationality. And what if someone refuses to accept the transcendental premise or the dictum to be rational with providing a rational argument for his or her position? Unfortunately the two remaining alternatives seem to be "live and let live" or fight. The former ends in relativism and the latter, which regrettably being the one humans have seemed to embrace, ends in war-a very dangerous solution at this point in history. And on that point I think Kantians and pragmatists would agree.

---

[35] Gewirth, Alan. (1978). *Reason and Morality.* Chicago: University of Chicago Press.

Part III
International Issues in Business Ethics

Chapter 6
Varieties of Corporate Social Responsibility

In 1997 I was present when a distinguished professor at the Harvard Business School announced that capitalism had won. Moreover that American capitalism had won and even more specifically that finance based American capitalism had won. The Harvard professor is one third right. Capitalism has won but I am not at all certain that the American finance based model will be the ultimate winner. I will elaborate on this point by distinguishing among several versions of capitalism that have very different views of corporate social responsibility. These versions of capitalism are the maximization of shareholder wealth made popular by Nobel prize winning Milton Friedman, the balance the interests of stakeholders view made popular by R Edward Freeman, and the sustainability model that is the official position of the European Union (EU). I will then consider the situation in Asia, specifically in Japan, and in countries like India and China that have what *The Economist*[1] calls a system of "state capitalism." I argue that the view of corporate social responsibility (CSR) held by the EU sustainability model of corporate social responsibility is morally superior. However, it is unclear, particularly at the time of writing this Chapter when the EU is in crisis, if the sustainability model has the best chance of succeeding in a competitive global capitalist marketplace. With respect to success we need to ask if the Chinese state based model of capitalism, which, at best, has a limited commitment to CSR, will ultimately prevail. We also need to ask whether the American finance based model of philanthropic CSR is economically adequate in the new international economic order. My contention is that it is not.

---

[1] *The Economist*, "State Capitalism," Special Report January 21, 2012, 3–18.

N.E. Bowie, *Business Ethics in the 21st Century*, Issues in Business Ethics 39,
DOI 10.1007/978-94-007-6223-7_6, © Springer Science+Business Media Dordrecht 2013

The Maximization of Shareholder Wealth Capitalism-American Finance Based Capitalism

The orthodox view in business schools, particularly in departments of finance and accounting is that the manager is an agent for the stockholders. The manager works for them and should do their bidding. Their bidding is profits and thus the purpose of a manager is to increase the wealth of the stockholders. As Milton Friedman has said

> There is one and only one social responsibility of business—to use its resources and engage in activities designed to increase its profits so long as stays within the rules of the game, which is to say, engages in free and open competition, without deception or fraud.[2]
>   and again
>   In a free enterprise, private-property system a corporate executive is an employee of the owners of the business. He has direct responsibility to his employers. That responsibility is to conduct the business in accordance with their desires, which generally will be to make as much money as possible while conforming to the basic rules of the society, both those embodied in law and those embodied in ethical custom.[3]

It is important to note that Friedman is not saying that managers ought to maximize profits even it is done in an unethical way. Friedman is very clear in saying that managers have a duty not to use deception and fraud in business. Business managers should engage in open competition. Price collusion would be a moral wrong for Friedman. Business managers ought to follow the law and they ought to obey the ethical customs embedded in society.

Corporate Social Responsibility as Charity

It would be a mistake to think that corporate social responsibility under this view is limited to increasing shareholder wealth. Many American business leaders think of social responsibility in terms of charity- of giving money away either directly or through a corporate foundation. Target Inc. gives 5 % of its pretax income to charity. Charitable giving has been a hallmark of the business community in Minneapolis/St Paul, Minnesota.

Advocates of Milton Friedman's position abhor such charitable giving on the part of corporations. They consider it tantamount to theft or perhaps more kindly put as taxation without representation. That charge seems overblown. Persons who buy Target stock are well aware of Target's policy of giving back to the community or they should be. People who own Target stock either endorse Target's program of corporate giving or they believe that it is either neutral or positive with respect to

---

[2] Friedman, Milton. (1982). *Capitalism and Freedom.* Chicago: University of Chicago Press, 133.

[3] Friedman, Milton. (1970). "The Social Responsibility of Business Is to Increase Its Profits." *New York Times Magazine*, September 13, 126.

Target's profits. Alternatively some CEO's give away their own money rather than that of the corporation. The Bill and Melinda Gates foundation and the gifts of Ted Turner come to mind. It should be noted that Friedman has no problem with successful business leaders giving their own money to charity. After all, it is their money. But corporate profits are not their money.

An Addendum to the Classical American View: Stakeholder Capitalism

R Edward Freeman is most closely associated with the view that management has a fiduciary duty to all its stakeholders and that the interests of the stockholders ought not to have priority over the interests of the other stakeholders. Freeman contends that management bears a fiduciary relationship to all stakeholders and that the task of the manager is to balance the competing claims of the various stakeholders.

> My thesis is that I can revitalize the concept of managerial capitalism by replacing the notion that managers have a duty to stockholders with the concept that managers bear a fiduciary relationship to stakeholders. Stakeholders are those groups who have a stake in or claim on the firm.[4]

Freeman distinguishes between a narrow use of the term "stakeholder" and a wide use of the term. On the narrow definition stakeholders are those groups who are vital to the survival and success of the firm. On Freeman's account these are the owners, employees, customers, managers, suppliers, and the local community. On the wide definition stakeholders are any group that affects or is affected by the firm.[5] In his own analysis, Freeman uses the narrow definition. I will follow Freeman in our analysis here.

Although the stakeholder theory is not as well developed and rigorous as the classical stockholder theory, it has, nonetheless, proven highly successful in the marketplace. Many-indeed one might now say most- corporations at least speak the language of stakeholder theory even if they do not always practice it.

It is important to note that in theory there need be no inconsistency between the wealth maximization view and the stakeholder view with respect to strategic management. Many argue that paying attention to corporate stakeholders is necessary for profit maximization. For example, if management does not insist that customers be treated well, the firm will not have customers or at least it will not have anywhere near as many as it could and ought to have. The view that in order to make profits, a firm must manage its stakeholder relations well is called instrumental stakeholder theory.

---

[4] Freeman, R. Edward. (1997, 2001). "A Stakeholder Theory of the Modern Corporation" in Tom L. Beauchamp and Norman E. Bowie (eds.), *Ethical Theory and Business*, 5th and 6th ed. Upper Saddle River: Prentice Hall Inc., 56.

[5] Ibid., 59.

Milton Friedman recognized that instrumental stakeholder theory was a smart management technique, but he had nothing but disdain for those who would call instrumental stakeholder theory corporate social responsibility.

> It may well be in the long-run interest of a corporation that is a major employer in a small community to devote resources to providing amenities to that community or to improving the government. That may make it easier to attract desirable employees, it may reduce the wage bill or lessen losses from pilferage and sabotage or have other worthwhile effects. Or it may be that, given the laws about the deductibility of corporate charitable contributions, the stockholders can contribute more to charities they favor by having the corporation make the gift than by doing it themselves, since they can in that way contribute an amount that would otherwise have been paid as corporate taxes.
>
> In each of these—and many similar—cases, there is a strong temptation to rationalize these actions as an exercise of "social responsibility."…It would be inconsistent of me to call on corporate executives to refrain from this hypocritical window-dressing because it harms the foundations of a free society.[6]

Before pointing out some of the misunderstandings in this quotation it is worth noticing that much of the general public has an attitude toward corporate philanthropy that is similar to Friedman: if philanthropic activity contributes to the bottom line the philanthropy is somehow tainted morally. However, both Friedman and the prevailing public attitude are mistaken here. First, as Friedman correctly points out, CEO's and top managers are agents of the stockholders and as agents have a moral obligation to make money. Seeking profit is a moral obligation. Second Friedman's view assumes a separation between business decisions and ethical decisions. My colleague R Edward Freeman refers to this viewpoint as the separation thesis, which he and his students have spent much time in the development of stakeholder theory refuting. Every business decision, they maintain, has ethical elements embedded in it. Third, Friedman seems to think that purity of motive is the essential ingredient in morality-a view that might be attributed to a simplistic understanding of the ethical theory of Immanuel Kant. As we saw in Chap. 4, I have developed a Kantian theory of capitalism that insists there is no contradiction when a business person claims that he or she is practicing corporate social responsibility both because it is right and it is profitable.

Some of Friedman's followers, most notably Michael Jensen, have adopted instrumental stakeholder theory without holding it in disdain.

> Enlightened value maximization recognizes that communication with, and motivation of, an organization's managers, employees, and partners is extremely difficult. What this means in practice is that if we tell all participants in an organization that its sole purpose is to maximize value we would not get maximum value for the organization….
>
> Indeed, it is obvious we cannot maximize the long-term market value of an organization if we ignore or mistreat any important constituency. We cannot create value without good relations with customers, employees, financial backers, suppliers, regulators, communities and so on.[7]

---

[6] Friedman, "The Social Responsibility of Business Is to Increase Its Profits," 124.

[7] Jensen, Michael C. (2002). "Value Maximization, Stakeholder Theory, and the Corporate Objective Function." *Business Ethics Quarterly*, 12(2), 245, 246.

In this quotation, Jensen recognizes that value maximization cannot be a motivator for corporate stakeholders. His view is consistent with what I have called "The Paradox of Profit:" The more a manager focuses on profit, the less likely he is to achieve it.[8] He also recognized that one cannot achieve value unless the firm also meets the needs of the corporate stakeholders. A manager treats stakeholders well because that treatment is necessary to achieve the goal of value maximization.

Social Responsibility Under the Stakeholder Model

The instrumental view stands in contrast to the more robust normative view that claims that management has moral obligations to stakeholders even if, when acting on these obligations profits are not maximized. Often this normative view is stated in terms of the rights of the various stakeholders-rights that create obligations or duties on the part of management.

Once the language shifts from instrumental stakeholder theory to a more robust ethical theory, there are some changes needed in the theory of corporate social responsibility. If stakeholders have rights and the local community is a stakeholder, then it looks like some attention to the needs of the local community is a moral requirement rather than a voluntary act of philanthropy. This shift from charity to obligations often goes unnoticed however. That is not the case in Europe.

The European Sustainability Version of Capitalism

In the "Green Paper,"[9] this strategic goal of sustainability is set out as a strategy of corporate social responsibility-CSR Europe as it is called. The European Union does not view the function of the corporation as maximizing shareholder value. Rather the EU argues that the corporation should be managed in a way that makes it sustainable and that sustainability is determined by financial success, environmental friendliness, and social responsibility. These are the three pillars of sustainability. An early definition of "sustainable development" was "development that meets the needs of the present without compromising the ability of future generations to meet its own needs."

These three factors of sustainability are measured by triple bottom line accounting. The goal of the European Union is "to become the most competitive and dynamic knowledge based economy in the world, capable of sustainable growth with more

---

[8] Bowie, Norman E. (1988). "The Paradox of Profit" in N. Dale Wright (ed.), *Papers on the Ethics of Administration.* Provo: Brigham Young University Press, 97–120.

[9] Commission of European Communities, *GREEN PAPER Promoting a European framework for Corporate Social Responsibility,* Brussels, July 18, 2001.

and better jobs and greater social cohesion."[10] The Green Paper elucidates the concept
as follows:

Corporate Social Responsibility is a concept whereby companies decide voluntarily to contribute to a better society and a cleaner environment. At a time when
the European Union endeavors to identify its common values by adopting a Charter
of Fundamental Rights, an increasing number of European companies recognize
their social responsibility more and more clearly and consider it as part of their
identity. This responsibility is expressed towards employees and more generally
towards all the stakeholders affected by business and which in turn can influence its
success.[11]

The official European Union position builds a theory of corporate social responsibility right into its macro-economic strategy. Within that strategy CSR includes
both concern for the environment and social responsibility. However, what is entailed
by the "social responsibility" criterion? To provide some specifics, here are some
items from the Green Paper. Being socially responsible means not only fulfilling
legal expectations, but also going beyond compliance and investing "more" into
human capital, the environment and relations with stakeholders. The internal dimension of corporate social responsibility includes enlightened human resources management, a concern with life-long learning for example, health and safety at work,
helping workers adapt to change, and more friendly management of environmental
impacts and natural resources. The external dimension includes cooperation with
supply chain firms to promote CSR throughout the supply chain, a commitment to
human rights, and a commitment to global sustainable development.[12]

As we see in Europe, corporate social responsibility means having the company
take a stand on certain social issues. The issue need not be an issue of charity at all.
In Europe it is often a commitment to human rights. The Green Paper is explicit in
that regard. "Corporate social responsibility has a strong human rights dimension,
particularly in relation to international operations and global supply chains."[13] In
addition, nearly all European companies that commit to sustainability also commit
to supporting a number of international human rights agreements both in their own
business and in the business activities of their supply chains. You seldom if ever see
such a commitment to human rights as part of an American company's statement of
business purpose. Let me make the point in another way. Under the sustainability
model, corporate social responsibility requires that the business leader makes sure
that his business activities do not violate human rights. He also has some responsibility to see that his stakeholders, particularly suppliers, also do not violate human
rights. Finally and perhaps most controversially corporations need to resist clear
violations of human rights by the governments where they do business. If they do
not wish to accept this obligation, then they should not be doing business in countries

---

[10] Ibid., 3.
[11] Ibid., 4.
[12] Ibid., 8–15.
[13] Ibid., 13.

with an extensive record of human rights abuses. American readers of *The Economist* will notice the importance that is given to business and human rights within the scope of that magazine. Although *The Economist* is considered a conservative publication within the U.S. meaning of "conservative", Americans associate the emphasis on human rights as a liberal cause as people in the U.S. use the term "liberal." As for specific examples, Royal Dutch Shell changed its policy with respect to intervention in political affairs when it was roundly criticized internationally for not intervening to save the life of Siro-Wiwa in Nigeria. And since all these issues we have discussed in this section are issues for the corporation, successful corporate leadership requires corporate social responsibility-not simply individual corporate charity. In Europe, stakeholder management is the means for determining what the third pillar of social responsibility requires. Basically the dictates of enlightened human resource management and respect for human rights are, in Europe, the bedrock of corporate social responsibility.

Philanthropy, the Safety Net, and Human Rights

The differences between the United States and the European Union with respect to CSR need further discussion. Why is there no tradition of significant philanthropy in Europe? I submit that one significant reason for the lack of a tradition of philanthropy is the fact that European countries including Great Britain have a much stronger safety net than is found in the United States. The Scandinavian countries in particular are especially generous. Europe has higher taxes, a more progressive tax system, and many more government services than the United States. Right wing politicians in the United States refer to socialist Europe. If the state provides many services for free and protects people who are unemployed, there is less need for charity. In the United States we think of social responsibility as helping to solve social problems. In Europe it is the job of government to solve social problems. Interestingly there is a common line of thinking here between Milton Friedman and "socialist" Europe. Both agree that it is the job of government rather than business to solve social problems.

As a generalization I think this statement is correct. However, it is a bit more complicated when a company actually contributes to a social problem. Thus the British Company, British American Tobacco, does view the health issues around smoking as an issue of social responsibility. It explicitly addresses the issue of how it can be a socially responsible manufacturer of cigarettes. They argue that as long as cigarettes are a legal product and there is no deception in marketing and no marketing to children, then they are being socially responsible. Of course many others disagree. The purveyors of fast food do have a social responsibility to consider the impact of their products on obesity-although obesity is less of a problem in Europe than in the United States. So with respect to social problems, the most accurate way to characterize European business philosophy is to say that social problems are the responsibility of government except in those cases where one's business activities contribute to the social problem.

Even this qualification is too simplified. Since all companies have an impact on the environment, then there is a general moral obligation as expressed in the second pillar for companies to aid in solving the environmental crisis. Companies do that by being more environmentally friendly.

With much of the responsibility for social problems in the hands of government, public sentiment and business practice have focused on human rights issues. Capital punishment is not permitted in the European Union. Labor rights are honored and the right to bargain collectively is seen as a human right. The contrast between the United States and Europe on the rights to unionize and bargain collectively is striking. I would argue that the United States is the most anti-union member of the G-20, the most hostile to unions of any advanced economy. Respecting labor and the right to bargain collectively does not involve philanthropy. Labor unions and their members have certain rights and managers have an obligation to accept and respect those rights. At least that is the view of the European Union.

A similar analysis can be given for a number of the examples of social responsibility mentioned above. In every one of these cases, the obligation is to a stakeholder in the firm. There is no general obligation to solve social problems. There are only obligations to respect the rights of stakeholders and an obligation to be a green firm in order to protect the environment.

The Business Case for Social Responsibility

One common feature of both the European view and the U.S. view is the belief on the part of American businesspersons committed to philanthropy and European businesspersons committed to sustainability that corporate social responsibility is good business. Sometimes paying attention to environmental and social issues is referred to as "the license to operate." Whether these partisans on both sides of the Atlantic are correct in arguing that CSR is good business is a matter of some controversy.

Corporate Social Responsibility in Asia

Japan

I am not sure which version of corporate social responsibility best captures the Japanese view. When I first contrasted Japanese management from American management in the early 1990s I borrowed the conceptual framework of Masahiko Aoki.[14] Many of the Japanese management practices he described and endorsed such as continuous improvement, just in time inventory, decreased specialization in

---

[14] See Aoli, Masahiko. (1990). "Toward an Economic Model of the Japanese Firm," *Journal of Economic Literature*, 28, 1–27.

job assignments, and the emphasis on quality with the ability of anyone on the line to stop the process have been adopted in the United States-especially in the automobile industry. These management practices have been viewed as more employee friendly than the more hierarchical anti-union practices in the United States. For example, in Japanese automobile plants, workers were encouraged to learn skills that enabled them to do a number of jobs on the assembly line. In that way Japanese workers had a greater understanding and appreciation of the final product. When you coupled these practices with a tradition of lifetime employment for regular workers, many experts thought they had an explanation for the perceived superior quality of Japanese products.

With this background in mind, I would characterize Japan as having cooperative capitalism. If competition is one of the main components of American culture, cooperation is one of the main components of Japanese culture including its economic institutions. You can see this in its Zaibatsu which consist of family owned firms that are linked to a network of supporting economic institutions that provide banking, trading, engineering, and logistical support. Each of the major family owned firms has such a supporting network. Japan has a stock market, of course, but major companies are not simply dependent on the wide public to raise capital. Each family firm is linked to a large financial institution that provides financial support. There is also vertical linkage as found in the keiretsu that provides integration in production and distribution. In addition there is a strong safety net in Japan provided by both the government and business. Until recently there was a tradition of life time employment for many employees of the larger firms. Although that tradition is eroding, employee layoffs are the last resort rather than the first resort as they are in the United States. Finally Japan has had a strong state supported industrial policy through MITI, The Ministry of International Trade and Industry. MITI is somewhat less important now, but the Japanese government still plays a role in economic policy that would be unacceptable in the United States. As I look beyond the individual economic institutions, what I see in Japan is a much more cooperative society internally although a society that competes vigorously in international trade. Some of this may be influenced by a Japanese religious and ethical tradition that believes that one has stronger ties and thus obligations to those close to one and weaker ties and obligations to those some distance from one such as foreigners. You see this in the auto industry where labor relations in the big auto firms are always peaceful but each auto company such as Honda and Toyota compete vigorously against each other as well as all others in the global marketplace.

As the Japanese economy went into recession and experienced bouts of deflation, many argued that Japan would have to change. Many of the so-called reforms were modeled on the finance based capitalism of the United States. I recall giving a talk to Japanese businessmen in which I criticized finance based capitalism and urged Japan not to embrace wholeheartedly the view of Milton Friedman. I remember distinctly one Japanese businessman coming up to me after the talk with tears in his eyes and saying how appreciative he was of the fact that I was the first American he had heard speak who did not tell him to maximize shareholder wealth. My impression is that Japan has taken relatively little from the finance based model and has, instead, adapted elements of the stakeholder model and the sustainability model into the Japanese system. For example a study by Ely and Pownall demonstrated how Japanese accounting standards take a broader stakeholder perspective than American firms with respect to accounting information.[15] The Caux Roundtable, an international group of business leaders, has adopted a set of principles known as the Caux Roundtable Principles of Business Ethics. These principles were adopted from a set of principles adopted by business leaders in Minnesota. The late chairman Ryuzaburo Kaku of Canon Corporation thought that the principles of stakeholder management in the Minnesota principles were similar to the spirit of the Japanese term keosi-living together in harmony. As a result many Japanese firms and eventually others around the world adopted the Caux Roundtable Principles. Other Japanese companies have adopted the philosophy of corporate social responsibility espoused by the European Union. However as with American firms, the social responsibility leg of sustainability has been focused on good deeds for stakeholders and a concern with social problems in Japanese society rather than emphasizing human rights.

Japanese firms have been more concerned with environmental issues. Its location on a major fault line subject to earthquakes has played a role in this environmental concern. A Japanese firm that early in the twenty-first century had emphasized its responsibility to the environment is Ricoh, a manufacturer of office equipment. Their corporate philosophy is refuse, return, reuse, reduce and recycle. Among the actions they have taken is to make uniforms from recycled plastic soft drink bottles. When updating the information on Ricoh for this Chapter, an examination of its website indicates that Ricoh has a comprehensive and contemporary philosophy of CSR. For example, Ricoh is committed to promoting social responsibility down its value chain.[16]

To this observer, Japanese companies, like their counterparts in Europe and the United States have a variety of corporate philosophies with respect to CSR. However, Japan has a culture that inclines it toward the sustainability model. In addition its position at a perilous point on earthquake fault lines makes it more sensitive to the environment than many other countries. My best guess is that Japan's economy will more and more resemble the sustainability model.

India

I confess that I have almost no expertise in discussing the Indian model of social responsibility and I have not visited the country. Any of us who teach in business school, however, are almost certain to have colleagues and friends who are Indian

---

[15] Ely, K.M. and Pownall, G. (2002). "Shareholder-versus Stakeholder Focused Japanese Companies: Firm Characteristics and Accounting Valuation," *Contemporary Accounting Research*, 19(4), 615–636.

[16] http://www.ricoh.com/csr/concept/index.html, Downloaded February 15, 2012.

and who can help us understand the norms of the Indian economy. I certainly have
benefited from my association with my Indian colleagues. Nonetheless my discussion
of India will be brief. First, it should be realized that India was for many years a
socialist country. Capitalism is a rather recent development in India. Second the
Indian government is notoriously inefficient and corrupt. The infrastructure in India
is terrible. A group of Indian Wharton students put the point succinctly. "India's lax
ethical standards, coupled with a rigid bureaucracy and weak enforcement mechanisms have certainly hurt the country in many ways."[17] Practicing business in that
environment is obviously a challenge. Indeed the Wharton students report that businesses in India both domestic and foreign must practice what the Indians call
"jugaad." The term "jugaad" roughly means "finding a way to your cheese." Whether
international corporations can conduct business in an ethical way-at least as defined
by Western standards is problematic. Some of the most skeptical students in my
classes have been Indian who report that bribery is essential if one is to succeed
in doing business in India. A recent article in *The Economist* discussing the latest
scandal in India, which involved scandals in the mobile phone industry, put it this
way: "Can a foreign firm ever be sure that its Indian partner is clean?"[18]

Under these circumstances, can India have a theory of corporate social responsibility and even if it had such a theory could it practice it? I think it is safe to say there
is no widely accepted theory of corporate social responsibility in India. However,
there are a number of Indian companies that practice corporate social responsibility
pretty much in line with the European model. Given the fact that India was a colony
of Great Britain until well into the twentieth century and given the fact that many
well known Indian companies have a long history as divisions of European companies, this should not be too surprising. One of the best examples here is Hindustan
Unilever. Hindustan Unilever is owned by the British Dutch company Unilever. It is
the largest consumer goods company in India. This company along with its parent
Unilever has completely accepted the sustainability view of CSR. You need only
tour its website to see the extensive sustainability programs that are in place and to
see the specific sustainability goals that it has set for itself.

An interesting question that deserves research investigation is whether the Indian
firms that are leaders in corporate social responsibility are either European owned
or were originally European owned. To the extent that there is a philosophy of social
responsibility in Indian capitalism, is it limited to firms that were not founded by
native Indians?

What does the future hold? Will more and more Indian companies adopt the
commitment to sustainability that is characteristic of Hindustan Unilever? Will
India gradually reform its rigid bureaucracy, weak enforcement mechanisms and
end its endemic practice of bribery? As India strives to be an economic power,
I think that the answer to the latter question has to by "Yes." Otherwise India's rise

[17] Anand, Ajay, Kavitha Cherian, Arpan Gautam, Roopak Mujmudar and Arzan Raimawala,
"Business v Ethics" The India Tradeoff?, Knowledge at Wharton, January 3, 2012.
[18] "Megahurts" *The Economist* February 11, 2012, 67–68. The actual quotation is on p. 68.

as an economic power will slow down and India may fall behind the other developing countries. An answer to the first question is less certain because it depends in part on the evolution of China's economy and to whether or not there really is a good business case for corporate social responsibility.

China

China is the most powerful member of those countries *The Economist* characterizes as examples of "state capitalism." Other examples include Russia and most of the oil rich countries in the Middle East. Brazil and Singapore could be included as well. These countries combine the power of the state with the powers of capitalism. The characteristics of state capitalism include having the government pick winners and having the government either own or be the major shareholder in major industries or companies. Yet these government controlled companies are capitalistic in the sense that they are listed on stock exchanges and are multinationals that compete globally.[19]

We might summarize Chinese political economy as follows: In the twenty-first century China's State Based Capitalism has become a serious challenger to both the American and European forms of capitalism. What makes the challenge particularly worrisome is that China is not a democratic country. On the economic front, the Chinese government sets goals for the economy, owns and operates some of the major economic enterprises, and has extensive regulation of the economy. This involvement of the government is an anathema to supporters of American based capitalism. Yet the Chinese economy is a growth powerhouse that has helped many industrial economies weather the recession that began in 2009. In addition the Chinese have provided extensive funding for America's borrowing. Recently, the Chinese government has been particularly critical of Western-and especially American economic institutions during the financial crisis of 2008–2009, the sovereign debt crisis in 2011 and the political impasse in the United States that lead to a credit downgrade of the United States by Standard and Poor's in 2011. As they survey the past decade, the Chinese have been increasingly vocal in doubting the superiority of both Western democracy and Western-especially American capitalism. One needs to ask whether ultimately Chinese state-based non-democratic capitalism will be the most successful economic system in the world. And if China does become the most successful economic system and does not practice corporate social responsibility, then what is the future for social responsibility in the rest of the world?

With respect to social responsibility, China is even more complicated than India or Japan. In 2005 I visited the People's Republic of China as a tourist with stops in Beijing, Shanghai, and Hong Kong. I then made two additional trips as an academic. In 2007 I gave a lecture at the Shanghai Academy of Social Sciences.[20] Some of the remarks that follow are from that lecture. One theme of that lecture was a critique

---

[19] *The Economist*, Special Report, "State Capitalism: The Visible Hand" January 21, 2012, 3.
[20] "Globalization, Business Ethics, and Business Strategy" for Shanghai Academy of Social Science, Shanghai, Peoples Republic of China, October 18, 2007.

of Chinese business practices. Much to my surprise the lecture was later published in Chinese. Then a year later in 2008, I took a group of American Executive MBA students to Shanghai and Guangzhou. Our focus on that trip was businesses-both Chinese and American firms doing business in China. Despite three extensive trips, it was extremely difficult for me to discern a philosophy of capitalism and of business ethics there. Given the fact that China's version of capitalism is still evolving, that should come as no surprise. At various international business ethics conferences and seminars I have met several colleagues in business ethics from the People's Republic of China. These colleagues have shown a great interest in sustainability and corporate social responsibility as articulated in the United States and especially in Europe. Many of the leading books in business ethics, including my *Business Ethics: A Kantian Perspective*, have been translated into Chinese. I should point out, however, that my academic hosts in China indicated that "capitalism" is still a dirty word in China. "Market economy" is the acceptable term. In summary, I think it is safe to say that Chinese academics endorse a sustainability view of CSR.

However when one turns from academic writings on Chinese business ethics and social responsibility to actual Chinese business practice and Chinese government policy, one wonders if China has a policy of social responsibility.

**Evidence That China Seems to Lack a Sense
of Corporate Social Responsibility**

At the macro-level we have to confront the fact that China has a non democratic form of government and thus both government policy and business practice contain values that are sharply at odds with the values of democratic countries. Specifically there is a lack of transparency, a lack of respect for privacy, censorship, and little concern for human rights within Chinese capitalism.

No matter what shape China's business system takes, there are certain factors that will be crucial to its success. Private property, including intellectual property must be protected. One need not have the same rules governing property rights as the United States or even the European Union. But the protection of property rights must be sufficient for other countries to be willing to invest in China and to trade with it. China must recognize that many in the West do not believe that China has gone far enough in protecting property rights. The piracy of movies and the manufacture of fake brand clothing, watches etc. which are sold as Nike or Levi Straus jeans, or Rolex watches are still perceived to be a major problem in China.

For example, BusinessWeek reports that the largest Chinese search engine, Baidu makes it easy to download illegal music. All you need to do is hit the MP3 player on Baidu's home page, type in the name of the song and click. A Chinese user is quoted as saying he and his friends aren't doing anything wrong. "I think it is the problem with the law, not with us users."[21]

---

[21] Einhorn, Bruce, and Xiang Ji. (2007). "Daft to Music Piracy: Chinese Search Engines Make It Easy to Steal Net Tunes," *BusinessWeek,* September 10, 42.

The Chinese economy is still tied strongly to the state. As with India there is a great deal of corruption and bribery. And as with India this corruption and bribery will act as a drag on its economic development. Corruption undermines both transparency and trust. Lack of transparency and trust undermine the possibilities for economic exchange.

Transparency is an essential requirement for a successful business environment. Building trust is essential for market success. Transparency and the building of trust are closely related. Indeed transparency is a necessary condition for trust. China has had difficulty with this in the past. During the SARS epidemic, China was widely accused of not providing information or sending samples to international health organizations. In the August 16, 2007, *The New York Times* reported on a pig virus that was decimating the pork industry in China. In reporting on the issue, he said,

> ...China's past lack of transparency—particularly over what became the SARS epidemic-has created global concern. They haven't really explained what the virus is, says Frederico Zuckermann, a professor of immunology at the University Of Illinois College Of Veterinary Medicine. This is like SARS. They haven't sent samples to any international body. This is really irresponsible of China. This thing could get out and affect everybody.[22]

In addition, China, unlike most of the other G-20 countries seems not to have developed a notion of stakeholder capitalism. Indeed many of the moral criticisms of Chinese capitalism are based on the fact that China has violated its obligations to various corporate stakeholders. One of the key stakeholders is the customer. For several years, China has been criticized for shipping poor quality goods overseas. Both the business press and the regular television and newspaper outlets have run featured stories on the numerous cases of toys, toothpaste, and pet food-to name a few products that have been dangerous and in some cases fatal to customers. A lengthy report in the *New York Times* indicates that every one of the 24 major recalls for dangerous toys in the United States involved toys made in China.[23] After publication of this report, Mattel had two massive recalls of toys made in China. In the case of the tiny magnets that could cause a child to choke, Mattel admitted that the Chinese had built the toys according to specification. However, millions of dolls had excessive lead in the paint-a situation that has been quite common in Chinese recalls. In the first recall of nearly a million toys on August 2, 2006 lead paint was the issue in Mattel's recall of Fisher Price toys made in China.

Another crucial stakeholder is the worker. Here again it appears to the outside world that China still has much work to do with regard to worker safety. News reports cite the August 17th 2007 flooding of a mine which drowned nearly 200 miners. Reuters reports that nearly 2,000 Chinese have died in mine accidents in the first 8 months of 2007.[24] Worker safety needs to be a priority for China.

---

[22] Barvoza, David. (2007). "Virus Spreading Alarm and Deadly Pig Disease in China," *The New York Times* August 16, C1,C4.

[23] Lipton, Eric S and David Barboza. (2007). "As More Toys Are Recalled, the Trail Ends in China," *The New York Times*, June 19, 1, C4.

[24] http://www.reuters.com/article/worldNews/idUSPEK22116420070823?feedType=RSS&feedName=worldNews

A second piece of the sustainability model is related to the environment. China has huge environmental issues. Some of these issues are the inevitable result of the rapid growth of the economy. Other issues result from poor policy decisions. Two recent articles, one by Asian Specialist Elizabeth Economy in the September/October 2007 *Foreign Affairs* and the other by Joseph Kahn and Jim Yardley in the August 26, 2007 *New York Times*,[25] speak to the direness of the situation.

Here are a two sample quotations:

> China's environmental problems are mounting. Water pollution and water scarcity are burdening the economy, rising levels of air pollution are endangering the health of millions of Chinese, and much of the country's land is rapidly turning into desert. China has become a world leader in air and water pollution and land degradation and a top contributor to some of the world's most vexing global environmental problems, such as the illegal timber trade, marine pollution, and climate change. As China's pollution woes increase, so too, do the risks to its economy, public health, social stability, and international reputation.[26]
>
> Environmental woes that might seem catastrophic in some countries can be seen as commonplace in China: industrial cities where people rarely see the sun; children killed or sickened by lead poisoning or other types of local pollution; a coastline so swamped by algal red tides that large sections of the ocean no longer sustain marine life.[27]

Given the growth in China's economy the last 5 years, you might think that the situation regarding worker safety and the environment would have improved markedly during this period. Alas, that has not been the case. *The New York Times* on January 26, 2012 had an extensive article on the total lack of concern for worker health and safety at an Apple iPad assembly plant in China.[28] That report was featured on page 1 and then continued for two full pages in the business section. The *Times* article was widely cited and provided evidence that there had been little progress in China on the issue of worker safety. The article also showed that American companies had not done enough to insist on better standards in its supply chains. Are American companies too weak to stand up to China? If so this has serious implications for the future of corporate social responsibility.

China has taken some action to improve its environmental standards, but the major cities in the county still suffer from severe air pollution[29] and the situation with maintaining an adequate supply of clean water has become dire in many parts of the country.[30] I am sympathetic to the argument that current developed countries paid little attention to the environment in the early stages of their development. Therefore countries that are moving from lesser developed to developed should

---

[25] Economy, Elizabeth. (2007). "The Great Leap Backward? The Costs of China's Environmental Crisis." *Foreign Affairs*, September/October, 38–59, and Joseph Kahn and Jim Yardley. (2007). "As China Roars, Pollution Reaches Deadly Extremes," *The New York Times*, August 26, 1, 10–11.

[26] Economy, op.cit. 2007, 38.

[27] Kahn and Yardley, op.cit. 2007, 1.

[28] Duhigg, Charles and David Barbozza. (2012). "In China, Human Costs Are Built Into an iPad," *The New York Times*, January 26, A1 and B 10–11.

[29] See for example, "Clearing the Air," *The Economist*, February 11, 2012, 80–81.

[30] http://www.channelnewsasia.com/stories/eastasia/view/1164079/1/.htm, Downloaded February 19, 2012.

have a pass at least for a while. Although there is merit to that argument, countries like China do have one advantage here. They can move directly to take advantage of the technological advances that protect the environment. In countries like the United States where new power plants are not being built (a huge mistake in my opinion), taking advantage of the new technology would require the retrofitting of every existing power plant. China is building new power plants. Why not build them up to the highest standard from the start? Ditto for all residential and commercial buildings in China, including factories.

Perhaps necessity will force China to do more to clean up the environment in China. However, China, along with the United States, shamefully, is often on the wrong side of international attempts to improve the environment. Recently the European Union passed regulation to reduce airline emissions. China is fighting the regulations as are airlines in the United States.[31]

The third pillar of sustainability is social responsibility. Of the three pillars this category is the most amorphous and the most controversial. As indicated, in the United States social responsibility has often been associated with philanthropy. In Europe the emphasis has been on human rights. Japan has yet to work out this category. To be candid, China's human rights record has been dismal and it seems to have gotten worse as the twenty-first century has progressed. China is responsible for repressive rule in Tibet and other western provinces. Demonstrations have been met with police violence. A number of Chinese victims of Chinese human rights violations have received the attention of the international community, including attention here in the United States. One of the best known victims is Liu Xiaobo, who won the Nobel Peace Prize in 2010. He was not permitted to leave China to accept the prize and was sentenced to a jail sentence of 11 years.[32] As of this writing there are reports he is being sent into exile. Another victim was Xu Zhiyong whose NGO, the Open Constitution (gong meng), was shut down despite the fact that he successfully ran for the People's Congress. Yet another was Hu Jia, who worked to raise awareness about AIDS and the environment. He was sentenced to jail, released, and then to start the New Year had his home raided.[33] Two other victims include the rural organizer and legal advocate Chen Guangcheng, who is blind and well known for his reports of forced abortions in China and although released from prison is now subjected to unlawful house arrest; and human rights lawyer Gao Zhisheng, who was reported at the start of 2012 as being imprisoned in a remote location.[34]

---

[31] "Trouble in the air, double on the ground," *The Economist*, February 11, 2012, 66.

[32] Bristow, Michael, "One year on: Nobel winner Liu Xiaobo still in jail," BBC News Asia-Pacific, October 6, 2011. http://www.bbc.co.uk/news/world-asia-pacific-15195263, Downloaded February 19, 2012.

[33] Simpson, Peter. (2012). "Chinese police raid home of human rights activist Hu Jia," *The Telegraph*, January, 12, http://www.telegraph.co.uk/news/worldnews/asia/china/9009763/Chinese-police-raid-home-of-human-rights-activist-Hu-Jia.html, Downloaded February 19, 2012.

[34] "Chinese rights lawyer Gao Zhisheng denied visitors in jail," *The Guardian*, January 10, 2012, http://www.guardian.co.uk/world/2012/jan/10/gao-zhisheng-denied-visitors-jail, Downloaded February 19, 2012.

It is abundantly clear that the Chinese do not accept the third pillar of sustainability. They do not accept corporate social responsibility when social responsibility is understood in terms of the protection and promotion of human rights. Given the importance that human rights have in the Western tradition, the failure of the Chinese to adopt the third pillar of sustainability raises questions about how western multinationals can or should do business in China. What is disconcerting to me is the ease with which so many American companies as well as other companies in the West have ignored the fact that China is a major violator of human rights and is quite unapologetic about it. Does this fact bode ill for the practice of corporate social responsibility when such practice urges the protection and promotion of human rights? In countries that produce oil or in a country like China with a potential market of two billion, I fear that it does. There does not seem to be a lot of will on the part of American companies to stand up to China. If a company does not stand up to China to promote social responsibility, will the support for social responsibility gradually diminish at home as well?

Which Version of Corporate Social Responsibility Should a Country Adopt?

I believe the sustainability version of corporate social responsibility should be adopted. One reason for adoption would be strictly pragmatic. If the EU strategy were economically superior to the American strategy, then there would be an economic reason to adopt it. The European Union believes that in the long run it is superior; they express these sentiments in what is called the business case for CSR. As the Green Paper indicates, "A number of companies with good social and environmental records indicate that these activities can result in better performance and can generate more profits and growth."[35]

Whether the EU can outperform the US in the long run is uncertain. Many in all countries believe that a commitment to social responsibility weakens economic growth rather than enables it. The business case for corporate social responsibility is received with great skepticism. I write this essay at a particularly difficult time for Europe. The sovereign debt crisis not only threatens to drive the European Union into recession. It threatens the very existence of the EU and its currency the Euro. Americans on the right look at Europe with disdain.

Although the European Union has a number of serious issues, it is a mistake to link all of Europe together. The economic problems are most severe in southern Europe especially in Greece and to a lesser extent in Italy, Spain and Portugal. The countries of northern Europe including Germany and the Scandinavian countries of Denmark and Sweden are doing well although these latter countries are the most "socialistic." The average standard of living in these countries is higher

---

[35] The Green Paper, op.cit., 7.

than that in the United States and there is far less income inequality. In the long run, I think it is a mistake to count Europe out. Time will tell.

There are other reasons I do not think Americans should be complacent. For several years in the early 2000s I took 25 MBA students to Brussels and London so that these students might have first hand experience with the sustainability model. Last year a senior executive of a major European company described the US has a high risk society. Although he did not elaborate on that comment, I began to think that he certainly had a point. American thinking is very short term. This is most obvious in financial markets. When I touted the long range planning (beyond the 70 years of remaining oil supply) of Shell and British Petroleum to my broker, he reminded me of the "realities" of the market. For the day trader, the long term is measured in seconds, for the momentum trader the long term is measured in days, and for the "long term investor" the long term is measured in months. There is no longer term. Even if this is a bit of an exaggeration, it is disturbing. How can we have sustainable investment in an environment where the long term is limited to a few months?

Further evidence of the pitfalls of a short term focus can be found in the unwillingness of Americans to plan for the future. We were the only major country not to sign the Kyoto Protocol. A greater percentage of American does not believe in climate change than in other industrialized countries and is more unwilling to take steps to mitigate global warming than any of the industrial countries. The state of our infrastructure is deplorable. Our rail system is primitive by contemporary standards. Our children have lower reading, math and science scores than most other industrial nations and the economic recession has only drained money from the public schools. Many fear we are a country in decline.

I have already described the economic power of China and shown that it has not made sufficient progress in stakeholder management, that its environment is still degraded and that China has no respect for human rights. But given its economic power, American firms as well as other Western firms are reluctant to stand up to it. These problems are compounded by what China considers to be our weaknesses. China has watched as the United States has lurched from one economic crisis to another in the past decade. The dot.com bubble collapsed as the twentieth century came to a close. Then right after the 9/11 attacks, we had the collapse of World Com, Arthur Andersen, and Enron among others. Then the financial crisis of 2008–2009. Rather than address problems, the radical tea party members of the Republican Party in the House were constant obstructionists, even to the point of bringing the United States to the brink of bankruptcy. To the Chinese neither American democracy nor American capitalism looked like a successful strategy.

The Moral Argument for Sustainability

The other argument for adopting the sustainability model of corporate social responsibility is normative or moral. A notion of leadership that measures legitimacy on achieving sustainability rather than simply on financial success is morally superior.

Everyone is subject to the general duty to do one's part to contribute to the common good. This duty is premised on the fact that a civil order is in the interest of all citizens and that citizens benefit from being in a civil society rather than in a state of nature. Think Hobbes here. If one partakes of the benefits of a civil society then one has an obligation based on fairness to support it. Otherwise one would be a free rider- a person who accepts the benefits of a system without accepting any of the burdens. This notion is most highly developed in the philosophy of John Rawls. Although Rawls provides a contractarian theory of justice, there is a place in his system for natural duties. One of the natural duties is the duty of justice. "This duty requires us to support and to comply with just institutions that exist and apply to us. It also constrains us to further just arrangements not yet established, at least when this can be done without too much cost to ourselves."[36] Since Rawls asserts that this principle is a natural duty, one might not think it needs justification. A natural duty is simply a duty we have without undertaking any voluntary act to be subject to the duty. However, the duty can be justified because it is coherent with principles chosen in the original position while alternative principles are not coherent. The details of Rawls' argument are beyond the scope of this Chapter (The interested reader should see section 51 in *A Theory of Justice*).

Rawls then applies the principle in a political context.

> For example, consider the case of a citizen deciding how to vote between political parties, or the case of a legislator wondering whether to favor a certain statute…. As a rational citizen or legislator, a person should, it seems, support that party or favor that statute which best conforms to the two principles of justice.[37]

Voting in this way is how one honors the obligations of the natural duty of justice. And it is rational to behave this way because the reasoning process in the original position shows that the two principles of justice are in the best interest of everyone and would be adopted in the original position. But acting on the natural duty of justice is rational in another way as well. So acting is mutually supporting. If others see one acting on a sense of justice, others are more inclined to act justly as well. In that way acting on a sense of justice leads to stability within the society. As Rawls said:

> We noted that in a well ordered society the public knowledge that citizens generally have an effective sense of justice is a very great social asset. It tends to stabilize just social arrangements.[38]

Rawls believes we will treat our friends and family justly. Psychologically wanting to treat our friends justly is on a par on wanting to be with them and of feeling sad when they suffer a misfortune. But why should we treat other members of a society who are not friends and family fairly? Rawls believes that behaving unfairly or

---

[36] Rawls, John. (1999). *A Theory of Justice*, Rev ed. Cambridge, MA: Harvard University Press, 99.

[37] Ibid., 294.

[38] Ibid., 295.

unjustly negatively affects the institutions of society and when these are negatively affected our family and friends are as well.

It certainly can be argued that many Americans have become free-riders. They are willing to take the advantages of just institutions but are unwilling to pay their fair share to see themselves as part of a wide community.

Let us now adapt this Rawlsian framework to a discussion of sustainable corporations or corporate social responsibility. First, it must be pointed out that Rawls assumed perfect compliance theory in his analysis. That is, he assumed that people in a just society would out of a sense of justice support just institutions. For the most part he did not theorize about how we ought to deal with conditions of partial compliance theory-that is in conditions where there is only partial compliance with the demands of justice. We of course are not assuming perfect compliance. However, this assumption should not hinder our analysis because I take seriously the second part of the natural duty of justice, namely that we are to "further just arrangements not yet established, at least when this can be done without too much cost to ourselves."

So how does this all apply to sustainability? I assume that some corporations are managed with a goal toward being sustainable and that others are managed in the traditional American way-to increase shareholder wealth as it is measured on a quarter to quarter basis. I further assume that it is morally better to manage with a goal to sustainability than to manage on the basis of short-term quarterly stock results. In making that moral judgment, I am assuming that the achievement of sustainability creates greater social value. After all if the sustainable corporation really protects environmental integrity, it seems obvious that social value is enhanced. I even assume that in the long run the sustainable corporation is more financially viable than corporations managed in the traditional American way. There is nothing radical about this assumption. It is the same assumption that drives the European Union's Corporate Social Responsibility initiative. As a Kantian I accept the notion that every person has dignity and that dignity is protected by asserting that every human being has certain natural rights that should be honored, protected, and enhanced. Respect for human rights is the third pillar of sustainability under the European model. Such respect should not be such a problem for Americans. We are a country founded on a philosophy of human rights. Why is there such resistance in the business community toward acting on the philosophical foundation of the American system?

Rawls's argument can be rephrased so that it provides an argument for supporting the sustainability account of corporate social responsibility. There is a natural duty to support sustainable corporations and where corporations do not behave in a sustainable manner, it is our duty to reform them when this can be done without too much cost to ourselves. The justification for this duty is similar to the justification given by Rawls for the natural duty of justice. Since a business community of sustainable corporations yields the most social good, it is rational to support that type of business community. To accept the benefits of sustainable businesses without accepting the burdens (such as paying a higher price) is unfair especially when this can be done with little cost to oneself. Acting on these obligations encourages similar actions by others and thus makes the achievement of a sustainable business culture more likely. This process supports sustainable business in a way similar to how the natural duty of justice supports stability in political life. Just as there is an obligation to support those institutions that really do contribute to a just society, there is a similar obligation to support businesses that seek sustainability. This argument is making a substantial claim. A minority of people desire to support sustainable business and many in that minority may go further and believe that there is a moral obligation to support sustainable business. I go further. I contend that there is a general and universal moral requirement that consumers support sustainable business-at least when that can be done without too much cost to oneself. Poor people are not under that obligation when the products of a sustainable business are more expensive than the products of a non-sustainable business.

Why Philanthropy Is Not Enough

One might argue that the goals of sustainability can be achieved through the traditional American system of philanthropy. Corporate foundations and successful businesspeople can support the environment and human rights and in such circumstances there would not be much difference between the American view of corporate social responsibility and the European one.

This argument cannot be sustained. First, philanthropy is always in danger of being considered an add-on, something that is not essential to the day to day running of the business and something that is done after the business is successful. But under the sustainability model, profits, environmental concern, and respect for human rights are all essential goals of management each and every day. They are achieved through stakeholder dialogues and measured by triple bottom line accounting. Sustainability is what business is all about. Unlike philanthropy it is not separate from the main task of running a business.

Does China Need Corporate Social Responsibility to Survive

I now return to a question we have raised before. Even if my moral argument on behalf of the sustainability model is correct, I may face a practical problem. If China is successful, then they may not accept the moral argument and both European multinationals and American multinationals might not challenge them. And if multinationals take that road, there is always the danger that the ideals of corporate social responsibility will weaken at home as well.

Rawls's theory of a social union is not an obvious fit in an American society that it highly individualistic. This talk of a social union probably seems strange to those in a society of rugged individualists. Rawls' idea of a social union might fit better in a society where solidarity is an important value. China is a highly collectivist society and one might think Rawls's theory might get a more sympathetic hearing in such a collectivist society. However, the Chinese are not likely to be influenced by Western political philosophy. Thus even if the moral argument is correct, if Chinese business practice runs counter to the argument and yet remains the most successful economy in the world, the correctness of the moral justification is a hollow victory.

There is some reason for optimism here despite the evidence cited above on the other side. China does realize it has an environmental problem and has made some moves to correct it. These moves in the right direction show that China already gives limited acceptance to the second pillar of sustainability-environmental concern.

Although Chinese capitalism does not focus on profits, it does need to be financially viable. And to be financially viable, China must subscribe to what I have elsewhere characterized as a minimum market morality.[39] China must reduce corruption, improve transparency, be committed to quality and safety if its economic system is to thrive. So China must accept the morality that goes with the first pillar of sustainability-financial success.

That leaves the third pillar-protection and support for human rights. At this point in its history China can be said to reject the third pillar. Progress here may be a long time in coming.

Is There a Future for Corporate Social Responsibility in the Twenty-First Century?

I think the answer to this question is "yes." Successful economies must subscribe to a minimum market morality as outlined above. Environmental issues cannot be ignored. So what of the third pillar of "social responsibility?" If social responsibility is understood in terms of solving social problems, then this pillar too will be honored. Unaddressed social problems if they become serious enough lead to social unrest. Business cannot thrive if countries are in social unrest. So business either by itself or in cooperation with government and non-profits will address social problems. Whether they will succeed is another question.

What about social responsibility understood as the protection and enhancement of human rights? I do not have a crystal ball here. However, over the past 200 years we have seen an expansion of human rights, to women and the disabled for instance. International bodies increasingly recognize human rights. And many countries that do not protect human rights, at least pay lip service to them. China, despite its vast economic power, may be on the wrong side of history on this issue.

With all this in mind, I think that both in terms of economic success and in terms of moral adequacy, the sustainability model of corporate social responsibility is the one that is best. I would hope that the United States would move closer to the sustainability model.

---

[39] Bowie, Norman E. (1988). "The Moral Obligations of Multinationals" in Steven Luper-Foy (ed.), *Problems of International Justice*. Boulder: Westview Press. I have maintained versions of the argument in that article in several of my writings.

Chapter 7
Constructing the Universal Norms of International Business

The most perplexing philosophical issue in international business ethics revolves around the question, "Should one do in Rome as the Romans do?" A universal affirmative response to that question seems to endorse ethical relativism and most philosophers are reluctant to go that route. On the other hand, philosophers would also admit that cultural circumstances often do matter, and that what is appropriate moral behavior in one circumstance may not be appropriate moral behavior in other circumstances. Thus philosophers writing in business ethics have tried to avoid ethical relativism on the one hand and, on the other hand, a kind of ethical absolutism in which there are right answers to moral issues independent of the culture.

In this chapter I argue that the only way to both legitimately and pragmatically resolve this "Should one do in Rome as the Romans do?" question is to enter into actual agreements. In developing my answer to this question I begin by contrasting my perspective with those of Thomas Donaldson and the late Thomas W. Dunfee in *Ties That Bind* and Patricia H. Werhane in "Exporting Mental Models."[1] Inspired by the contractualism of John Rawls and the theoretical work of the group of political theorists known as deliberative democracy advocates, I will argue that the universal norms of international business should be constructed. I urge this course of action even if there are universal moral norms that could be discovered by reason (Kant) or empirically (the hypernorms of Donaldson and Dunfee). My approach is dictated by the logic of construction rather than the logic of discovery. I will argue that not only is the construction approach appropriate philosophically but that as a practical matter this approach is being carried out in the practice of international business ethics and in international diplomacy. However, there are so many international agreements we

An early version of this paper was presented at the annual meeting of The Academy of Management, Social Issues in Management Division, August 7, 2001. I appreciate the many helpful comments I received at that time.

[1] Donaldson, Thomas and Thomas W. Dunfee. (1999). *Ties that Bind*. Boston: Harvard Business School Press, and Werhane, Patricia H. (2000). "Exporting Mental Models: Global Capitalism in the 21st Century," *Business Ethics Quarterly*, 10(1), 353–362.

N.E. Bowie, *Business Ethics in the 21st Century*, Issues in Business Ethics 39,
DOI 10.1007/978-94-007-6223-7_7, © Springer Science+Business Media Dordrecht 2013

may be approaching a crisis of legitimacy. Which of the multitude of agreements should a company endorse? I propose criteria for answering that question based on the work of the deliberative democrats. I then apply those criteria to several international agreements and find several of them, despite good intentions, to be wanting. In my view the UN Global Compact has, at this moment, the greatest claim to legitimacy.

The Donaldson/Dunfee Approach

Thomas Donaldson's *Ethics in International Business*[2] appeared in 1989 and like most philosophical discussions of business ethics at that time gave more weight to universal norms and conceded less to cultural conditions. The centerpiece of that book is the ten international human rights that all international businesses must honor to varying degrees. A second key element of the book is an algorithm that tells a corporation in situations not revolving around human rights issues when it should and when it should not do as the Romans do. Despite the widespread praise the book received, many objected that all the international rights were not and perhaps should not be universally accepted. Other critics raised objections to the algorithm. These detailed criticisms and objections will not be reviewed here but I find many of them persuasive. Rather I wish to point out that Donaldson's work is a project of discovery and not a project of construction. By that I mean that Donaldson takes his ten international rights as a starting point without much argument. They are based on intuition and reason although Donaldson believes they are accepted universally. Thus Donaldson discovers them. They are not arrived at through a contractual process-somewhat surprisingly given that Donaldson's earlier and later work is contract based. His algorithm is his own creative contribution and it seems fair to say that he discovered it. In either case neither his list of universal human rights nor his algorithm were constructed from dialogue with others, philosophers, international business leaders, or diplomats. I shall argue that such discovered norms are weaker in the sense of being less justified than norms that are constructed. And I think this is true even if Donaldson is right in his choice of international rights and his algorithm-something that most critics doubt.

Donaldson then entered a creative and productive partnership with Thomas Dunfee that resulted in a series of important articles based on contract theory. The resulting theory is known as integrated social contracts theory (ISCT) and both ISCT and two of the key concepts of the theory, hypernorms and moral free space entered the business ethics literature. Eventually the articles evolved into the important book, *Ties That Bind*. I believe that the book is an interesting compromise between the universalist Donaldson of 1989 and the more relativist oriented legal scholar Dunfee. This book gives much more space to differences in culture and much more

[2] Donaldson, Thomas. (1989). *The Ethics of International Business*. New York: Oxford University Press.

latitude for a "do in Rome" answer to the "When in Rome should you do as the Romans do?" question than does Donaldson's (1989) book. The first principle of the macro contract is: "Local economic communities possess moral free space in which they may generate ethical norms for their members through micro-social contracts."[3] However, Donaldson and Dunfee are no relativists because any authentic micro-social norm can only be legitimate if it is consistent with universal norms. In *Ties That Bind* the true universal norms are the hypernorms.

How are hypernorms discovered and what are they? Hypernorms are universal precepts that can be used to test authentic micro-social norms for moral legitimacy. Donaldson and Dunfee want to keep their epistemological assumptions to a minimum so they remain agnostic as to whether these norms are given in nature, through reason, or revealed by God. To maintain that agnostic position, they endorse a convergence approach to hypernorms. We are told to look to the sages in philosophy, particularly moral theory, and religion. We are told to look at cultural practice and we are told to look at international agreements. Donaldson and Dunfee optimistically believe that we would discover a convergence from these sources on certain procedural, structural and substantive hypernorms. It is significant to note that international agreements are an important source to examine for hypernorms, but the mechanics of these international agreements are not discussed. This is still a theory based on discovery rather than construction. We search for hypernorms in certain places and with luck we may discover that ethical theory, religious tradition, cultural practice and collective agreements might overlap. When such overlaps occur we have a hypernorm.

The difficulty with this approach can be seen when we look at some of the examples that Donaldson and Dunfee provide. Particularly instructive is their discussion as to whether or not there is a hypernorm regarding gender discrimination. Suppose a global express delivery firm regularly employs women drivers in their worldwide operations. However, in Saudi Arabia women are not allowed to drive and the issue facing the express delivery firm is whether the firm should honor this authentic[4] norm and not hire women drivers in Saudi Arabia. (I realize as a practical matter they can't.) However, should they morally be permitted to hire women drivers? Donaldson and Dunfee argue that they should; they believe there is a hypernorm against such gender discrimination. They say:

> Prohibitions of this selective type of gender discrimination can be found in standards of the United Nations, the ILO, the laws of many countries, major philosophies and religions. The evidence appears to meet the standard establishing a presumption. On the other hand the Saudi norm is based upon a religious interpretation; but the vast majority of other Muslim countries does not share this interpretation. Again the hypernorm is established.[5]

I assume that we must conclude from this analysis that the Saudi norm on this matter is not legitimate and that morally the express delivery company should hire

---

[3] Donaldson and Dunfee, op.cit., 46.

[4] For Donaldson and Dunfee a norm is authentic if the vast majority of the community accepts it. See Ibid., 39.

[5] Ibid., 61–62.

women drivers. As a practical matter it means, I think, that the express delivery service should withdraw from Saudi Arabia, since the Saudis will not permit women drivers. However, it is important to recognize that the Saudis emphatically deny that they are doing anything wrong. They believe that their culture does respect women and that such respect requires that women not be permitted to drive.

What move can Donaldson and Dunfee make? How can such a dispute be settled? And such disputes are hardly figments of the philosopher's imagination. China is a signatory to the UN Declaration on Human Rights, but they do not interpret those rights the way Americans do. China also acknowledged certain human rights norms in order to gain entrance into the World Trade Organization but China protested bitterly when it believed the U.S. was shoving its interpretation of these norms down its throat. Ditto with winning U.S. Congressional approval for Most Favored Nations status for trade with the United States. Thus when writers like me and Donaldson and Dunfee look to international agreements and say that country x or country y signed, we are taking an overly simplified approach. Their interpretation of what they signed may be very different from the interpretation that Western countries may put on those same principles. Lee Kuan Yew the former prime minister of Singapore has been most ada- mant in expressing that point of view. Singapore thinks it has a better handle on human rights than American society does. What is needed in these cases is further dialogue to see where the areas of agreement about human rights lie and where the disagreements lie. One can then work to narrow the disagreement. But to move, as Donaldson and Dunfee seem to do in the case above is too quick. There is a hypernorm for respect for women, but is there really a hypernorm about gender discrimination?

Finally one can argue that the discovery of convergence is not enough. Const- ruction must both precede discovery and follow discovery. Suppose we agree with Donaldson and Dunfee that there is a hypernorm against bribery. However there is no hypernorm that bribery is wrong everywhere in international business transac- tions. Transparency International has pointed out that some of the countries that have few bribe takers have a large number of bribe givers. It is not enough that each country has a norm that bribery not be permitted in its country. We need a norm that says that bribery everywhere in business is wrong. We need an actual contract where representatives from business and government agree what is to count as bribery and further agree in a collective action that bribery so defined is wrong. In this way a universal norm against bribery is constructed rather than merely discovered. To put it another way the best way to justify the universal norm against bribery is not to simply appeal to the fact that all countries have laws against it, but that all countries have laws against it and that the signatories have signed a contract where they agree that bribery is wrong everywhere in the context of international business and further the signatories have publicly endorsed that view. And the good news is that every international agreement that has recently been developed or is in the process of being formulated does endorse such a view with respect to bribery. Thus I am argu- ing that we need an approach to hypernorms that emphasizes construction rather than discovery.

I now turn to Patricia Werhane's warnings about the dangers that attend those who would argue for universal standards.

The Patricia Werhane Approach

The danger that universalists face is that the norms or concepts claimed to be universal are in fact parochial. Manny Velsaquez puts it this way. "All of the absolutist approaches that contemporary ethics has set before us (utilitarianism, justice principles, and human rights theories), and that aspire to universal validity are in fact parochial."[6] One reason for the parochial nature of universal claims is that we are trapped by what Professor Patricia Werhane calls our mental models.[7] Mental models are conceptual frameworks through which we structure the world of our experiences. It is a way we humans have of organizing our experiences and giving them meaning. What concerns Werhane is that a mental model of free enterprise American capitalism is being exported uncritically to the rest of the world. She then provides several cases where the uncritical acceptance of this mental model was socially disastrous. Mental models are not limited to conceptions of economic organization. As Werhane says, "Abstract ideas such as autonomy, equality, private property, ownership and community create mental models that take on different meanings depending on the situational and social context."[8]

Professor Werhane is certainly right to raise such concerns but don't Werhane's concerns run the danger of cultural relativism and the conclusion that when in Rome one ought to do as the Romans do. Werhane at times comes dangerously close to relativism. For example, Werhane says, "One needs to examine one's own mental models and try to fathom which models are operating in the community in which a company is planning to operate. In particular, it is important to find out what the operative social structures and community relationships are, what it is that this community values as social good, and try to imagine how those things might be different given the introduction of a new kind of economic system."[9] Werhane tries to avoid the relativistic implications of her position by arguing that there is a "thin thread of universal agreement about "bads" which cannot be tolerated or should not be permitted in any community (what Walzer calls moral minimums).[10] Werhane then identifies these universal "bads" as deficient or despicable living conditions, indecencies, violations of human rights, mistreatment, and other harms."[11]

But surely what counts as a bad is itself determined by our mental model. As mentioned previously, several Asian thinkers such as Lee Kuan Yew have argued that they accept human rights, but not the western version of human rights. Such thinkers, it seems to me are taking the mental model methodology seriously.

---

[6] Velasquez, Manuel. (2000). "Globalization and the Failure of Ethics," *Business Ethics Quarterly,* 10(1), 346.

[7] Werhane. op.cit.

[8] Ibid., 357.

[9] Ibid., 358.

[10] Ibid. The reference to Walzer is Walzer, Michael. (1994). *Thick and Thin.* Notre Dame: Notre Dame University Press.

[11] Ibid.

Also Velasquez argues that the notion that people ought to be treated equally would not carry weight in societies that are organized by what they believe to be a natural hierarchy. The egalitarian mental model would not appeal to those whose mental model is organized around a natural hierarchy or caste system.[12] Thus I would argue that Werhane cannot escape relativism by appealing to these universal "bads."

It also seems to follow from Werhane's analysis that international companies doing business or setting up subsidiaries in host countries should sacrifice their own norms and adopt the norms of the host country unless doing so were to involve the company in a universal bad. But could such a priority rule be justified? Should a Japanese company doing business in the US adopt the employment at will doctrine- a doctrine that Werhane has roundly criticized in many of her own writings? Unless Werhane can show that the employment at will doctrine is a universal bad, I believe her arguments would require the Japanese to follow the American norm here. I see no conclusive reason why national norms should trump the norms of international business. More about that later.

Thus Professor Werhane's injunction to engage our moral imagination on the when in Rome question is not enough. What is needed is equal dialogue that results in agreement. Imagination may be a necessary first step, but what is ultimately needed is a social contract.

International Agreements

The rapid growth of international business and the limits of international law leave business enterprises at sea as they navigate through the various moral and legal norms of the countries in which they do business. Business transactions would be smoother if there were at least some common rules or at least common understandings. Interestingly enough there is considerable international activity devoted toward developing such norms. As evidence that this approach has some promise one can cite the numerous agreements that have either been adopted or are being worked out as we speak. After a number of exposes regarding sweatshop conditions in supplier plants to the apparel industry, both the Fair Labor Association (FLA) and Social Accountability International developed industry wide standards for supplier firms. By the way most university labeled apparel is governed by the FLA. One hundred one countries met in late October 2000 to discuss an international treaty regulating tobacco and curbing smoking by teenagers.[13] Here is a partial list of international institutions that promulgate principles on the conduct of business across geographic boundaries: The OECD Guidelines for Multinational Enterprises, The ILO Tripartite Declaration concerning Multinational Enterprises and Social Policy, The Caux

---

[12] Velasquez, op.cit., 348.
[13] *The New York Times* October 15, 2000, 4.

Principles, The Global Sullivan Principles, The ICC Rules of Conduct on Extortion and Bribery in International Business Transactions, The ICC Business Charter of Sustainable Development, various ICC marketing and advertising codes, The Responsible Care programme (chemical industry) and the Coalition for Environmentally Responsible Economics (Ceres) Principles. There is also Amnesty International's Human Rights Guidelines for Companies and the ICCR, ECCR, TCCR Principles for Global Corporate Responsibility.[14]

The attempt by international organizations is just the approach I think is needed to get international standards of business conduct that all parties that sign on to the agreements believe are justified and once agreed to have a chance of being practically effective. What provides the justification and practicality is the fact that the standards are constructed by agreement among the parties. This is what I mean by saying that the norms of international business should be constructed rather than discovered.

Some might object that it is possible that the constructed standards violate a higher morality-a hypernorm if you wish. However, how would the person arguing this persuade the participants to the agreement that what they had done was morally mistaken. The person could enter into a dialogue with them to convince the participants that they are mistaken. That is the correct way to proceed. The constructivist position encourages such dialogue. But if the person criticizing the agreement cannot convince them, then the only path open is for the critic not to participate in activities covered by the agreement. If there had been an international agreement that companies could stay inside South Africa during Apartheid so long as they had engaged the South African government with respect to Apartheid, a corporation that thought the agreement was morally incorrect should not do business in South Africa. (This example is purely hypothetical since the international agreement went the other way. However, companies like IBM that did not agree with the Sullivan principles as the agreement was known, did remain in business in South Africa.) Constructing international agreements is the way to resolve the, "When in Rome should you do as the Romans do?," problem. The way to answer the question is by constructing an agreement rather than by discovering the "right" answer.

A Problem: The Multiplicity of Agreements

Which, if any, of the above agreements should a corporation sign? The response of a senior corporate official on this issue surprised me. He indicated that companies did not see this as a major issue. They would sign any agreement so long as it did

---

[14] This list is representative rather than exhaustive. The January 2011 issue of *Business Ethics Quarterly* contains a special section on "Accountability in a Global Economy." There are 5 excellent articles in this collection. I especially recommend the article by Gilbert, Rasche, and Waddock, "The Emergence of International Accountability Standards", 23–44.

not conflict with the company's core values. In other words, there was an issue of legitimacy but that issue was not about the multitude of ethics codes but rather it was about whether the codes were consistent with the authentic moral norms of the company. There are a number of reasons for this. First, upwardly mobile managers in international firms gain the experience they need by managing subsidiaries in a variety of countries. If the core values of the company change from country to country, these managers will suffer from the phenomenon of cognitive dissonance. They will no longer know what the company is and what it stands for. For those companies that have made a strong ethical commitment part of their core values, there is even a greater reason to try to maintain consistency across cultures. To change one's moral stripes would undermine the moral reputation of the company.[15] For example if a corporation has become known as environmentally friendly in the US and indeed increased its profits as a result of that reputation, then it would be foolish for that company to simply meet the legal minimum in countries where it does business and the environmental laws are not as strict. Once that became known its reputation in the U.S. would suffer as well. That is why the Dupont Company has the following principle with respect to health and safety: "If our safety standards are higher, we use ours. If the other country's are higher, we use theirs." So there are a number of business reasons why an international company would not want to adopt the local host country's authentic micro-social norms. And often I do not see any moral reason why, when the host country norms conflict with the core values and the core values do not conflict with genuine universal norms why they should. My position here is very different from both Donaldson/Dunfee and Werhane who seem to give preference to host country norms.

Consider the previously mentioned issue of whether a Japanese company with a subsidiary in the United States should adopt the U.S. practice of employment at will. I do not see the logic of a requirement that the Japanese should adopt U.S. practice. After all many international companies have economic resources that exceed the GDP of many countries. I do not see why the norms of nation states should necessarily take precedence over the norms of multinationals. For example, I see nothing wrong with a Japanese company refusing to adopt the American principle of employment at will when doing business in the U.S. In addition, as pointed out above, there are also good business reasons for the Japanese to stick with their own practice even in the United States. Thus the practices of international companies seem at odds with Werhane's seeming preference for following host country norms.

What of Donaldson/Dunfee? I frankly find their advice inconsistent here. On the one hand they seems to say that when an international company confronts a legitimate and authentic micro-social norm in another country that differs from its own

---

[15] A colleague and I have elaborated this argument and defended it in detail. See Bowie. Norman E. and Paul Vaaler. (1999). "Some Arguments for Universal Moral Standards" in Georges Enderle (ed.), *International Business Ethics: Challenges and Approaches*. Notre Dame: University of Notre Dame Press, 160–173.

core values, then in that case it should do as the Romans do. Morally an international company ought to respect the legitimate norms of the countries where it does business. After all their Rule of Thumb 1 for settling conflicts of norms says:

1. Transactions solely within a single community, which do not have significant adverse effects on other human beings or communities, should be governed by the host community's norms.

And rule of thumb number 4 says:

4. Norms essential to the maintenance of the economic environment in which the transaction occurs should have priority over norms potentially damaging to that environment.[16]

Those two norms seem to give preference to the host country over the norms of the multinational. Several of the examples that Donaldson and Dunfee cite seem consistent with those two rules of thumb. For example, on page 45 they say "To the extent that the moral rules pertaining to public auctions are different in Australia from Indonesia, the Indonesian manager should follow the Australian auction norms so long as doing so has consequences primarily confined to Australia."

On the other hand consider their discussion of Rule of Thumb #2, Donaldson and Dunfee cite with approval the "corporate imperialists" AT&T, Levi Strauss and Motorola, that in times of conflict have followed their own core values (internal norms) rather than the norms of the host country.[17] They seem to think that Levi Strauss has a procedure for settling value conflicts that trump rules of thumb 1 and 4?[18] But why do the corporate values prevail in this case but not in other cases?

In any case to the extent that Donaldson and Dunfee would require international companies to adopt host country standards there is a significant disagreement between what their moral theory requires and the standard practice of US multinationals. At this point it is sufficient to point out that most international companies would not accept the priority rules that Donaldson and Dunfee endorse. And more importantly, I do not think they would be necessarily wrong.

Negotiated Agreements and Questions of Legitimacy

On my theory such conflicts need to be resolved by actual social contracts, that is, international agreements. When relevant both international companies and the representatives of nation states ought to be parties to the agreement. A discussion of these issues leads us directly to a discussion of legitimacy. The legitimacy issue can

---

[16] Donaldson and Dunfee, op.cit., 184, 187.

[17] Ibid., 185.

[18] Ibid., 186.

be illustrated with the Caux Roundtable Principles for Business. These principles are heavily indebted to the Minnesota principles and the work of Kenneth Goodpaster. However, regardless of their meritorious content, there was no chance that the Minnesota Principles could become the standard for international business. Even if everyone accepted the contents of the Minnesota principles, it would seem parochial to have truly international standards that had "Minnesota" in the title. This may seem like a small issue, but recall that my position is committed to the existence of actual contracts. When Chairman Kaku of the Canon Corporation introduced the Japanese notion of Kyosei into the principles, the contents had a bit more of an international flavor. But this content could only become the Caux Roundtable Principles when the Caux Roundtable endorsed them. And I can tell you that the members of that body did discuss the principles and had input into the final document.

However, the Caux Roundtable is itself a self-appointed un-elected group of businesspersons. Its original purpose was to support free trade. Its meetings are not open to non-members. It makes no claim to be truly representative of the variety of business interests around the world. Indeed when the principles were endorsed there were no representatives from Latin America, Australia, Africa, or any other Asian country except Japan. No business entity need honor those principles until it endorses them. To those who have not endorsed them, they carry no authority whatsoever. None of this should be taken as critical of the Caux Roundtable. Indeed they should be commended for physically taking the Principles to various parts of the world and getting them endorsed. As a result of their efforts the Principles have been translated into 12 languages and presented to the United Nations World Social Summit.

There are of course regional agreements but they have limited legitimacy as well. The European Community has spoken as one on a number of issues including outlawing bribery. Indeed their anti bribery provisions may be even stronger than those of the Foreign Corrupt Practices Act in the U.S. And unlike the Caux Roundtable Principles, they are binding on members of the European Community and on anyone doing business in the European Union. That is because that body is duly and legally representative of the members of the European community and has been given the authority to do the things it does. But they are regional agreements and by definition their claims to legitimacy are limited.

Also compare the Caux Roundtable with the International Chamber of Commerce (ICC) that has been working in this area for over 20 years and which describes itself at its website as the world business organization. The ICC claims that it is a world business organization rather than a regional one. Is it more representative than the Caux Roundtable (which also claims to be a world business organization?)? It was founded much earlier, 1919 vs. 1986 and over 2,300 companies have signed its statements on the environment. Also it is now working in partnership with the United Nations having been granted highest-level consultative status. As a kind of philosophical position piece, the ICC states the following:

> Self-regulation is a common thread running through the work of the commissions. The conviction that business operates most effectively with a minimum of government intervention inspired ICC's voluntary codes. Marketing codes cover sponsoring, advertising practice, sales promotion, marketing and social research, direct sales practice, and marketing on the

Internet. Launched in 1991, ICC's Business Center for Sustainable Development provides 16 principles for good environmental conduct that have been endorsed by more than 2,300 companies and business associations.[19]

Do the ICC principles have a greater claim to legitimacy than those of the Caux Roundtable? If number of signatories is accepted as one indication of legitimacy and I think it should be, then the ICC principles have an edge over the principles of the Caux Roundtable.

Let us do another comparison-this time using the AA 1000 standards and the SA 8000 standard. The December 1999 issue of *Ethical Performance* had as its feature story the standards launched by the Institute of Social and Ethical Accountability that are designed to help companies improve their overall ethical performance. The standards, which are known as AA 1000, are designed to guide businesses on "how they should talk to stakeholders, develop performance indicators, carry out social audits, produce social reports, and measure ethical standards." But their appeal is meant to be universal. A spokesperson for the group says, "We have designed it as a foundation standard that offers a common currency of principles and processes and a common language."

The AA 1000 accounting measure is under the sponsorship of The Institute of Social and Ethical Accountability. It was launched at a meeting in Copenhagen in November 1999. It claims to be the first global standard for the ethical performance of organizations-a claim that could be disputed by the backers of SA 8000 discussed below. The Accountability web site points out that AA 1000 is focused on securing the quality of social and ethical accounting, auditing, and reporting. Moreover, the organization is in the business of training and certification. The organization seems to be in the ethics business. A visit to its website will give an overview of the ASA 1000 in read only format. On what grounds should a company accept the AA 1000 standard? More importantly can an organization that is in the ethics business have a claim to legitimacy over a negotiated agreement by all the relevant stakeholders to the agreement? After all the standards were created by the organization and then put out there for companies to accept or not.

Social Accountability International inaugurated the SA 8000 standard in October 1997. It came about as a result of a meeting of interested parties where originally it was agreed that the standard should be under the direction of the Council for Economic Priorities, a high profile NGO with headquarters in New York and London. The standard is a third party code which can be applied internationally across all commercial sectors to evaluate whether companies and other organizations are complying with basic standards of labor and human rights practices. Although certification was originally with the Council for Economic Priorities, certification is now controlled by Social Accountability International itself. As of December 31, 2010 SA 8000® certification covers over 2,700 facilities in 62 countries, across 65 industries, and over 1.6 million employees.[20]

---

[19] Found at website www.iccbo.org/home/icc_and_unitednations/history_of_the_icc.asp

[20] From the Social Accountability International website at http://www.sa-intl.org/index.cfm?useaction=Page.viewPage&pageId=472

It should be noted that the standard itself is based on a series of international conventions and agreements, particularly those of the ILO and the UN Declaration on Human Rights. These agreements provide what is referred to as the normative elements. Many UK and U.S. companies have used the standard to audit suppliers. It is generally admitted, however, that these standards are subject to different interpretation and that the standard cannot be applied dictatorially. The certification activities as well as other activities related to corporate social responsibility have expanded greatly since 1999.

I would argue that the SA 8000 standards have a slightly greater claim to legitimacy compared to the AA 1000 standards. The fact that they are sponsored by a NGO gives them better claim to neutrality than a for profit business that might be tempted to mold its code to appeal to the businesses that are likely to sign them. However, this advantage has lessened as the organization has greatly expanded the services for which it collects a fee. The fact that their normative content is derived by international agreements is a stronger factor in their favor. Finally, they have already been accepted by a number of firms and a number of firms use them to monitor supply chains. All of these factors give an edge to the SA 8000 standards.

Despite initial appearances I think the SA 8000 standard does not command the legitimacy of another attempt to provide universal standards for business-the UN Global Compact. The SA 8000 standard does not meet the conditions of legitimacy that I think should be required. The initial SA 8000 standard resulted from conversations between a SGS Director and other interested parties. The Council for Economic Priorities does not have the international representation of a number of other bodies. As of now the relation of Social Accountancy International to the Council for Economic Priorities is unclear. Neither mentions the other on its respective website. Nonetheless the perspective of Social Accountability International is still primarily Western. The greatest use of the standard has been by Western companies to audit Asian suppliers. Even though its normative content is based on international agreements, some of its provisions contain language that will limit its acceptance. For example, on discrimination, the language is as follows:

5. No discrimination based on race, national or social origin, caste, birth, religion, disability, gender, sexual orientation, union membership, political opinions and age. No discrimination in hiring, remuneration, access to training, promotion, termination, and retirement. No interference with exercise of personnel tenets or practices; prohibition of threatening, abusive, exploitative, coercive behaviour at workplace or company facilities; no pregnancy or virginity tests under any circumstances.[21]

It seems clear that as we saw in the earlier discussion of the treatment of women in Saudi Arabia, the anti-discrimination requirement is far too broad to get genuine consent from many parties. There certainly is no hypernorm or much in the way of voluntary international agreement that would justify a standard of non-discrimination

---

[21] Social Accountancy Website http://www.sa-intl.org/index.cfm?fuseaction=Page.viewPage&pageId=1140&parentID=473&nodeID=1, Downloaded February 20, 2012.

as extensive as the one articulated in SA 8000. Please note that I am not disagreeing with the standard. Rather what I am saying is that we cannot currently get universal agreement to accept such a standard. And such universal agreement should be our goal.

It seems to me that the most wide-ranging comprehensive and legitimate organization for constructing the norms of international business is the UN Global Compact. After all the United Nations is the recognized international body with the most member countries. In addition the organizations that accept the Global Compact each must actually endorse it. By that I mean that an international corporation is only bound by the agreement if it actually signs it. Thus the fact that a nation belongs to the United Nations does not mean that multinationals with home offices in that nation are thereby bound to the Compact. The Compact is a compact between the United Nations and the signatory companies. As former Secretary General Kofi Annan said, "The Global Compact is an initiative to safeguard sustainable growth within the context of globalization by promoting a core set of universal values which are fundamental to meeting the socioeconomic needs of the world's people today and tomorrow."[22] The universal values are expressed in nine principles grouped under human rights, labour, and environment. These principles will need to be implemented through dialogue and an agreed upon Global Reporting Initiative. The UN will work through the International Labour Organization, Business for Social Responsibility and the Prince of Wales Business Leaders Forum. as well as other partners. The International Chamber of Commerce has endorsed this approach. Thus the UN Global Compact has a greater claim to legitimacy than most international organizations because (1) of the range of member countries, (2) the fact that acceptance of the Compact is voluntary on the part of each signatory, (3) that each signatory is entering a contract with a truly international body and (4) that the implementation of the nine principles is through dialogue.

Philosophical Grounding for Constructing Universal Norms

Part of the theoretical basis for my account of legitimacy comes from the work of a group of scholars called deliberative democrats who have been influenced by the work of Habermas.[23] These scholars argue that majority voting is not sufficient to justify democratic decision-making. What is needed in a democracy is adequate voice. What is impressive about the UN Global Compact is the amount of voice that is given to NGO's and corporations as the General Reporting Initiative and the Code of Conduct are developed. I believe the UN Global Compact has a better claim for providing voice than the other international agreements.

---

[22] United Nations Document.

[23] See for example, Thompson, Dennis and Amy Gutmann. (1996). *Democracy and Disagreement.* Cambridge: Harvard University Press.

However, acceptance of the provisions of the contract does commit the signatories to specific actions. To ensure accountability signatories are being asked to endorse the Global Reporting Initiative (GRI). GRI's vision is to create a voluntary framework within which corporations worldwide publicly disseminate information that is comparable, consistent and credible-in short to elevate sustainability reporting to a level equivalent to financial reporting. Current information on the GRI can be obtained by going to https://www.globalreporting.org/Pages/default.aspx

The construction of these norms-at least in so far as they apply to human rights issues- is now underway. The Commission on Human Rights sponsors the effort, which is under the Economic and Social Council of the United Nations. In an earlier version of this paper, I said the following about the work of the Commission.

"The drafting group is called the Working Group on the Methods and Activities of Transnational Corporations. I have been privileged to see and comment on the drafts of the two documents, Principles Relating to Human Rights Conduct by Companies, and Principles Relating to Human Rights Conduct by Companies with Source Materials. As drafted, I think the principles are too broad to gain acceptance and are subject to some of the criticisms that I made against the SA 8000 principles. However, there are clear provisions for revising the document in light of input from the myriad of cooperating organizations. If I am right in claiming greater legitimacy for the UN Global Compact, the message to these other organizations is that they should work together with the UN Global Compact. The UN welcomes cooperative participation."

My reservations at that time were well founded. The draft guidelines have been abandoned. What we now have before us is what is known as the Ruggie Principles, named for John Ruggie, special Representative of the Secretary-General on the issue of human rights and transnational corporations and other business enterprises. One quotation will give you the flavor of the document:

> The Framework rests on three pillars: the State duty to protect against human rights abuses by third parties, including business, through appropriate policies, regulation, and adjudication; the corporate responsibility to respect human rights, which means to act with due diligence to avoid infringing on the rights of others and to address adverse impacts that occur; and greater access for victims to effective remedy, judicial and non-judicial.[24]

This Chapter is not concerned with an explanation and evaluation of the responsibilities of business with respect to human rights.[25] Also it is important to point out that the content of these guidelines is limited to the responsibilities of corporations with respect to human rights. The guidelines are not an exhaustive set of guidelines that apply to all issues of business ethics. What is important here is that the process of devising the guidelines involves the kind of construction of universal norms that I support. In addition the guidelines take notice of the work of others in this field.

---

[24] Ruggies, John, Guiding Principles For The Implementation Of The United Nations 'Protect, Respect And Remedy' Framework, p. 3.

[25] For that task see, Munchlinski, Peter. (2012). "Implementing the New UN Corporate Human Rights Framework," *Business Ethics Quarterly,* 22(1), 145–177.

The Guiding Principles' normative contribution lies not in the creation of new international law obligations but in elaborating the implications of existing standards and practices for States and businesses; integrating them within a single, coherent and comprehensive template; and identifying where the current regime falls short and how it should be improved.[26]

This kind of construction of international norms is slow and laborious but it seems to me that this process is the only way to have norms of international business ethics obtain something close to universal legitimacy. There is nothing wrong with philosophers and others who propose international norms and who argue for them. But the legitimacy of these norms is best achieved through collective dialogue. The Ruggie principles were achieved by the right process.

A Difficulty

One of the common requirements for legitimacy has been omitted from the discussion thus far. The other constituent of legitimacy is the requirement that it be non-coercive. Most moral and political philosophers would argue that coerced agreements lose some or all of their binding force. Donaldson and Dunfee agree.

It seems to me that the problem with many collective agreements is that the signatories believed that economic or political circumstances forced them to sign. They were in fact (on at least some definitions of coercion) coerced. For example in human rights debates with the Chinese, some might try to score points by reminding the Chinese that they are signatories to the UN Declaration on Human Rights. The Chinese cannot deny that they are signatories, but they argue that their interpretation of human rights is very different from the way they are interpreted in the West. In the debates surrounding their admittance to the World Trade Organization and to Most Favored Nation trade status, the Chinese deeply resented the fact that the United States seemed to force its interpretation of human rights down their throats. Some in the Mideast feel the same way about the interpretation of international non-discrimination statutes. How can it be argued that an international agreement is legitimate on my terms if a country or corporation believes that it must sign or accept a certain interpretation of the agreement in order to achieve economic benefits? The non-coercion condition would not be met.

For the initial corporate signatories I believe the UN Global Compact and the Ruggie principles do well on the non-coercion score as well. Greater voice and broader representation are more likely to lead to more universal agreement. But should more and more corporations sign on, not only to the nine principles, but also to the Global Reporting Initiative, what position would those last holdouts be in? If there are real business benefits to being a signatory and if nearly all other corporations, including their competitors, are signatories, wouldn't they feel forced to be a signatory as well?

---

[26] Ruggles, op.cit., 4.

Quite frankly I see no way out of this difficulty. As a voluntary agreement gains acceptance, there is greater pressure on those who have not agreed to accept it. All that can be done is to give as much opportunity for voice as one can and for the majority signatories to take seriously any arguments by those who have still not signed on.

Summary

As I have analyzed these international agreements, I have tried to take the idea of the social contract seriously. I have tried to avoid the metaphor of discovery and focus instead on the metaphor of construction. By focusing on construction, I am not denying that there are universal principles to be discovered. However, even if these principles were self-evident to all, there are still issues of implementation across diverse cultures. And besides these principles are not universally self-evident. Thus as a practical matter, both the principles and their implementation must be constructed. Moreover, justification requires construction as well. On some issues, such as bribery, agreement on the principles may be easy although agreement on implementation may be more difficult. On other issues, e.g., agreement on a non-discrimination norm, will almost certainly be contentious. However, if we are to have universal standards for business that pass the requirements for legitimacy, we have little choice in the matter. The arduous task of construction must be undertaken. At this point, I believe that the United Nations Social Compact is the best positioned to undertake a construction that passes the tests of legitimacy. The Ruggie principles are already a significant step in the right direction.

Part IV
Specific Business Ethics Issues

Chapter 8
Morality, Money, and Motor Cars Revisited

Background

My 1990 article Morality Money and Motor Cars is, as many critics have pointed out strikingly at odds with the rest of my published work. How did I come to write such an anomalous piece? Both Kenneth Goodpaster and I were invited by Michael Hoffman and his colleagues to address the Eighth National Conference on Business Ethics at Bentley College in the fall of 1990. Goodpaster and I were to be on the program together and we jokingly referred to each other as the Minnesota Twins. However, I thought for this occasion I should differentiate myself from Goodpaster and indeed from most of the philosophers who were writing on business and/or environmental ethics. I decided to write a sort of pro Friedman like piece on the environment. I succeeded and to my amazement this piece may be the most anthologized piece that I have written.

Not surprisingly the article has been rather roundly criticized by my colleagues and friends. It would be easy to simply dismiss the article as an attempt to be provocative but not really a statement of my real position. However, I actually do believe much of what I said in that early article. Some claims need to be softened. Some of the arguments need to be tighter. This chapter represents my latest thinking on the ideas expressed in the original article and takes into account much of the critical scholarship surrounding the article. I also will explain and comment on the attempt by Marc Cohen and John Dienhart to change the orientation of the article so that it fits more naturally into my Kantian project in business ethics.

This is an updated version of the article that appeared in W. M. Hoffman, R. Frederick, and E. S. Petry Jr., eds. *Business Ethics and the Environment* (*New York*: *Quorum Books*), *1990, 89–97*, Material from the original article is reprinted with permission of the Center for Business Ethics, Bentley College, Waltham MA: and its director Michael Hoffman. Several paragraphs are also taken from "A Reply to My Critics" in *Kantian Business Ethics*: *Critical Perspectives*, Denis G Arnold and Jared Harris eds. Edward Elgar Publishing 2012. Reprinted by Permission of Edward Elgar Publishing.

Environmentalists frequently argue that business has special obligations to protect the environment. Although I agree with the environmentalists on this point, I do not agree with them as to where the obligations lie. In the original article I made the following rather bold claims that need to be softened. One of the more important ones was the following: "Business does not have an obligation to protect the environment over and above what is required by law; however, it does have a moral obligation to avoid intervening in the political arena in order to defeat or weaken environmental legislation."[1] Even in the original article, I conceded that business may have an obligation to educate consumers about the environmental impact of the decisions they make. I now argue that for some companies there is a moral obligation to educate. To be credible, I also need to consider the practical aspects of my claim that companies should not lobby in order to defeat or weaken environmental legislation. In this article I will consider some moral constraints on such lobbying. Thus I do not think that all business attempts to lobby in order to weaken environmental legislation are wrong, but I do think there are moral limitations on the process of such lobbying.

Some readers of the original article thought that I was endorsing the principle, "If it's legal, it's ethical." Nothing could be further from the truth. Indeed, Chap. 1 of this volume contains an update of my article, "Fair Markets" that shows convincingly that such a doctrine is inconsistent with what we know about legal decision making. In the original article business had a moral obligation with respect to lobbying that was more demanding –far more demanding-than its legal obligations with respect to lobbying. These moral obligations remain in this article although they are less restrictive than the obligations in the original article. I did argue then and I continue to argue here-with two important exceptions- that business has no moral obligation to go beyond the law with respect to the products they put in the market place. The exceptions are that business has a moral obligation to educate consumers about their environmental choices and that business is limited in the way they can lobby about environmental issues. What is the reasoning for this claim?

Distinguishing Special Obligations to the Environment from Other Moral Obligations

In developing this thesis, several points are in order. First, many businesses have violated important moral obligations, and the violations have had a severe negative impact on the environment. For example, toxic waste haulers have illegally dumped hazardous material, and the environment has been harmed as a result, One might argue that those toxic waste haulers who have illegally dumped have violated a special obligation to the environment. Isn't it more accurate to say that these toxic

---

[1] Bowie, Norman E. (1990). "Money, Morality, and Motor Cars" in W.M. Hoffman, R. Frederick, and E.S. Petry (eds.), *Business Ethics and the Environment*. New York: Quorum Books, 89.

waste haulers have violated their obligation to obey the law and that in this case the law that has been broken is one pertaining to the environment? Businesses have an obligation to obey the law—environmental laws and all others. Since there are many well-publicized cases of businesses having broken environmental laws, it is easy to think that businesses have violated some special obligations to the environment. In fact, what businesses have done is to disobey the law. Environmentalists do not need a special obligation to the environment to protect the environment against illegal business activity; they need only insist that business obey the laws.

Business has broken other moral obligations besides the moral obligation to obey the law and has harmed the environment as a result. Consider the explosion and sinking of British Petroleum's (BP) Deepwater Horizon in the Gulf of Mexico in the summer of 2010. This event cost 11 lives and resulted in the worst environmental spill in American history. It was a true environmental disaster. Various investigations have cited lax safety procedures at BP as one of the causes, Moreover, BP had a long history of safety violations in the United States before the Deepwater Horizon explosion. A BP refinery explosion in Texas resulted in the largest fine ever levied at that time-21 million dollars. Moreover, BP had been cited for numerous safety violations even after the explosion-some 700 safety violations.[2]

A reasonable position in this matter is to claim that BP's policies were so lax that the company could be characterized as morally negligent. In such a case, BP would have violated its moral obligation to use due care and avoid negligence. Although its negligence was disastrous to the environment, BP would have violated no special obligation to the environment. But it would have violated a straight forward moral obligation to avoid being negligent.

Environmentalists, like government officials, employees, and stockholders, expect that business firms and officials have moral obligations to obey the law, avoid negligent behavior, and tell the truth. In sum, although many business decisions have harmed the environment, these decisions violated no special environmental moral obligations. If a corporation is negligent in providing for worker safety, we do not say the corporation violated a special obligation to employees; we say that it violated its obligation to avoid negligent behavior.

Why Business Has Few Special Obligations to Protect the Environment

The crucial issues concerning business obligations to the environment focus on the excess use of natural resources (the dwindling supply of oil and gas, for instance) and the externalities of production (pollution, for instance). The critics of business

---

[2] Lyall, Sarah. (2010). "In BP's Record, A History of Boldness and Costly Blunders," *New York Times*, July 12.

want to claim that business has some special obligation to mitigate or solve these problems. I believe this claim is largely mistaken. It is largely but not completely mistaken because there is an important exception to my general claim. If business does have a special obligation to help solve the environmental crisis, that obligation results from the special knowledge that business firms have. If they have greater expertise than other constituent groups in society, then it can be argued that, other things being equal, business's responsibilities to mitigate the environmental crisis are somewhat greater. Absent this condition, business's responsibility is no greater than and may be less than that of other social groups. What leads me to think that the critics of business are mistaken?

William Frankena distinguished obligations in an ascending order of the difficulty in carrying them out; avoiding harm, preventing harm, and doing good.[3] The most stringent requirement, to avoid harm, insists no one has a right to render harm on another unless there is a compelling, overriding moral reason to do so. Some writers have referred to this obligation as the moral minimum. A corporation's behavior is consistent with the moral minimum if it causes no avoidable harm to others.

Preventing harm is a less stringent obligation, but sometimes the obligation to prevent harm may be nearly as strict as the obligation to avoid harm. Under what conditions must we be good Samaritans? Some have argued that four conditions must exist before one is obligated to prevent harm: capability, need, proximity, and last resort.[4]

The least strict moral obligation is to do good—to make contributions to society or to help solve problems (inadequate primary schooling in the inner cities, for example). I have argued elsewhere that corporations have imperfect duties of this sort.[5] Although corporations may have some minimum obligation in this regard based on an argument from corporate citizenship, the obligations of the corporation to do good cannot be expanded without limit. An open-ended injunction to assist in solving societal problems makes impossible demands on a corporation because, at the practical level, it ignores the impact that such activities have on profit.

It might seem that even if this descending order of strictness of obligations were accepted, obligations toward the environment would fall into the moral minimum category. After all, the depletion of natural resources and pollution surely harm the environment. If so, wouldn't the obligations business has to the environment be among the strictest obligations a business can have?

Suppose, however, that a businessperson argues that the phrase "avoid harm" usually applies to human beings. Polluting a lake is not like injuring a human with

---

[3] Frankena, William. (1973). *Ethics*, 2nd ed. Englewood Cliffs: Prentice Hall, 47. Actually Frankena has four principles of prima facie duty under the principle of beneficence: one ought not to inflict evil or harm; one ought to prevent evil or harm; one ought to remove evil; and one ought to do or promote good.

[4] Simon, John G., Charles W. Powers, and Jon P. Gunneman. (1972). *The Ethical Investor: Universities and Corporate Responsibility*. New Haven: Yale University Press, 22–25.

[5] Bowie, Norman E. (1999). *Business Ethics: A Kantian Perspective*. New York: Blackwell Publishers, Chapter 4.

a faulty product. Those who coined the phrase *moral minimum* for use in the business context defined harm as "particularly including activities which violate or frustrate the enforcement of rules of domestic or institutional law intended to protect individuals against prevention of health, safety or basic freedom."[6] Even if we do not insist that the violations be violations of a rule of law, polluting a lake would not count as a harm under this definition.

The environmentalists would respond that it would. Polluting the lake may be injuring people who might swim in or eat fish from it. Certainly it would be depriving people of the freedom to enjoy the lake. Although the environmentalist is correct, especially if we grant the legitimacy of a human right to a clean environment, the success of this reply is not enough to establish the general argument.

Consider the harm that results from the production of automobiles. In 2009 there were 30, 797 deaths from automobile accidents in the United States.[7] These deaths – or at least many of them-are avoidable. If that is the case, doesn't the avoid-harm criterion require that the production of automobiles for profit cease? Not really. What such arguments point out is that some refinement of the moral minimum standard needs to take place. Take the automobile example. The automobile is itself a good-producing instrument. Because of the advantages of automobiles, society accepts the possible risks that go in using them. Society also accepts many other types of avoidable harm. We take certain risks—ride in planes, build bridges, and mine coal—to pursue advantageous goals. It seems that the high benefits of some activities justify the resulting harms. As long as the risks are known, it is not wrong that some avoidable harm be permitted so that other social and individual goals can be achieved. The avoidable-harm criterion needs some sharpening.

Using the automobile as a paradigm, let us consider the necessary refinements for the avoid-harm criterion. It is a fundamental principle of ethics that "ought implies can." That expression means that you can be held morally responsible only for events within your power. In the ought-implies-can principle, the overwhelming majority of highway deaths and injuries are not the responsibility of the automaker. Only those deaths and injuries attributable to unsafe automobile design can be attributed to the automaker. The ought-implies-can principle can also be used to absolve the auto companies of responsibility for death and injury from safety defects that the automakers could not reasonably know existed. The company could not be expected to do anything about them.

Does this mean that a company has an obligation to build a car as safe as it knows how? No. The standards for safety must leave the product's cost within the price range of the consumer ("ought implies can" again). Comments about engineering and equipment capability are obvious enough. But for a business, capability is also a function of profitability. A company that builds a maximally safe car at a cost that puts it at a competitive disadvantage and hence threatens its survival is building a safe car that lies beyond the capability of the company.

---

[6] Ibid., 21.

[7] http://www-fars.nhtsa.dot.gov/Main/index.aspx

The decision to build products that are cheaper in cost but are not maximally safe is a social decision that has widespread support. The arguments occur over the line between safety and cost. What we have is a classical trade-off situation. What is desired is some appropriate mix between engineering safety and consumer demand.

Let us apply the analysis of the automobile industry to the issue before us. That analysis shows that an automobile company does not violate its obligation to avoid harm and hence is not in violation of the moral minimum if the trade-off between potential harm and the utility of the products rests on social consensus and competitive realities.

As long as business obeys the environmental laws and honors other standard moral obligations, most harm done to the environment by business has been accepted by society. Through their decisions in the marketplace, we can see that most consumers are unwilling to pay extra for products that are more environmentally friendly than less friendly competitive products. Nor is there much evidence that consumers are willing to conserve resources, recycle, or tax themselves for environmental causes.

Since safety standards for automobiles has increased greatly, the main criticism of the automobile industry today is that it has not focused on manufacturing cars that give high gas mileage. Too many SUV's and trucks are produced, the critics argue. However, automobile manufactures simply respond to consumer demand. When gas prices rise substantially, consumers shift to more fuel efficient vehicles. When they decline, they go back to their old ways and buy more gas guzzlers. If an automobile company produces small fuel efficient cars when people want gas guzzlers it will go out of business. Now I agree with the environmentalists that these purchasing decisions are unsustainable and damaging to the environment. But whose fault is that? I would not blame the automobile companies so much as the consumers. After all these companies are just responding to consumer choice. I would place the moral obligation to protect the environment in this case on the consumers. If consumers would honor their obligation to buy more fuel efficient cars, automobile manufacturers will respond.

Some would say that we need to change people's attitudes toward the environment. Those with a liberal political philosophy have the right attitude toward the environment. However, liberals often do not act consistently with what they profess to believe. Liberals have consistently opposed having windmills, large solar panels, recycling plants, and mass transit in their neighborhoods.[8] There has even been a backlash against bike paths.

It gets worse. In fact consumers sometimes frustrate and undo the good things that a company does to protect the environment. Frito Lay, which is owned by PerpsiCo, redesigned the packaging for all its Sun Chip products. The packaging was totally biodegradable and thus was extremely environmentally friendly. However, consumers complained bitterly that the packaging was too noisy. Sales fell precipitously

---

[8] Rosenthal, Elisabeth. (2011). "Not in my "Liberal" Backyard," *The New York Times,* March 13, WK 3.

and Frito Lay went back to its old packaging for all but one of its Sun Chip products. Too noisy! Consumers won't even accept a little more noise to help the environment. Check out You Tube on the subject.[9]

Data and arguments of this sort should give environmental critics of business pause. Despite all the green talk, there is a lot of evidence that consumers, even liberal ones, will not make sacrifices to protect the environment. Many people will not even make minor sacrifices as we see with the biodegradable Sun Chips packaging. When consumers act in ways that protect the environment, companies will respond. In many cases, the moral obligation to protect the environment rests on the shoulders of the consumers.

An Environmentalist's Response: The Public Goods Aspect of Consumption

Nonetheless, these environmental critics of business are not without counter-responses. For example, they might argue that environmentally friendly products are at a disadvantage in the marketplace because they have public good characteristics. After all, the best situation for the individual is one where most other people use environmentally friendly products but he or she does not, hence reaping the benefit of lower cost and convenience. Since everyone reasons this way, the real demand for environmentally friendly products cannot be registered in the market. Everyone is understating the value of his or her preference for environmentally friendly products. Hence, companies cannot conclude from market behavior that the environmentally unfriendly products are preferred.

Suppose the environmental critics are right that the public goods characteristic of environmentally friendly products creates a market failure. Does that mean the companies are obligated to stop producing these environmentally unfriendly products? I think not, and I propose that we use the four conditions attached to the prevent-harm obligation to show why not. There is a need, and certainly corporations that cause environmental problems are in proximity. However, environmentally clean firms, if there are any, are not in proximity at all, and most business firms are not in proximity with respect to most environmental problems. In other words, the environmental critic must limit his or her argument to the environmental damage a business actually causes. The environmentalist might argue that Frito Lay ought to do something about its packaging; I do not see how an environmentalist can use the avoid-harm criterion to argue that Frito Lay should do something about acid rain. But even narrowing the obligation to damage actually caused will not be sufficient to establish an obligation to pull a product from the market because it damages the environment or even to go beyond what is legally required to protect the environment. Even for damage actually done, both the

---

[9] One example can be found at http://www.youtube.com/watch?v=FQb7ULO_l7c

high cost of protecting the environment and the competitive pressures of business make further action to protect the environment beyond the capability of business. This conclusion would be more serious if business were the last resort, but it is not.

The Obligation Not to Lobby Against Environmental Legislation

Before dealing with the obvious practical difficulties in making a suggestion that business has an obligation not to lobby against environmental legislation, let me lay out the theoretical case for an obligation not to lobby.

Traditionally it is the function of the government to correct for market failure. If the market cannot register the true desires of consumers, let them register their preferences in the political arena. Even fairly conservative economic thinkers such as Milton Friedman allowed government a legitimate role in correcting market failure.[10] Perhaps the responsibility for energy conservation and pollution control belongs with the government.

Although I think consumers bear a far greater responsibility for preserving and protecting the environment than they have actually exercised, let us assume that the basic responsibility rests with the government. Does that let business off the hook? No. Most of business's unethical conduct regarding the environment occurs in the political arena.

Far too many corporations try to have their cake and eat it too. They argue that it is the job of government to correct for market failure and then use their influence and money to defeat or water down regulations designed to conserve and protect the environment. They argue that consumers should decide how much conservation and protection the environment should have, and then they try to interfere with the exercise of that choice in the political arena. Such behavior is inconsistent and ethically inappropriate. Business has an obligation to avoid intervention in the political process for the purpose of defeating and weakening environmental regulations. Moreover, this is a special obligation to the environment since business does not have a general obligation to avoid pursuing its own parochial interests in the political arena. Business need do nothing wrong when it seeks to influence tariffs, labor policy, or monetary policy. Business does do something wrong when it interferes with the passage of environmental legislation. Why?

First, such a noninterventionist policy is dictated by the logic of the business's argument to avoid a special obligation to protect the environment. Put more formally:

1. Business argues that it escapes special obligations to the environment because it is willing to respond to consumer preferences in this matter.
2. Because of externalities and public goods considerations, consumers cannot express their preferences in the market.
3. The only other viable forum for consumers to express their preferences is in the political arena.

---

[10] Friedman, Milton. (1982). *Capitalism and Freedom*. Chicago: University of Chicago Press, 30–32.

4. Business intervention interferes with the expression of these preferences.
5. Since point 4 is inconsistent with point 1, business should not intervene in the political process.

The importance of this obligation in business is even more important when we see that environmental legislation has special disadvantages in the political arena. Public choice theory reminds us that the primary interest of politicians is being reelected. Government policy will be skewed in favor of policies that provide benefits to an influential minority as long as the greater costs are widely dispersed. Politicians will also favor projects where benefits are immediate and where costs can be postponed to the future. Such strategies increase the likelihood that a politician will be reelected.

What is frightening about the environmental crisis is that both the conservation of scarce resources and pollution abatement require policies that go contrary to a politician's self-interest. The costs of cleaning up the environment are immediate and huge, yet the benefits are relatively long range (many of them exceedingly long range). Moreover, a situation where the benefits are widely dispersed and the costs are large presents a twofold problem. The costs are large enough so that all voters will likely notice them and in certain cases are catastrophic for individuals (e.g., for those who lose their jobs in a plant shutdown).

Given these facts and the political realities they entail, business opposition to environmental legislation makes a very bad situation much worse. Even if consumers could be persuaded to take environmental issues more seriously, the externalities, opportunities to free ride, and public goods characteristics of the environment make it difficult for even enlightened consumers to express their true preference for the environment in the market. The fact that most environmental legislation trades immediate costs for future benefits makes it difficult for politicians concerned about reelection to support it. Hence it is also difficult for enlightened consumers to have their preferences for a better environment honored in the political arena. Since lack of business intervention seems necessary, and might even be sufficient, for adequate environmental legislation, it seems business has an obligation not to intervene. Nonintervention would prevent the harm of not having the true preferences of consumers for a clean environment revealed. Given business's commitment to satisfying preferences, opposition to having these preferences expressed seems inconsistent as well.

The Cohen-Dienhart Perspective[11]

The argument above for an obligation not to lobby on environmental matters is based primarily on certain economic facts. Issues of neighborhood effects drive the analysis. In a recent article, Marc Cohen and John Dienhart have provided a moral

---

[11] Cohen, Marc A. and John C. Dienhart. (2012). "Citizens, Kant and Corporate Responsibility for the Environment" in Denis G. Arnold and Jared Harris (eds.), *Kantian Business Ethics: Critical Perspectives*. Cheltenham: Edward Elgar Publishing.

argument based on Kantian ethics-an argument that fits well with my larger project of bringing Kantian ethics to bear on issues of business ethics.

Cohen and Dienhart begin by endorsing the idea of Mark Sagoff that we should distinguish between our preferences as consumers and our preferences as citizens. In a series of brilliant articles,[12] Sagoff shows how we are often at two minds on environmental issues. As consumers we might want more ski slopes and theme parks, but as citizens we might want more regulations that could prohibit these kinds of things when they destroy pristine raw beauty or bring commercial activities into historically sacred areas. If applied to my argument, a corporation should not interfere with the rights of citizens to express their preferences as citizens. Kant never talks about the rights of consumers, but in his political philosophy, he does talk about the rights of citizens.

Cohen and Dienhart point out that this line of argument might show that business has obligations to individuals and he points to two Kant scholars who take such an approach-Onora O'Neill[13] and Allen Wood.[14] Suppose both those accounts are correct. They would show that there is an obligation to protect the environment that is derivative on protecting the rights of citizens, but it might not show that business has an obligation to the environment per se. Cohen and Dienhart expand on a remark by Wood that persons and institutions should not interfere with a citizen's autonomy as citizen. Cohen and Dienhart put it this way:

> But in the context of Bowie's work, in the context of the political process, interference by business could also compromise autonomy, it could compromise the freedom persons have to make decisions about the environment and the common good. Put another way, by interfering with the social contract and the political process, business fails to treat persons as ends, and business therefore has a Kantian obligation to stay out of the political process. Bowie's proviso, therefore, understood in terms suggested in the previous section, as protecting citizens' ability to shape the social order and business practice with respect to the environment, has a fully Kantian justification. In other words, there is still no direct obligation on the part of business to protect or repair the environment, though there is a positive duty to permit citizens the space to do so. This line of thought follows the strategy Wood suggests.[15]

I fully endorse this argument but there is more. Cohen and Dienhart also contend that a similar argument can be based on the requirements for property rights. They argue as follows:

> For Kant property rights in an object limit the freedom of others who might have some interest in that object; so holding property is a matter of consensus. Market transactions

[12] Sagoff, Mark. (1981). "At the Shrine of Our Lady of Fatima, or Why Political Questions Are Not All Economic," *Arizona Law Review,* 23, 283–1298, and Sagoff, Mark. (2000). "At the Monument to General Meade, or on the Difference Between Beliefs and Benefits," *Arizona Law Review,* 42, 433–462.

[13] O'Neil Onora. (1998). "Kant on Duties Regarding Nonrational Nature-II," *Proceedings of the Aristotelian Society, Supplementary Volumes* 72, 211–228.

[14] Wood, Allen W. (1998). "Kant on Duties Regarding Nonrational Nature-II," *Proceedings of the Aristotelian Society, Supplementary Volumes* 72, 189–210.

[15] Cohen and Dienhart, op.cit., 106.

depend on such rights, and therefore on consensus, but consensus will not be possible when there are costs that are externalized—the party bearing those costs will not participate in the scheme of property rights, it would not be rational to permit others to benefit while bearing an externalized cost. Guyer emphasizes this point: "a system of property rights can be freely agreed to by rational beings only if it is equitable to some suitable degree" (2000, p. 251). An economic system with externalities would violate this requirement. So the system of property and the market depend on eliminating externalities, and business must stay out of the process by which this is done.[16]

Again, I fully endorse the Cohen Dienhart approach and I am most appreciative of an analysis that supports my larger Kantian project and brings the original, "Money, Morality, and Motor Cars" more into line with my overall position. We now have three arguments on behalf of an obligation on behalf of business to avoid lobbying against environmental legislation. There is an argument based on economic analysis that shows that business would be acting inconsistently if it lobbies in that way and there are two Kantian arguments that I adopt from Cohen and Dienhart. (I will not develop the idea that the inconsistency argument may ultimately be Kantian as well.)

Dealing with Practical Realities

The extent of this obligation to avoid intervening in the political process needs considerable discussion by ethicists and other interested parties. As stated, there is no practical way that a moral norm prohibiting business from lobbying on environmental issues would be accepted. There are even some reasonable arguments that business could make against such a moral norm. Businesspeople will surely object that if they are not permitted to play a role, Congress and state legislators will make decisions that will put them at a severe competitive disadvantage. For example, if the United States develops stricter environmental controls than other countries do, foreign imports will have a competitive advantage over domestic products. Shouldn't business be permitted to point that out? In theory business people have a point, but the reality is that many industrial nations have stricter environmental regulations than the United States. This is particularly true in Europe. Even China, which is often maligned over pollution, is doing more than the United States. It is just that in China, the growth of the economy has been so rapid, environmental issues that result from rapid growth are overwhelming the progressive steps the Chinese have or are taking. (What is so disturbing about China's response to the environmental crisis is that they are not honest with their own citizens about how serious the situation is. I recall vividly when I visited China in 2008, the sun appeared as a red globe through a haze. You could actually briefly look at the sun. My hosts thought that this experience was normal. They did not realize the sky is supposed to be blue.)

---

[16] Ibid., 106–107. The Guyer book cited in the quotation is *Kant on Freedom, Law and Happiness.* New York: Cambridge University Press.

The current political climate in the United States seems to indicate that the United States is likely to fall further behind other countries with respect to environmental regulations. Business concern on this competitive issue seems quite out of place.

Other arguments focus on issues internal to the United States. For example, the fact that any legislation that places costs on one industry rather than another confers advantages on other industries. The cost to the electric utilities that primarily use coal from regulations designed to reduce the pollution that causes acid rain will give advantages to natural gas and perhaps even solar energy. Shouldn't the electric utility industry be permitted to point that out?

These questions are difficult, and my answer to them should be considered highly tentative. I believe the answer to the first question is "yes" and the answer to the second is "no." Business does have a right to insist that the regulations apply to all those in the industry. Anything else would seem to violate norms of fairness. Such issues of fairness do not arise in the second case. Since natural gas and solar do not contribute to acid rain and since the costs of acid rain cannot be fully captured in the market, government intervention through regulation is simply correcting a market failure. With respect to acid rain, the electric utilities do have an advantage they do not deserve. They are imposing a cost on society without compensating society for that cost. Hence they have no right to try to protect it. But try and protect it they will.

Although the theoretical arguments based on a combination of economic and ethical analysis provide a powerful argument for a moral rule than forbids companies from lobbying, such a rule is not practical in the United States where the current legal environment is to give corporations the same free speech rights that fall on individuals. Legally the right to free speech trumps any moral obligations that prohibit lobbying. This is especially true after the United States Supreme Court decision in *Citizens United v. Federal Election Committee.*

Before tackling the no prohibition argument directly, I should point out that my analysis would not prohibit all lobbying. It would only prohibit lobbying for laws which would give a firm or industry an unfair advantage. This limitation of the no lobbying rule is a restriction on the broader moral norm against lobbying that I made in the original article.

The new moral rule is as follows: Firms are prohibited from lobbying against environmental legislation and regulations that would give those firms an unfair advantage in the market place. If a firm or industry reasonably believes that proposed legislation or regulations will put it or them at an unfair disadvantage and the proposed legislation is not correcting a negative externality that the firm or industry has benefited from, then there is no absolute moral prohibition on their lobbying against it.

Even in those cases, there are constraints on the kind of lobbying that can be done. Using campaign contributions to gain access- a device that many of my foreign students see as bribery- would not be morally permitted. Also the lobbying must be based on scientifically verifiable evidence. Working on the government relations chapter with my co-author Meg Schneider for *Business Ethics for Dummies* resulted in some additional moral constraints on lobbying. In that work, we focused on the concept of fairness as the central value. We argued that lobbyists and government affairs officers had to play fair.

"In government relations, playing fair means avoiding behaviors and situations that give you an unfair advantage over other people-who also are trying to get their voices heard in the halls of power. Unfair advantages can come in the form of personal relationships (such as former lawmakers who become lobbyists and try to capitalize on their earlier relationships with people in elected or civil service positions) or misuse money and gifts."[17]

In addition to the exhortation to play fair, we have some specific suggestions as to what fairness in the context of lobbying would require:

1. Accurately represent the company's interests and concerns
2. Truthfully disclose relationships with the represented client
3. Recognize and accurately report alternative viewpoints
4. Give fair consideration to diverse needs and wants.
5. Consider the common good.[18]

To that list I would emphasize again the requirement that the lobbyist's appeal must be based on scientifically verifiable evidence.

However, even in the lobbying arena, the moral obligations to play fair do not fall solely on corporations. They fall on government as well. Legislators should neither propose nor oppose environmental legislation simply because powerful people in their districts support or oppose it. Indeed they should not support or oppose legislation simply because of the positive or negative impacts it might have in their districts. The common good must be taken into account. Moral demands of fair play fall on legislators and regulators as well as on corporations. Legislative bodies and regulatory agencies need to expand their staffs to include technical experts, economists, and engineers so that the political process can be both neutral and highly informed about environmental matters. The requirement that decisions on the environment be made on scientifically verifiable grounds applies as much to legislators and regulators as it does do corporations. And many believe that our legislators and regulators have not done well in that regard. To gain the respect of business and the public, performance needs to improve.

One of the main criticisms of environmental regulation at present is the fact that the two parties are in a virtual war about the environment. As a result whenever there is a change of political power in the White House or in Congress, the rules change. This creates great uncertainty and many businesses would rather have an environmental rule that it finds unfair then have uncertainty. It would be my hope that more scientific evidence and less politics would lead to better laws which would in turn lead to more certainty for business. Of course the Republican Party will have to rediscover the value of science.

[17] Bowie, Norman E. and Meg Schneider. (2011). *Business Ethics for Dummies*. Hoboken: Wiley Publishing Inc., 115.
[18] Ibid. The first four in the list are on p. 115. The fifth is extracted from the material on 117–118.

Some believe that in the struggle among interest groups each vigorously lobbying government and bound by few constraints, the best environmental legislation will emerge. I see no evidence that such a claim is true. Given all the externalities that surround environmental issues, I see no more reason to trust the invisible hand in the marketplace of ideas than I do in the normal marketplace. The law of the jungle will not produce the best results. Political activity like business activity needs moral constraints.

The Obligation of Business to Educate Consumers

Ironically business might best improve its situation in the political arena by taking on an additional obligation to the environment. Businesspersons often have more knowledge about environmental harms and the costs of cleaning them up. They may often have special knowledge about how to prevent environmental harm in the first place. In other words it is often the case that there is rather heavy information asymmetry between the public and business with respect to potential harm to the environment. In the original paper, I argued that perhaps business has a special duty to educate the public and to promote environmentally responsible behavior. In making that point, I recognized that I was making an exception to my claim that business has no special obligation to protect the environment. In this revised paper, I make a much stronger claim. I believe that business does have a moral obligation to educate the public when the following conditions obtain.

1. The business has a set of products some of which are more environmentally friendly than others.
2. Consumers disproportionately choose the least friendly environmental products
3. Because of information asymmetry, consumers are not aware of the adverse environmental impact of their choices.

When these conditions are met, businesses have a obligation to educate consumers about the adverse consequences of their choices on the environment. This obligation may be more robust than it seems. For example, if a manufacturer of fertilizers manufactures both a traditional fertilizer and a biodegradable fertilizer and consumers favor the traditional fertilizer because of its lower cost, the manufacturer should focus its research and development dollars on manufacturing a cheaper biodegradable alternative.

Business has no reticence about leading consumer preferences in other areas. Advertising is a billion-dollar industry. Rather than blaming consumers for not purchasing environmentally friendly products, perhaps some businesses might make a commitment to capture the environmental niche. I have not seen much imagination on the part of business in this area. Far too many advertisements with an environmental message are reactive and public relations driven. Recall those by oil companies showing fish swimming about the legs of oil rigs. And BP's Beyond Petroleum mantra rings hollow after the Deepwater Horizon disaster. An educational campaign that encourages consumers to make environmentally friendly decisions in the marketplace would limit the necessity for business activity in the political arena. Voluntary behavior that is environmentally friendly is morally preferable to coerced behavior. If business took greater responsibility for educating the public, the government's responsibility would be lessened. An educational campaign aimed at consumers would likely enable many businesses to do good while simultaneously doing very well.

In addition to the obligation to educate under certain conditions, I add an additional obligation. When a business has at least two products where one is more environmentally friendly than the other but the least environmentally friendly product is cheaper, business has an obligation to try to bring the costs of the more environmentally friendly product down. For example, in the firm's research and development efforts, more money and effort should be spent in reducing the cost of the more environmentally friendly product rather than the less environmentally friendly product.

Concluding Thoughts-An Expanded Set of Moral Obligations for Business with Respect to the Environment

How far does my current thinking deviate from my thinking in the original "Money Morality and Motor Cars?" I continue to maintain that a lot of harm business does to the environment violates straightforward general ethical obligations of any business. It just happens that some violations of these obligations harm the environment. I also continue to place a lot of responsibility for protecting the environment on consumers. In many cases, action by consumers would be the quickest way to change business behavior. However, the wide-ranging existence of externalities, complicates the analysis. On both economic grounds and grounds of consistency, there is an argument that business should not lobby against environmental regulations. This original argument is buttressed by the citizenship and autonomy arguments of Cohen and Dienhart. However, in the original article I did not even consider the practical issues that stand in the way of the adoption of this ethical obligation. Nor did I consider the special nuances involved. In this chapter, I recognize that the moral ban on lobbying needs to be restricted to a special case. **Firms are prohibited from lobbying against environmental legislation and regulations that would give those firms an unfair advantage in the market place**. The unfair advantage I am speaking of occurs, when a firm or industry imposes a negative cost on the environment without the market having any way to compensate for this cost. In the absence of that unfairness, lobbying is permitted. Specifically, if a firm or industry reasonably believes that proposed legislation or regulations will put it or them at an unfair disadvantage and the proposed legislation is not correcting a negative externality that the firm or industry has benefited from, then there is no absolute moral prohibition on their lobbying against it. I have also imposed some other fairness conditions on lobbying, but these conditions would apply to all lobbying and not just to lobbying about environmental regulations.

In the original article I suggested that business may have an obligation to educate consumers about environmental issues. Here I have specified that under certain conditions business does have such an obligation. In addition I have added an additional obligation-an obligation to reduce the costs of products that benefit the environment rather than the costs of products that harm the environment, wherever possible.[19] Thanks to my critics this revised version of "Money, Morality and Motor Cars," is a better fit with my overall philosophy of business ethics. It does impose more robust moral obligations on business. But it maintains the insight that the moral obligations do not rest on business alone. All stakeholders have a responsibility to act in an environmentally friendly way.

---

[19] When a firm has no competing products that it produces, it is always in the firm's interest to lower costs when it can increase profits by doing so.

Chapter 9
Ethics in Financial Services: Systems and Individuals

> *Some turn every quality or art into a means of getting wealth;*
> *this they conceive to be the end, and to the promotion of the end*
> *they think all things must contribute.*
>
> –Aristotle, Politics, Bk. 1, Ch. 9.1258a13-14

Introduction

Few, if any, major catastrophic events result from a single cause. This financial crisis is not different. The existence of multiple causes explains why various self-interested parties focus on causes that are unrelated to their own contribution to the crisis. In addition, certain parties receive blame for the crisis when the party is either innocent or its contribution is negligible. Let's try to sort this out. As we sort this out we will focus our attention on the ethical lapses that helped cause the crisis. We begin by mentioning a few factors in the crisis that may have contributed but the role played by these factors was not significant.

Some have faulted the federal government for a policy decision that encourages people to own their own homes. In other words government policy supports home ownership over renting. This is clearly seen in tax policy that permits interest and real estate tax deductions but provides for no deductions for rental costs. Although the policy may have been pursued overzealously, we see nothing morally wrong with the policy per se. It is a policy that has wide support among the American public. Many argue that home ownership contributes to family stability. Others argue that neighborhoods characterized by high levels of home ownership are more stable and less susceptible to social problems than neighborhoods with a high concentration of renters.

Another factor often cited is the dishonesty of mortgage applicants. It is true that some mortgage applicants lied on their applications. How large that number was is a

This chapter is a cooperative effort with my friend and colleague Ronald Duska.

matter of dispute. And getting an accurate count here is complicated by the fact that some-perhaps many- of the cases of dishonesty were actively encouraged by the lenders themselves. Blaming this crisis on mortgage applicants is downright silly. Stories abound of recently hired mortgage brokers working out of hotel rooms processing mortgage applications with no background checks. Let's stop blaming the victim.

In this Chapter, we begin with a discussion of the purpose of the financial system and then ask whether the financial services industry engaged in activities that undermined the purpose of the financial services industry. Engaging in such activity would itself be unethical. In discussing these activities we will do the following: (1) Investigate what the legitimate purpose of financial markets is; (2) Show how financial markets lost sight of their purpose; (3) Spell out more extensively the meaning of "corruption"; (4) Inquire to what extent greed played a role in the corruption; and (5) Consider the ethical role that individual financial services professionals play in the markets and their consequent role responsibility.

The Purpose of Financial Markets

The ultimate purpose of markets is the production and exchange of goods and services. For any market to succeed, there need to be sectors, which provide services necessary for the effective functioning of the market. There must be producers, consumers, traders and any number of other actors fulfilling the roles necessary to have a vibrant and healthy market. Corporations or sectors of the economy can only survive in the long run if they provide a good or service that is needed. For example, we no longer need firemen on trains with diesel engines. Not everything needs to be sustained. Things that fulfill no purpose should die out.

The needs of society determine the purposes of financial markets. People need capital, loans, and money with which to purchase necessary items. To fulfill these purposes society has invented banks, insurance companies, stock markets and any number of other agents, as well as financial instruments that are developed and sold by various actors in the financial markets. When the various sectors of the financial markets forget they are in business to provide those goods and services for clients, and concentrate solely on income generation, they fail to live up to their responsibility and become corrupted.

It is important to note that different sectors of the financial markets fulfill different needs. The responsibility of those in these sectors is to perform their role in such a way that they fulfill the specific needs of the clients. Let's examine a few.

One of the purposes of banks is to loan money. Banks make money doing that, but making money is not their purpose. Making money is the incentive to perform the business of servicing clients and customers well. For banks to persist they need to evaluate risk. It is unfair to their depositors to lend (depositors') money to those who are not credit-worthy. Certified public accountants exist to help give accurate and useful pictures of the financial holdings of companies. Rating agencies exist to give evaluations of the soundness of companies. It is unfair to the investing public for certified public accountants to be swayed by the fact that the companies that they audit pay for the audit. It is also unfair to the investing public for the rating agencies to be swayed by the fact that companies pay fees to these very same agencies. Could you help but notice how fast rating agencies lower the scores of political entities like the United States and several European countries but failed to notice the financial issues that surrounded the mortgage companies and the major banks and insurance companies before the financial crisis hit?

The fundamental goods in the financial services market are financial instruments. But instruments are things that are useful for other purposes. What is their basic purpose? What are they used for? Life insurance policies, annuities, securities, mutual funds, CDs and other instruments are used to manage risk and provide financial security. The purpose of the hedge fund is to "hedge" or balance the risk of an investment when one's investments seem to be too extended. These financial instruments do not exist to be manipulated and arbitraged for the simple purpose of making more money for advisers or companies.

According to Robert Schenk,

> … the primary purpose of financial markets is to allocate available savings to the most productive use. A well-functioning financial sector increases economic growth. If an economy does not allocate savings to the most productive uses, it will grow more slowly than it can grow.[1]

Joseph Stiglitz maintains that there are three important functions the financial markets serve[2]: to allocate scarce capital more efficiently to benefit the rest of the economy; to manage risk; and to direct resources to the activities with the highest returns (i.e. run the payment mechanism at low transaction costs). For Stiglitz, the stock market, as one area of the financial market place, is "first and foremost, a forum in which individuals can exchange risks. It affects the ability to raise capital (although it may also contribute to management's shortsightedness.) However, Stiglitz laments what it has become for "in the end, it is perhaps more a gambling casino than a venue in which funds are being raised to finance new ventures and expand existing activities… new ventures typically must look elsewhere."

In summary, the financial system is the complex array of financial markets, securities, and institutions that interact in facilitating the movement of capital among savers and borrowers. That financial system is also used for mediation of risk among parties. In the best possible model, this is all accomplished in a very efficient and hopefully ethical manner. But underlying all this is the belief that the other party can be trusted in the exchange. Once trust is gone, the market will not operate.

Losing Sight of the Purpose of Financial Markets

We take it as a fundamental ethical principle that: Any social system is legitimated only if it serves the common good. We would argue that from society's point of view the fundamental purpose of business is not to maximize profit, but to create goods

---

[1] Schenk, Robert. htpp://ingrimayne.com/econ/Financial/Overview%ma.html

[2] All three Stiglitz quotations in this paragraph are from Stiglitz, Joseph E. (1993). "The Role of the State in Financial Markets," *Proceedings of the World Bank Annual Conference on Development Economics*, 21.

and services, i.e. value.[3] Since financial services and financial markets are a subset of business activity, they must serve business' ultimate purpose, or else the tail will wag the dog. But, recently, financial markets have had a tendency to become independent entities of their own and subvert the common good.

In an important 2003 book, *Infectious Greed*,[4] Frank Partnoy gives a host of stunning examples, which eerily remind us of the situation today, where fundamental purposes were forgotten, and hence the balance required by justice was lost. As far back as 1987 at Banker's Trust, Andy Krieger was successful in using currency options to manipulate unregulated currency markets with over the counter transactions. Krieger's success at Banker's Trust lead Charles Sanford, the CEO, to encourage traders to speculate with the bank's capital. Why did he speculate in that way? He did it for the sake of ever increasing profits. What began as an investment that exploited inefficiencies in the market lead to speculation once the inefficiencies were discovered and eliminated, In other words the inefficiencies effectively dried up and the speculation ensued. Speculation is never the primary business of a bank and engagement in it can lead to the downfall of a bank, as it did in the case of Banker's Trust. In that case, as Partnoy points out, "Investment positions (were) even hidden from investors at Banker's Trust...(but) there was nothing illegal about it."[5]

Another example is Gibson's Greetings, Inc. a company that produced and sold greeting cards. Gibson's Greetings got involved in interest-rate swaps on their loans, which at the time, in early 1992, yielded a profit of $260,000. The swaps were used to hedge debt and became, for a short time, profit generators. That is until interest rates went up. In 1993 Gibson got involved in $96 million worth of swaps. According to Partnoy, Banker's Trust, which took no risk, "made about $13 million from the swaps with Gibson, all of which supposedly began as an effort to find a low-cost hedge for a simple fixed-rate debt."[6] Gibson, instead of concentrating on the production of greeting cards, the purpose of its company, became an outright gambler for the sake of easy profits. Banker's Trust, instead of looking out for the interest of its client, Gibson, looked to its own bottom line.

Jaime Jaramillo, was prescient, when he observed in 1994, long before the financial market melt-down, that:

Today's financial economy is nothing more than a "great big fantasy," where promises made by people, firms, or even computers are taken so seriously that they are regarded as wealth. This fantasy eases economic transactions and enhances efficiency only to the extent that the instruments used in it are trusted by economic agents, and the entire system ceases to function when faith in these instruments collapses. The state's role in financial markets is necessary because of the "fiat" nature of monetary and financial instruments.[7]

---

[3] Duska, Ronald. (2007). "The Why's of Business Revisited" in *Contemporary Reflections on Business Ethics*. Dordrecht: Springer.

[4] Partnoy, Frank. (2003). *Infectious Greed*. New York: Henry Holt and Co., 184.

[5] Ibid., 19, ft nt. 24.

[6] Ibid., 53.

[7] Jaramillo-Vallejo, Jaime. (1993). Comment on "The Role of the State in Financial Markets," By Stiglitz, *Proceedings of the World Bank Annual Conference on Development: Economics Supplement* (Washington, DC) Downloaded from http://www-wds.worldbank.org/servlet/WDSContentServer/WDSP/IB/1994/03/01/000009265_3970702134931/Rendered/INDEX/multi_page.txt, February 25, 2012.

To claim that the financial economy is a "great big fantasy" is to say the least a strong claim. But consider. A large portion of the earnings of hedge fund managers was made from dealing with Credit Default Swaps, Collateralized Debt Obligations and other exotic financial instruments in the sub-prime mortgage market, and in some cases from shorting the very financial packages these hedge firms assembled for others.

It is an interesting and related fact, that in December 2007, the Bank for International Settlements reported derivative trades tallying in at $681 trillion—ten times the gross domestic product of all the countries in the world combined. As the author said, "Somebody is obviously bluffing about the money being brought to the game, and that realization has made for some very jittery markets".[8]

Let us examine certain elements of this fantasy and see how these elements run contrary to the primary purpose of financial institutions. The basic responsibility to serve the ends and purposes of the good of society was undermined by individuals in financial institutions pursuing self-interest without constraints or regard for fulfilling their professional purpose. Ultimately, there seemed to be little concern for the good of the whole. In short, the pursuit of self-interest turned into selfishness which is the unconstrained pursuit of self-interest at the expense of and without concern for others.

One might then propose the thesis that the problem with financial markets is that they have turned into gambling casinos where wealth accumulation is the be all and end all of their activity, and hence they are not fulfilling their purpose. This is detrimental to the economies of the world, because while financial markets create no goods, 40 % of all profits are made in the financial sector. This straying from the basic purpose creates an opportunity for simply creating the fantasy world of financial instruments that Jaramillo warned about; where there is no "there" there.

Numerous critics have zeroed in on problems created by derivatives

"Derivatives" are complex bank creations that are very hard to understand, but the basic idea is that you can insure an investment you want to go up by betting it will go down. The simplest form of derivative is a short sale: you can place a bet that some asset you own will go down, so that you are covered whichever way the asset moves[9]

Derivatives are useful hedging instruments and are widely used in the financial services industry. However, they are somewhat complex and can be misused and be misunderstood even by people who are relatively sophisticated about financial matters. The use of derivatives became fairly common around 1978. The first blow-up occurred in Orange County California. In 1991 the Orange County treasurer had invested over $14 billion in derivative contracts- primarily contracts issued by Merrill Lynch. When the Federal Reserve began to raise interest rates in 1994, Orange County lost $1.5 billion of its investment, could not pay back a loan and was forced to declare bankruptcy. At the end of a string of lawsuits, Merrill Lynch made

[8] Bank for International Settlements BIS 77th Annual Report June 2007. Downloaded from http://www.bis.org/publ/arpdf/ar2007e.htm, February 25, 2012.
[9] Brown, Dr. Ellen "Credit Default Swaps: Evolving Financial Meltdown and Derivative Disaster Du Jour," *Global Research* April 11, 2008 Downloaded from http://www.globalresearch.ca/index.php?context=va&aid=8634, February 25, 2012.

$70 million in payments to Orange County and in fines to the SEC. The Orange County treasure went to jail.

Even Proctor and Gamble, a company that is hardly a novice in the financial markets owed Bankers Trust $195.5 million more than predicted on derivative contracts when interest rates rose. How did Bankers Trust handle the issue? They convinced Proctor and Gamble to purchase more derivatives. Proctor and Gamble sued and in the end Bankers Trust forgave most of the $200 million that Proctor and Gamble owed the bank. No wonder Warren Buffett called them "financial instruments of mass destruction."[10]

Short sales can increase the efficiency in markets because they signal that there are individuals who believe the economic value of a firm will go down in the future. An increase in short sales can serve as a warning to managers to improve performance or at a minimum to improve communication. However, in the financial crisis short sales exacerbated the extent and speed of the crisis. Markets were flooded with sellers and there were few buyers. In a short sale, the law technically requires that you own the stock you are selling. In practice that rarely happened. In market terms the short sales were "naked." During the height of the crisis short sales were banned and the debate about the role of short sales and how extensively short sales should be regulated continues.

It may be the case that complex financial instruments make the market more like a casino than a model of efficiency. We are not experts in these matters and so we leave the controversy to the experts. But if we did have a casino, did we have a corrupt casino as well? Did the mob take over the casino?

What Is Corruption?

Corruption can be viewed, as a state of affairs, which occurs when an individual, entity or system does not perform as it was intended to perform, i.e. does not fulfill its purpose. According to Aristotle, all things aim at some good. Entities and activities come into existence for a reason. They have some purpose or use. Since goals energize and keep entities and activities alive and animated, not fulfilling that original purpose leads to a loss of vitality or the animating principle, which derives from the Latin word *animus*, which means "soul". Now, any living entity, (be it a system, institution or individual) which fails to fulfill its purpose or function becomes corrupt and eventually dies away. That's why we associate the word "corruption" with rot and putrefaction. The recent market crisis shows the corruption in both government and financial markets.[11]

---

[10] Buffett, Warren. (2002). *Berkshire Hathaway Annual Report.*

[11] We would suggest that in this matter we can see similarities between the twentieth century philosopher Ludwig Wittgenstein and Aristotle. Two central claims for which Wittgenstein is famous are the claim that "The meaning is the use" and the claim that there are "forms of life" which constitute sociological relationships. According to Wittgenstein, we know what something is by knowing

This corruption of markets, though, is not easy to recognize because it is abetted by a misconception of the true purpose of markets. Too often people think that the purpose of markets is to make profits for individuals. That view is not new. Markets do help people gain wealth, but that is not their societal purpose. While it is clearly the case that gaining wealth is an incentive to produce and exchange, incentives are not the same as purposes. The father of capitalism, Adam Smith, rightly noted, that we would not get much market activity if there were no appeal to self-interest. He writes, "It is not from the benevolence of the butcher, the brewer or the baker, that we expect our dinner, but from their regard to their own interest."[12]

While Smith points out the obvious fact that self-interest is a great motivating factor and shows that self-interest is a great incentive to get people engaged in market activity, we should not confuse that incentive with the real purpose of the market. To confuse incentives with purposes is similar to confusing the engine of a plane with the destination of a plane. The engine is what drives you to your goal. It is not the goal. Accumulating wealth is what drives the market, but it is not the ultimate goal of markets. It is only a means to other more essential goals.

Becoming overleveraged, through buying short and long, is not the purpose of markets—it is out and out gambling. If the solitary quest for profit in these sectors deflects the market from fulfilling those functions, it is corruption.

Given the above, it should be clear that there was rampant corruption leading to the economic crisis of 2008. Rating agencies failed in performing their tasks. Lending institutions failed by giving out loans to non-credit worthy individuals, thereby jeopardizing other clients. Accountants and auditors failed in their duty to make sure financial statements reflected the worth of the companies they were reporting on or auditing. Investment advisers like Bernie Madoff failed to fulfill their fiduciary duty. One's duty is not simply to be clever in doing something. One's duty is to fulfill one's role, which means fulfilling the purposes of that role. A clever financier can game the market and use his clients. An ethical financier will perform his or her function for the sake of the clients and public he or she serves.

---

its use—what it is for, and that use constitutes a "form of life". Max Weber, in *Christianity and the Spirit of Capitalism*, talks about the spirit of capitalism as being an ever renewed search for profit. To tie these notions of Weber and Wittgenstein together, let us suggest that such a spirit (Geist) as Weber refers to constitutes for Wittgenstein a "form of life". The identification of form (formal cause) and purpose (final cause) is not only manifested in amorphous social organizations, it is also manifested in individual human beings. A person's purpose or ends are, in a sense, his or her soul, since those ends define what the person is. A person's mission (a collection of his or her ends) is the result of the person's commitments to particular projects and ideas. The mission one chooses defines their identity in a more meaningful manner than a description of their aggregate physical characteristics.

[12] Smith, Adam, *An Enquiry into the Nature and Causes of The Wealth of Nations*, I, ii, 2. Hereinafter referred to as WN.

Is Greed a Factor in the Corruption?

The present crisis has been aptly described as the perfect storm-too easy credit, too much leveraging, not enough information, over optimistic ratings, easy money and the desire on the public to acquire without the requisite thrift. But was the cause of all that simply greed or avariciousness or are the causes more subtle?

Let us investigate the ethical claim that greed was the cause. Greed may have been one of the causes, but we think that the claim that greed is the cause is too simple. To make our case we need to be more precise in defining "greed". First, it is important that greed not be confused with self-interest.

As we noted above, Adam Smith recognized the power of self-interest in his famous quote:

> It is not from the benevolence of the butcher, the brewer or the baker, that we expect our dinner, but from their regard to their own interest... (Thus in economic matters) .... We address ourselves not to their humanity but to their self-love, and never talk to them of our own necessities but of their advantages.[13]

It is this addressing of people's advantages that makes capitalism so successful. But by addressing people's self-love, are we promoting greed? Not necessarily. Smith's point is that self-love or self-interest can work for the benefit of the public good. However, when self-interest becomes so paramount that it is expressed at the expense of the public good, then self-interest can be transformed into greed. We believe this is what happened in the financial crisis. The meltdown was the consequence of the promotion and adoption of an acquisitive form of life across all sectors of the economy. Human nature is what it is. Human beings look out for their own advantage. But in the financial crisis the ethic that constrained that pursuit of self-interest was moribund.

If one looks at Max Weber, we can see that in many ways the recent collapse of the markets can be attributed to what he, in his classic work *The Protestant Ethic and the Spirit of Capitalism*, identified as the spirit of capitalism, a spirit that looks awfully much like greed. For Weber, capitalism is involved in "the single minded pursuit of profit and forever renewed profit."[14] According to Weber, such a pursuit is what gives the capitalist society its shape or form of life. For him any business operating in a wholly capitalistic society, which does not always take advantage of opportunities for profit making, is doomed to extinction. But, we would argue that such single-mindedness is monomaniacal and that such an unchecked pursuit of profit as a goal is an extreme, leading one to corruption.

Aristotle, the always temperate philosopher, would assert that virtue is always a golden mean and a vice is always an extreme. Oftentimes, in financial market transactions the unfettered pursuit of wealth for its own sake is paramount. How else can one explain, not the millions, but the billions of dollars of profit? Aristotle describes

---

[13] Smith, ibid.
[14] Weber, Max. (1958). *The Protestant Ethic and the Spirit of Capitalism*. New York: Scribners, 17.

the practice of accumulating wealth for the sake of accumulating wealth, as greed. He deems greed unnatural and inordinate (out of order) in the sense that it is against the purpose of human beings, because the purpose of human beings is to live well, and the single-minded quest for wealth cannot be sufficient for living well. Rather, it corrupts the human being. Aristotle took note of those who "…turn every quality or art into a means of getting wealth; this they conceive to be the end, and to the promotion of that end they think all things must contribute." Clearly for Aristotle, this is a picture of someone corrupt. Like Midas, those who accumulate wealth for its own sake are, "intent upon living only, and not upon living well."[15]

This would be analogous to the for-profit corporations if the sole purpose of existence of a corporation is the ever increasing reach for more and more profit. In that case, the corporation loses its main purpose—the reason society allows it to flourish and exist—which is produce goods and/or services. The pursuit of profit overrides concerns for those for whom the good or service is provided. This explains clearly what happened at places like Enron, and perhaps at some of the large commercial banks.

Thus we can see that in some respects greed certainly was a cause of the financial crisis. Business ethicists by and large have been highly critical of the current level of executive compensation. It is not uncommon for those looking to apportion blame for our current financial predicament to point to "greedy CEOs" and corporate "fatcats" as the culprits who place our nation in the bind that it currently finds itself. It is interesting to note who the top income earners were before the collapse of the financial markets in 2008. According to *The New York Times*, reporting on an *Alpha Magazine* study of hedge fund managers, that distinction would go to John Paulson who earned an estimated $3.7 billion in 2007 and $2 billion in 2008. The second highest earner was James Simons of Renaissance Technologies with estimated 2008 earnings of $2.5 billion and estimated 2007 earnings of $2.8 billion. George Soros of Soros Fund Management had estimated 2008 earnings of $1.1 billion and estimated 2007 earnings: $2.9 billion. John D. Arnold of Centarus Energy made an estimated $1.98 billion in 2007 and 2008, while Ray Dalio of Bridgewater Associates made a mere $1 billion in those 2 years.[16]

What's more, *The Financial Times* pointed out that the 10 best-paid hedge fund managers in 2007 earned more than the combined GDP of Afghanistan and Mongolia. "John Paulson, who topped the list with $3Bn, could have purchased Bear Stearns almost three-times over out of his gross earnings that year! Forget that $100 m or so Goldman CEO Lloyd Blankfein is said to have earned in 2006- these guys wouldn't get out of bed for that."[17]

At the time of the financial collapse many were complaining about the unfairness of CEO's salaries. It was thought they were being overcompensated. Yet, if we compare Paulson's $3 billion income to the income of Goldman Sach's CEO,

[15] Aristotle, Politics, Book I, Ch. 9, 1258a.
[16] http://www.nytimes.com/2009/03/25/business/25hedge.html
[17] http://news.hereisthecity.com/2008/04/08/and_the_billy_big_bonus_of_200/

Lloyd Blankenfein, we see that Paulson made 30 times more money in 2007 than Blankenfein's comparatively measly $100 million. Clearly, if there is something inordinate about CEO's salaries, there is certainly something inordinate about the earnings of some hedge fun managers.

But the greed of individuals themselves was not the only cause of the corruption of the markets. There were systemic factors at work which lead to widespread conflicts of interest, conflicts of interest that incentivized selfish behavior either on the part of individuals or companies. Thus along with greed, there were systemic ethical lapses within financial institutions. And regrettably these systemic ethical lapses were incentivized by the widespread existence of conflicts of interest.

A conflict of interest can be either actual or apparent. One has a conflict of interest when one has an interest of his own or another that may conflict with the interest of the institution or person (s) for whom he is an agent. When faced with an actual conflict of interest, one invariably acts on behalf of his own interest or the interest of another at the expense of the interest of an institution or person(s) for whom he is an agent. For example, a stock broker has a conflict of interest when he recommends a stock initial public offering (IPO) to the public where his bank is the financial institution doing the IPO deal. That conflict goes from being perceived to being actual if the broker recommends the stock to the public while believing that it is not an attractive investment for the general public. That is precisely what Jack Grubman did. The Enron scandal of 2001 exhibited a number of conflicts of interest. Arthur Andersen was the auditor of Enron and had a duty to the investing public to make an objective assessment of Enron's financial statements. However, Arthur Andersen took in much more revenue selling consulting services to Enron than it did in getting paid for auditing them. Arthur Andersen had a personal interest that interfered with their duty to the public and since they acted on that interest Arthur Andersen was guilty of an actual conflict of interest. (Professor Bowie has argued that the auditing function of CPA's rests on at least a perceived conflict of interest because the auditors are paid by the firms they audit. However, most of these conflicts of interest are perceived rather than actual After all most audits of publicly held firms are legitimate even though the firm that is audited pays for the audit so the conflict of interest involved is most often perceived rather than actual.) With Arthur Andersen's auditing of Enron, the perceived conflict of interest became actual. Auditors who are certified public accountants have a strong obligation to the public to certify that the accounts they are auditing are trustworthy (comply with generally accepted accounting practices) In the Enron case, Arthur Andersen's interest in serving the client that paid it-Enron-interfered with and overrode its duty to the public to provide an accurate audit. In addition some Andersen personnel worked for Andersen as Andersen accountants, which again is a clear conflict of interest. You cannot work for the company you audit. In that case even perceived conflicts of interest are not acceptable.

When we look at the financial crisis the entire system was riddled with conflicts of interest. The rating agencies are paid by the companies they regulate. Thus they have an interest that can and, in the financial crisis, did conflict with their duty to the public to provide accurate objective evaluations of the credit-worthiness of these mortgage security tranches. The employees of the mortgage companies had their income determined by the number of mortgages they processed regardless of quality. Thus mortgage brokers had a personal interest in maximizing their income that interfered with their obligation to only grant mortgage approval to those who could afford the mortgages and to make sure that each person had the mortgage that was appropriate for him or her. Five year adjustable ARM's with a balloon payment are not appropriate for most borrowers.

Some of the most egregious conflicts of interest involved Goldman Sachs and Company. One article by the *New York Times* focused on conflict of interests at Goldman Sachs.[18] Among the incidents cited in the *New York Times* article were the following:

1. Goldman Sachs was selling the public mortgage related securities issued by its client Washington Mutual. At the same time Goldman Sachs believed that Washington Mutual was engaged in activities that put it at risk and actively bet against (shorted) Washington Mutual stock.
2. Goldman Sachs took out bets against longstanding clients of Goldman Sachs. It wagered against Bear Stearns and Countrywide Financial as well as American International Group (AIG). AIG was the insurer of Goldman Sachs mortgage bonds. Documents show that Goldman was buying protection against a possible default by AIG even as Goldman Sachs pressured AIG to put up more cash as collateral. Goldman Sachs also bet against National City, a Cleveland bank the firm had advised. In the Bear Stearns case, Bear Stearns was encouraged to buy a portion of a one billion dollar package of mortgage related securities called Timberwolf. At the same time Goldman Sachs was betting against Bear Stearns shares. Bear Stearns was merged into JPMorgan Chase to avoid bankruptcy. If Bear Stearns had gone bankrupt as Goldman Sachs hoped the profits for Goldman Sachs would have been 33 million dollars.
3. The State of New Jersey had Goldman Sachs as one of its main investment bankers. To its chagrin New Jersey discovered that Goldman Sachs was encouraging speculators to bet against New Jersey's debt in the derivatives market.
4. Goldman Sachs has a best practices statement to which it is supposed to adhere. Principle 1 says "Our clients' interest always come first." As item 2 above shows, that principle was not observed. Principle 14 says "Integrity and honesty are at the heart of our business." Hardly.
5. Goldman Sachs encouraged rather than discouraged conflicts of interest. Some former employees of Goldman Sachs report that there was a 15th best practice principle. "If you are not embracing conflicts, you are not being aggressive enough in generating business."

In commenting on these details, *The New York Times* said, "…potential conflicts of interest inherent in Wall Street's business model are at the core of many of the

---

[18] Morgenson, Gretchen and Louise Story. (2010). "Clients Worried About Goldman's Dueling Goals," *New York Times*, May 18.

investigations that state and federal authorities are conducting." But the situation at Goldman Sachs involves more than conflict of interest.

One of the most controversial collateral debt obligations issued by Goldman Sachs was the Abacus 2007-ACI deal. That deal looks fraudulent. According to a Wharton study, "Goldman Sachs and Abacus 2007-AC1: A Look Beyond the Numbers," investors lost one billion dollars in the deal but the deal produced one billion dollars in profits for a Goldman collaborator the hedge fund Paulson and Company that was betting that the housing bubble would collapse. Investors in Abacus knew nothing of the relationship that Goldman Sachs had with Paulson and Company. They lacked the following information. Goldman Sachs sold a Mortgage Collatorized Debt Obligation (CDO) to customers, the development of which was heavily influenced by John Paulson. However, in the marketing materials used to promote the transaction to investors, Goldman Sachs failed to disclose that Paulson had played a role in the portfolio selection process and also failed to disclose that Paulson had adverse economic interests. As a matter of fact, knowing it was largely "junk" Paulson shorted the CDO he helped put together.[19]

At that point we have a clear conflict of interest and the possibility of fraud. Larry Kudlow of CNBC in musing about the case said the following.

> All this... raises the key question of whether Goldman Sachs' decision not to disclose Paulson's involvement was a correct judgment, or whether it was a material omission. It just seems to me that Goldman Sachs should have named Paulson in the offering circular for the CDO. They didn't. Is it because they didn't want investors to understand that this was a bear-market, short-the-bond CDO?[20]

It has been argued that the Abacus CDO was created to unravel quickly. It has been pointed out that this CDO constructed by Goldman Sachs lacked sufficient cash; its covenants were weak; and it afforded less investor protection than usual in order to provide higher yields. Needless to say this is troubling since, it appears that the CDO was designed to fail and that those marketing the CDO knew that. To market such a product in those circumstances seems to involve deliberate fraud although no one involved has been criminally charged nor are they likely to be. Creating something that's designed to fail? What kind of brokerage service is this?

This is not mere carping by two business ethicists. The SEC charged Goldman Sachs with misconduct and Goldman paid a record $550 million to settle the charges. In paying the fine Goldman made the following statement:

> Goldman acknowledges that the marketing materials for the ABACUS 2007-AC1 transaction contained incomplete information. In particular, it was a mistake for the Goldman marketing materials to state that the reference portfolio was "selected by" ACA Management LLC without disclosing the role of Paulson & Co. Inc. in the portfolio selection process and that Paulson's economic interests were adverse to CDO investors. Goldman regrets that the marketing materials did not contain that disclosure.[21]

---

[19] http://www.scribd.com/doc/30032645/Goldman-Sachs-complaint, April 16, 2010 11:22 EDT. For more on this we recommend three books: *The Big Short*, by Michael Lewis; *Reckless Endangerment*, by Gretchen Morgenson and Joshua Rosner; and *Money and Power*, by William D. Cohan, among others.

[20] http://kudlowsmoneypolitics.blogspot.com/2010/04/case-against-goldman-sachs.html

[21] http://www.sec.gov/news/press/2010/2010-123.htm

Tying It All Together

Many commentators on the financial crisis who focus on the causes of the crisis begin and end with greed. We agree that greed is certainly an important element in understanding the financial crisis. But ending the analysis by citing greed as **the** cause is too simplistic. The fact that people refused to recognize and in some cases even seemed to endorse conflicts of interest is especially troubling. Even more troubling is the fact that some people and some financial institutions abused information asymmetry and deliberately sold products to an unsuspecting public-products that they had reason to believe would fail. Thus we moved from greed-a vice- to conflict of interest, deception and fraud that are unethical and illegal. How did this happen? Our larger thesis is that this happened because people forgot that self–interest must be constrained and it happened because these individuals and institutions lost sight of the larger purpose of business in general and of financial institutions in particular.

Let's return to our earlier discussion of Aristotle and Adam Smith. As we saw, with Aristotle, where greed rules, there are no limits. What begins as a necessary service in a financial world became corrupted by forgetting what the service was about and what it was for. If the only goal is to maximize wealth or profit, by definition there is no end–no place to stop. To maximize means there is never enough.

And counter to the belief of many, Adam Smith never promoted self-interest without any limits. He asserted that the pursuit of self-advantage is indeed a good thing, so that

Every man,..., is left perfectly free to pursue his own interest his own way, and to bring both his industry and capital into competition with those of any other man, or order of men.

But he puts a limit on that: "as long as he does not violate the laws of justice."[22]

If we take justice to mean everyone gets his or her due, or if justice is balance, then one achieves the balance by doing what is to one's advantage, but always keeping in mind and being constrained by the purpose of one's pursuit.

It is just this balance that was lost and it was lost because many of the players in the financial markets lost sight of the purpose of one's pursuit. Forgetting the major purpose of financial markets, financial market players took on projects simply to accumulate wealth—for the company and the executives. This forgetting led to inordinate greed, which led to the corruption of many financial institutions.

At this point it is important to re-emphasize the purpose of business in general and of financial institutions in particular. Commercial pursuits are necessarily societal. They involve others and the purpose of working for others. What does a lender owe the borrower? What is a mortgage company for? Is giving someone a mortgage they cannot afford, giving them their due? Is providing someone who is non credit worthy with credit giving them or the other stakeholders their due? Is failing to appraise securities properly giving those who trust the ratings their due? What is a

---

[22] WN, IV, ix, 51.

bank for? What is a rating agency for? What are financial markets for? Is helping to destroy trust by failing to disclose crucial information including possible conflicts of interest giving society its due?

The crucial question at this point is this. Are Aristotle's and Smith's views of limited pursuits of self-interest constrained by societal purposes to be the defining ethical principle of markets or is Weber right in his judgment of capitalism that we quoted earlier correct? Is the collapse into greed a necessary aspect of the free market system? One would hope not, and the constant notion that certain behavior is scandalous, underlies the fact that there is still an ethos that seeks human fulfillment, and recognizes that it won't be achieved by the pursuit of wealth for its own sake.

Aristotle pointed out that there are more things necessary to living well than the solitary pursuit of wealth. Businesses which discover the importance of serving their stakeholders will not only flourish as outstanding corporate citizens, they will provide a model of integrity for all to follow and be the foundation of trust that is necessary for markets to operate efficiently for the benefit of society. However, given the propensity of human beings to look out for their own advantage, we need to set up incentives that reward responsible behavior with worthwhile goals.

To summarize: Financial markets have a role and purpose in society, but when that purpose is distorted because of greed and the proper role is abandoned for the sake of profit, the entire system gets corrupted. What has happened over and over again is that the markets have been manipulated and financial instruments misused. There are legitimate uses and purposes for hedges, SPE's, derivatives, and Swaps, such as to handle risk management. But, when accumulation is pursued and rewarded for its own sake, those purposes are forgotten.

Financial Services Professionals

Up to this point we have looked at the corruption of the system of financial markets. In spite of the systemic risks and corrupt practices, there are groups of financial services professionals who sell the various financial instruments and products. We will complete this Chapter by looking briefly at their ethical responsibilities. Clearly, if Goldman's Mortgage CDO was defective and a broker knew that, he should not have sold it.

There are various types of micro behavior within the market system that need to be examined. Generally there is agreement that a number of practices such as fraud, stock manipulation and churning are unethical. However, there are also practices in financial dealings where it is unclear whether and how those practices are unethical. Questions can be raised about the following sorts of practices such as: insider trading, tax shelters, income smoothing, some appearances of conflict of interest, independence, de-mutualization, confidentiality and privacy, conflicting loyalties between clients and companies, and the responsibilities of professionalism among others.

Is insider trading really wrong? If so, what exactly is wrong with it? How much disclosure is necessary in sales of financial instruments? How much disclosure is necessary in financial statements that show the financial strengths and weaknesses of a company? Should mutual fund managers put themselves in unwarranted conflict of interest situations by engaging in private purchases of stocks their company trades in? Should banks be able to sell insurance and investment products, and does such a capability create unnecessary conflicts of interest for them? Should one demutualize? What should the limits of privacy be in the credit industry? What climate should be created so that the interests of the broker do not conflict with those of his client? Do we need fee based advising only, or is commissioned based selling with an agent's responsibility to give a client the best possible advice? Are financial service personnel professionals or simply sales people, and what are their responsibilities as such?

Once again, the needs of society determine the purposes of the financial markets. Not everything needs to be sustained. Things that fulfill no purpose should die out. The ethical rules in the market place, even in the market place of money, that individuals should follow are fairly straightforward. Market transactions between individuals ought to be carried on without using others and without engaging in deception or fraud in accordance with one's role. However, human beings, being what they are, will for a variety of reasons fall short of fulfilling their responsibilities (in the worst cases, greedily and selfishly use others for their own gain). What follows is a list of ethically problematic ways of behaving in the financial services industry.

Perhaps the easiest form of being unethical is by lacking integrity. Ways of being deceitful or dishonest in the financial services industry include misrepresenting the financial product, including deceptive illustrations of possible returns, concealing of risk factors, withholding full disclosure, misrepresenting one's ability, and other activities. Fraud is a legal concept and has specific meanings in specific instances, but generally involves "intentional misrepresentation, concealment, or omission of the truth for the purpose of deception or manipulation to the detriment of a person or organization."[23] Beyond deception and fraud, there are other ways of using a client, particularly in exchange situations, but possibly elsewhere, which involve coercing or manipulating the client, by fear mongering or other means.

As we have already shown. a central concern in financial services arises from conflicts of interest. There is conflicting interest when either the broker or agent's interest is served by selling a product the client does not need or is inferior to another product, typically a product that provides less remuneration to the sales person. There is also conflict when an agent has two clients, and service to one will be detrimental to the other. If the interests in conflict are the interests of the agent against those of the client, professionalism demands that the agent subordinate his or her interests to those of the client. When the interests in conflict are those of two parties, both of whom the agent serves, solutions are more complex.

There are particularly difficult conflict of interest situations for accounting firms arising from providing external audit function for a publicly held firm while simultaneously selling consulting services to the same firm. Also, the audit function

[23] Downes, John and Jordan Elliot Goodman. (1985). *Dictionary of Finance and Investment Terms* (Barron's Finance and Investment Handbook). Woodbury: Barron's, 148.

has inherent conflicts balancing confidentiality to the client and their duty to inform the public of possible illegal practices. The SEC has historically been concerned about the latter problem, but it is the mixing of auditing and consulting that concerns the SEC even more.

Financial planners routinely run into conflicts between the interests of their clients and the structure of fees for their services. There is an interesting juxtaposition in the field between fee only planners and planners that sell a product. A fee only planner charges for their advice, but receives no commission from the client's implementation of that advice. Most planners are not fee only. They do not overtly charge for their advice, but are remunerated through a commission on the implementation of that advice. This creates an interesting dilemma—does my advice purely service the needs of the client or do I shade my advice depending on the structure of a commission schedule?

In money management and investment banking, there are numerous examples of potential unethical practices. For example, money managers who trade personally in the securities their firms hold in portfolio. A manager with large holdings in a security can easily influence the price of that security as they buy and sell; therefore why not enter the market for a personal transaction before placing the firm's transaction? Investment bankers have ample opportunities to engage in practices that are either clearly a conflict of interest, and often illegal, or border on a conflict of interest. Free riding and withholding securities from the public in an initial public offering is illegal, but the temptation to compromise this rule is powerful when the issue is "hot"; that is everyone knows the price will increase once the security begins to trade in the secondary market. In December 2000 the SEC commenced an investigation against three prominent investment banking firms for selectively providing shares of "hot" IPOs to certain clients. The investigation centered on a "quid pro quo" arrangement where the client is charged higher fees for other services in exchange for IPO shares that will surely rise in value.

Another unethical practice which occurs in the financial services industry is the scalping of securities: for example an investment advisor who buys a security before recommending it, then selling out after the price has risen based on the recommendation. The most prominent case occurred in the 1980s involving the Wall Street Journal's "Heard on the Street" column. This column was widely read and carefully followed by investors. The articles were very specific and often listed companies and recommendations resulting in many to buy upon the written recommendations. The author was accused of tipping off certain individuals about the contents of articles before they were published.

Cornering the market is obviously unethical and often illegal, especially when it is in direct violation of government regulations, as was the well-publicized case against Salomon Brothers in 1991. Salomon was one of the major primary dealers in US government securities. These dealers bid in the auctions for Treasury bills, notes and bonds. The government has regulations concerning the percentage of successful bids that may go to individual firms, but firms may also bid for their customers. In one auction in early 1991 Salomon received over 80 % of the offering under the pretense that a sizeable amount of the bids were for customers. In the subsequent investigation they were charged with illegal activity, but there was also evidence to suggest that Salomon had used agreements with customers that technically may not have been illegal, but surely bordered on the unethical given the intent of the government rules.

Companies can get involved in activities such as: illegal dividend payments, where "dividend payments come out of capital surplus or that make the company insolvent;"[24] incestuous share dealing- buying and selling of shares in each other's companies to create a tax or other financial advantage,[25] compensation design, where they set up alternative forms of payment to allow agents to avoid rebating violations; discrimination in hiring and promoting; misrepresentation to new hires; invasion of privacy ; and dubious claim settlement policies.

In insurance sales, there is needless replacement, and defective illustrations, which have been the basis of billion dollar lawsuits against Prudential, New York Life and Metropolitan Life among others. Brokers and agents get involved in churning accounts that benefit the agents at the expense of the clients. Some attempts have been made to counteract these unethical practices. For broker/dealers there is insistence on suitability rules, which demand you know and act in behalf of the best interests of the client you are selling to. There is the prohibition for financial planners and for those with control over clients' monies, either as trustees or brokers or advisers against commingling those funds with the financial service agents.

For those on the exchanges, there is insider trading, which is, as the name implies, engaging in trading on the basis of inside information. This practice is viewed as unfair to other traders who do not have the information as it makes for an unequal playing field. There is free riding, in the form of withholding a new securities issue to resell later at a higher price, or in the form of buying and selling in rapid order without putting up money for the sale.

Finally, there are prohibitions against schemes such as pyramiding that build on non-existing values, such as a Ponzi Scheme, rigging the market, manipulation, or running ahead i.e. an analyst buying a stock before making the recommendation to buy to his or her client.[26]

Most of these unethical practices have in common, if not downright deception, the use of one's customers or clients for the benefit of the firm, the officers of the firm or the financial services professional. This litany should help us begin to understand the tremendous range of possible conflicts of interest and out right possibilities of fraud in financial interaction. What can be done to avoid such problems?

---

[24] Ibid., 174.
[25] Ibid., 175.
[26] Ibid., 352.

Basic Ethical Principles: A Call to Reexamine Purpose

We have just provided a list of only some of the types of ethical misbehavior to occur in the financial services industry. Given the huge diversity of issues, what is the practical way to approach them? First, it would seem useful to come up with some general principles to follow. Second, it would be helpful to examine the various kinds of regulation governing financial services. Finally, it would seem helpful to examine how to make the environment more susceptible to ethical behavior. There is not time to deal adequately with the last issues, but we will briefly lay out some general principles.

Our experience show there are three valuable and overarching ethical principles that can be applied to the majority of issues in financial services: (1) avoid deception and fraud, and (2) honor your commitments. (3) fulfill the true purpose of your professional role. Note that the different sectors of the financial markets fulfill different needs. The responsibility of those in these sectors is to perform the role in such a way that it fulfills those needs.

One can use the knowledge of financial markets to make predictions about what instruments will do, and that knowledge is important for the financial adviser. However, that knowledge can be used for good or ill. Integrity demands that one fulfill one's purpose. It demands aligning the cleverness or skill of the professional with ends that serve those whom the professional is committed to serve. In the case of financial services professionals, that is the client. The primary purpose of the financial adviser is to give advice. That means determining and serving the needs of the advisee not the adviser. The adviser has a fiduciary responsibility to put the interests of the advisee first. Giving advice that is geared to enrich the adviser more than the advisee is not advice. It is corrupt behavior. It is the manipulation, by deceptive words, of the person for whose interests the adviser is supposed to look out.

It should be clear that there was rampant corruption leading to the economic crisis of 2008. Rating agencies failed in performing their tasks. Lending institutions failed by giving out loans to non-credit worthy individuals, thereby jeopardizing other clients. Accounting and auditing failed in their duty to make sure financial statements reflected the worth of the companies they were reporting on or auditing. Investment advisers like Madoff failed to fulfill their fiduciary duty. One's duty is not simply to be clever in doing something. One's duty is to fulfill one's role, which means fulfilling the purposes of that role. A clever financier can game the market and use his clients. An ethical financier will perform his or her function for the sake of the clients and public he or she serves.

That basic responsibility to serve the ends and purposes of the good of society was undermined by pursuing self-interest without constraints and without a concern for the good of the whole. In short, the pursuit of self-interest turned into selfishness, which is the unconstrained pursuit of self-interest at the expense of and without concern for others. That is the underlying corruption.

Chapter 10
Stakeholder Board Representation as a Means of Governance

After over 10 years of unending financial scandals, scandals that have continued well beyond the passage of Sarbanes-Oxley (SOX) and Dodd-Frank, perhaps it is time to look at some out of the box proposals to improve corporate governance. My suggestion which rests on the theoretical work of R Edward Freeman and more recently of Patricia Werhane is to suggest that many governance problems could be resolved if the corporate boards of publicly held companies were composed of representatives of the most important stakeholders of that corporation. This chapter consists of four parts. In "Section One: Proposals for Reform" I mention some of the reforms that have taken place and point out that although these reforms may be necessary for a system of appropriate corporate governance, they will not be sufficient. In "Section Two: Stakeholder Theory" I briefly review stakeholder theory with a special emphasis on Freeman's suggestion that corporate boards consist of stakeholder groups. In "Section Three: Stakeholder Governance", I explain my model of stakeholder governance. In the final section, "Section Four: Objections and Replies", I will consider some objections to stakeholder governance and provide some suggestions as to how these criticisms can be answered.

Section One: Proposals for Reform

Regulatory Reform

Certainly the most ambitious reforms in response to the wave of corporate scandals were changed laws and expanded regulations. The first in response to the scandals of 2001 was the Sarbanes-Oxley Act, now known affectionately as SOX. Among

This chapter is a greatly revised version of a paper I read at the Transatlantic Business Ethics Conference, Wharton, University of Pennsylvania, April 6, 2006.

N.E. Bowie, *Business Ethics in the 21st Century*, Issues in Business Ethics 39,
DOI 10.1007/978-94-007-6223-7_10, © Springer Science+Business Media Dordrecht 2013

the reforms of that time SOX was the most comprehensive. However, in addition during this time the Securities and Exchange Commission created a new set of regulations as did the New York Stock Exchange. Finally, the influence of New York State Attorney General Eliot Spitzer's aggressive enforcement of existing law cannot be underestimated. The second response in response to the financial crisis of 2008–2009 was the Frank-Dodd act that is still being implemented.[1]

I am not one to quarrel with these new laws, regulations, and more vigorous enforcement of current law. I am not overly concerned about the alleged increased costs they impose on business since business has brought this on itself. For decades I have reminded my students that one of the advantages of ethical conduct on the part of corporations is less regulation. Bad apples create more regulation and much of the regulation that is enacted ignores unintended consequences and overreaches. I think Dodd-Frank is a perfect example of this phenomenon of overly complicated and onerous response to unethical behavior. However, even these laws on their most draconian interpretation will not go far enough to improve corporate governance.

The first point to make is that the laws do not work. A number of excellent papers presented at the U of Minnesota conference Ethics in the Financial Services Industry (April 2004 and published in a special issue of *Business and Professional Ethics Journal)* made this point. Two of the most developed critiques were by Daryl Koehn and Karim Jamal.[2]

Koehn, who was especially prescient when one looks at the 2008–2009 financial crisis, pointed out that many of the new financial instruments and processes are so complex that the regulators do not understand them. She cites one example where bank officials who had devised new models to monitor and assess risk had to explain them to the regulators. In addition there are simply not enough regulators. As part of the Republican strategy to reduce the size of government, the regulatory agencies have been starved for personnel. In addition, regulators, although supposedly independent, are political beings. They are aware of the election returns. Also regulators quarrel among themselves-sometimes over turf and sometimes over content. New York State Attorney General Eliot Spitzer and the Securities and Exchange Commission (SEC) had had public disagreements over regulatory issues on a number of occasions as federal and state regulators responded to the Enron and other debacles of 2001. For a more complete discussion of these matters see Koehn's complete paper.

Jamal asks the following pertinent question: "Seventy years after the Securities Acts of 1932 and 1933, which set up a regulatory body called the Securities and Exchange Commission (SEC), why do we think more regulation will lead to better

---

[1] For more on the ethical issues surrounding the financial crisis of 2008–2009, see Chap. 9 written with Ronald Duska.

[2] Koehn, Daryl. (2004). "What Form of Business Regulation is Workable?" *Business and Professional Ethics Journal,* 12(1 and 2), 43–63 and Jamal, Karim. (2004). "After Seven Decades of Regulation, Why is the Audit Profession in Such a Mess?" *Business and Professional Ethics Journal,* 12(1 and 2), 65–92.

auditor behavior?" Jamal's basic negative answer is that the actions of regulators often exacerbate the conditions that lead to fraud rather than limit fraud. Why is that? Jamal begins by pointing out there is a fundamental conflict of interest in the way that publicly traded firms hire auditors. That conflict of interest results because firms hire and fire the auditor firms that do the audit. When I did my first research into accounting ethics, this conflict of interest jumped out at me yet the auditing profession seems to steadfastly ignore the problem.[3] Jamal recommends a third party intermediary to hire the auditors. Another of Jamal's salient criticisms of the rules based approach is that a kind of game, I would say choreographed dance, takes place. Jamal describes it this way. "We appear to be getting into a game of escalating rule-writing, followed by creative games by management to get around the new rules." The third problem is that the regulators have eliminated the professional norms and rules that restrain competition among auditors. Auditing may provide an example of a case where restraint of competition is a good thing. Jamal argues that we need less commercialization of auditing and he praises SOX for eliminating some of the consulting services that an auditing company can offer to client firms.

Other scholars have focused on the topic of direct concern in this Chapter-the failures of governance by corporate boards. Several scholars have shown that Boards cannot act at arms length and protect shareholder interests due to managerial power. Many have noted that there is often an inverse relationship between profitability of the firm and the amount of executive compensation. A good summary of many of the issues along with recommendations for greater transparency can be found in an article by Bebchuk and Fried[4] With respect to the Board's use of stock options to reward executives, Jamal[5] argues that we should revise Section 162n of the US tax code that has permitted the abuse of stock options in publicly held companies. Later work by Harris and Bromiley has shown that the likelihood of an accounting restatement due to misrepresentation is statistically proportional to the amount of stock options granted to the CEO.[6] Thus the greater the amount of the stock options the greater the likelihood of misrepresentation. It is interesting to note that excessive executive compensation is recognized as a major problem in business ethics yet despite various attempts at reform it remains intractable. I believe one of the strengths of my proposal for stakeholder Board voting representation is that the problem of excessive executive compensation can finally be meaningfully addressed. I provide much more discussion of this issue later in the Chapter since I use executive compensation as a test case for the effectiveness of stakeholder representative boards.

---

[3] Bowie, Norman E. (1988). "Accountants, Full Disclosure, and Conflicts of Interest." *Business & Professional Ethics Journal*, 5(3 and 4), 59–73.

[4] Bebchuk, Lucian A. and Jesse M. Fried. (2006). "Pay Without Performance: Overview of the Issues," *Academy of Management Perspectives*, 5–24.

[5] Jamal, op.cit.

[6] Harris, Jared and Philip Bromiley. (2007). "Incentives to Cheat: The Influence of Executive Compensation and Firm Performance on Financial Misrepresentation," *Organization Science*, 18(3), 350–367.

Limitations of the Compliance-Based Approach

The emphasis on solving business ethics issues by regulation is an example of a compliance-based approach. Proponents of regulation argue that a stiff climate of compliance is an appropriate element in preventing corporate malfeasance. Even if the arguments discussed above concerning the pitfalls of the regulatory approach could be circumnavigated, even the best regulatory approach cannot be sufficient. Arguments against the sufficiency of compliance have been made by such scholars as Weaver and Trevino and Reynolds and Bowie.[7] In their empirical research Weaver and Trevino showed that a values- based program, unlike a compliance based program, was positively correlated with greater commitment to the organization, was more supportive of employee integrity, and with the willingness of employees to deliver bad news to a superior. In their normative research, Reynolds and Bowie emphasize the importance of motive or good intentions in ethics. Simply following the law or checking the boxes is not acting from a moral motive and as a result there is no real buy-in to ethical integrity. Laws are seen as an imposition whereas acting on ethical principles is agent determined and indicates both rational and emotional commitment to ethics. With compliance, ethical conduct can be or seem forced. With a values-based program, ethical conduct feels authentic or in the popular phrase, "real."

Board Reforms

There have been a number of calls for Board reforms with the aim of improving governance. The Board of Directors was a prime target of SOX. Companies listed on the major stock exchanges need to have a majority of the Board consist of independent directors. The nominating committee and staff compensation committee of the board must consist entirely of independent directors. However, achievement of true independence has been difficult. After all, most Board members are CEO's or high officials of other corporations. Thus there is a common outlook on management since there is a tendency for the CEO's to think alike. There is also a natural tendency to get along with one's colleagues. There is the danger that the Board becomes a kind of club or, in more scholarly terms, that it suffers from groupthink. These criticisms help explain why even after the Board reforms that were required by SOX, there is still a serious issue of excessive executive compensation.

---

[7] See Weaver, Gary R. and Linda K. Trevino. (1999). "Compliance and Values Oriented Ethics Programs: Influences of Employee Attitudes and Behavior," *Business Ethics Quarterly,* 9(2), 315–335 and Reynolds, Scott J. and Norman E. Bowie. (2004). "A Kantian Perspective of the Characteristics of Ethics Programs," *Business Ethics Quarterly*, 14(2), 275–294.

Even when the heads of non-profits or former political leaders are appointed to the Board, there is a strong management orientation. The Board still primarily consists of managers. To put the issue in stakeholder terms, current corporate boards are composed almost exclusively of one stakeholder-managers. Other corporate stakeholders are either not represented or at most have minimal representation. By having the Board be composed of stakeholder representatives, I believe real independence could be achieved.

I am not alone in calling for reforms. Additional reforms have been called for. For example, Bebchuk and Fried[8] want to make it easier for stockholders to replace directors, to eliminate staggered board terms, and to force managers to honor majority backed stockholder resolutions. However, these reforms have not been forthcoming. Business interests led by the Business Roundtable have successfully fought these reforms during the entire decade of crises. I have always found it interesting that many of those corporate executives who embrace the philosophy of Milton Friedman that the purpose of business is to create shareholder wealth continue to fight any attempt to give the shareholder greater voice in the management of the corporation.

However, it should be pointed out that even if these reforms were successful, they would only improve the position of one stakeholder constituency,-the stockholders. The interests of the other stakeholders are not touched by these reforms. Having made that criticism, I want to emphasize nonetheless that one of the major failures of current Board governance practice is that Boards have failed to protect the interests of the stockholders, as they are legally and morally required to do. That is why, as we shall see, I advocate voting representation on the Board for stockholder interests. Current Boards have failed as agents of the stockholders.

Principles Rather than Rules

One idea, which is prominent in debates surrounding accounting and auditor independence, is the suggestion that the focus should be on principles rather than on rules. In the philosophical literature this distinction between rules and principles is most prominent in the work of Ronald Dworkin. Using that distinction Dworkin[9] has argued that there is one and only one correct decision regarding any legal case because even in the absence of a legal rule to settle the case, there is an applicable principle that will do so. Whereas rules are highly specific, principles are not. We all know what a rule is. Rules are highly specific and usually codified or at least written down. Dworkin defines a "principle" as follows: "I call a "principle" a standard that is to be observed ... because it is a requirement of justice or fairness or some other dimension of morality."[10] In the absence of a rule to cover an ethical issue, look for a principle.

---

[8] Bebchuk and Fried, op.cit.
[9] Dworkin, Ronald. (1977). *Taking Rights Seriously.* Cambridge: Harvard University Press.
[10] Ibid., 22.

In debates surrounding international accounting standards much has been made of the distinction between the American system of elaborate rules and the European system based on principles. A principle might be something like: Make sure the financial information fairly reflects the financial position of the company. It is more general than a rule. With a rule-based approach, the auditors try to use rules to reflect the financial position of the company. However, sometimes carefully following the rules will not provide the best indication of the financial health of the company. A number of scholars including Jamal[11] have spoken on behalf of the principles based approach.

Other scholars have gone on to suggest a conceptual framework for maintaining auditor independence which relies on principles rather than rules but is much more extensive than just providing a list of principles. For example, The Independence Standards Board commissioned a group to provide such a conceptual framework. The late Thomas Dunfee was one of the members of that task force. That task force used a risk assessment strategy. Of particular concern were threats to auditor independence, the type and adequacy of the safeguards put in place to mitigate the threats, and a perception measure of independence risk which was "the likelihood that an auditor's objectivity (a) would be compromised or (b) reasonably would appear compromised to well-informed investors and other users."[12] The task force then developed basic principles of auditor independence. One of those principles was "considering the views of investors and other interested users...."[13] This principle provides an opening to the kind of stakeholder governance I endorse in this paper.

Governance by principles rather than rules may well be an improvement over the current rules based approach. However, a change in orientation from rules to principles will not get to the heart of the matter. I maintain that the current problems of Board governance result from a homogeneity of interests on the part of Board members. The perspective of the Board is primarily a management perspective. If the various stakeholders are to be protected, then real live representatives of stakeholders need a place on the Board. Since the suggested reforms will not get us where we need to be with respect to governance, I suggest a strategy of stakeholder representation with voting rights on Boards of Directors of publicly held corporations.

Section Two: Stakeholder Theory

In the business ethics literature, the father (perhaps now grandfather) of stakeholder theory is R Edward Freeman. As we have seen earlier, in developing stakeholder theory, Freeman and his colleague the late William Evan distinguished a broad definition of stakeholder from a narrow definition. Under the narrow definition,

---

[11] Jamal, op.cit., 74.

[12] Staff Report, "A Conceptual Framework for Auditor Independence" Independence Standards Board, July 2001, 6.

[13] Ibid., 9.

stakeholder groups are "those groups who are vital to the survival and success of the corporation." On the broad or wide view, stakeholder groups or individual stakeholders "include any group or individual who can affect or is affected by the corporation."[14] That distinction will be important as I develop my proposal for stakeholder Board representation.

In some of his early work with William Evan, Freeman explicitly endorsed a "Stakeholder Board of Directors" where the Board would consist of representatives of five stakeholder groups: employees, customers, suppliers, stockholders, and members of the local community.[15] In addition there would be a board member who would be the metaphysical director who would speak for the corporation. These directors would be sure that the corporation was managed for the benefit of the corporate stakeholders. With the exception of the metaphysical director, much of this is plausible and deserves serious consideration. Unfortunately, from my perspective, Freeman seemed to have abandoned his advocacy of a stakeholder board-at least until very recently.

In a later version of the aforementioned essay in his own name, Freeman adopted a Rawlsian perspective so that rather than an actual stakeholder board, there was an original position where the stakeholders acting under a partial veil of ignorance adopted the basic principles of corporate governance. There were six such principles: (1) The principle of Entry and Exit, (2) The Principle of Governance, (3) The Principle of Externalities, (4) The Principle of Contracting Costs, (5) The Agency Principle and (6) The Principle of Limited Liability.[16] I endorse these principles and point out that they function as principles rather than rules and thus are consistent with the observations made for governance reform discussed in "Section One: Proposals for Reform". However, for the purposes of this chapter, I am less concerned with the principles and more concerned with the actual participants on stakeholder Boards of Directors. I will have more to say on this shortly.

A stakeholder board of directors disappeared from Freeman's writing for over 15 years- at least to the best of my knowledge. However In his most recent book, *Stakeholder Theory: The State of the Art*, Freeman and his colleagues have continued to flirt with the idea of stakeholder representatives on the Board of Directors. In discussing the nascent idea of a stakeholder board of overseers mentioned by some transaction cost economists, Freeman calls the idea of such a board "intriguing." He indicates that such a board could function as a governance mechanism and has assigned the board the following tasks: "(1) To reduce information asymmetry among key stakeholders so that management could more easily create even more value,

---

[14] Evan, William M. and R. Edward Freeman. (1988). "A Stakeholder Theory of the Modern Corporation: Kantian Capitalism" in Tom L. Beauchamp and Norman E. Bowie (eds.), *Ethical Theory and Business*, 3rd ed. Englewood Cliffs: Prentice Hall Inc., 100.

[15] Ibid., 104.

[16] Freeman, R. Edward. (1997). "A Stakeholder Theory of the Modern Corporation" in Tom L. Beauchamp and Norman E. Bowie (eds.), *Ethical Theory and Business*, 5rd ed. Englewood Cliffs: Prentice Hall Inc., 74.

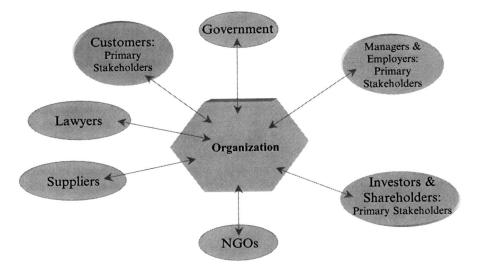

Fig. 10.1 Standard stakeholder "map"

(2) to view the interest of financiers, customers, suppliers, communities, and employees as joint, and (3) assume the continuation of the corporation through time."[17]

Later in the same work, Freeman and his colleagues say, "For this function [providing a firm with resources] stakeholder theory would advocate appointing external stakeholders to the board."[18] And there is empirical support that appointing external stakeholders would provide the firm with greater resources. Freeman and his colleagues cite studies by Johnson, Daily and Ellstrand as well as Stearns and Mizruchi that appointing representatives from financial institutions facilitates capital acquisition.[19]

I have criticized current Board governance procedures on the grounds that the Board represents a homogenous management perspective. Early stakeholder theory made a similar error when the typical stakeholder map always showed management at the center of the stakeholder wheel with spokes out to the other stakeholders. The conversation centered on the obligations management had to these other stakeholders. However, as George Bush would put it, on this model management is the decider. Patricia Werhane has characterized the traditional stakeholder map as follows (Fig. 10.1):

---

[17] Freeman, R. Edward, Jeffrey S. Harrison, Andrew C. Wicks, Bidhan L. Parmar and Simon E. DeColle. (2010). *Stakeholder Theory: The State of the Art.* Cambridge: Cambridge University Press, 19.

[18] Ibid., 112.

[19] For details see Johnson, J.L., C.M Daily, and A.E. Ellstrand. (1996). "Boards of Directors: A Review and Research Agenda," *Journal of Management,* 22(3), 409–438. See also, Stearns, L.B. and M.S Mizruchi. (1996). "Board Composition and Corporate Financing: The Impact of Financial Institution Representation on Borrowing," *Academy of Management Journal,* 36(3), 603–618.

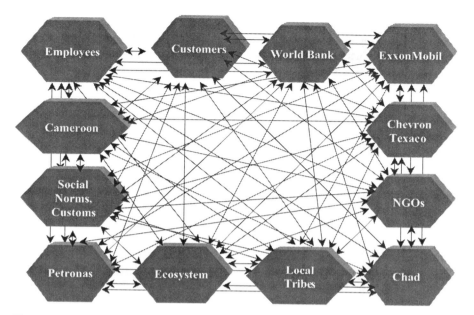

Fig. 10.2 ExxonMobil stakeholder networks

Patricia Werhane's significant contribution to stakeholder theory is to point out that our perspective and hence the perspective of management would change if management were not at the center of the wheel. Werhane has teased out the implications of putting various stakeholders at the center. In doing this work, the wheel disappears as Werhane develops a systems approach of stakeholder alliances. One example of her re-characterization is provided here (Fig. 10.2).

Werhane's contribution will become important as I develop my suggestion of a stakeholder Board of Directors.

Section Three: Stakeholder Governance

Among the advantages of this proposal is that it is consistent with some of the more enlightened approaches to corporate strategy. Just after the turn of the century I took 25 MBA students to Europe to give them the opportunity to hear first hand corporate executives explain their corporate social responsibility programs. As the public has grown more skeptical of corporate behavior, major companies have recognized the need to change how they communicate with stakeholders. Officials at Shell put it this way: We have had to move from "trust me" to "tell me" to "show me" to "engage me." The obvious way to engage is through stakeholder dialogues, which is exactly what Shell has done. British American Tobacco has said that its old strategy was "decide, deliver, and defend." Its new strategy is "listen, understand, decide, and deliver." Listening and understanding require stakeholder dialogues. In Europe, there is constant reference to managing for the 3 P's, people, planet, and profits. How is a manager to do that, unless he or she engages in dialogue with stakeholders?

I should point out that stakeholder management or stakeholder engagement is hardly new. It might seem so to many business ethicists because we have been so concerned about how managers could possibly prioritize stakeholder interests and then harmonize them for win-win situations. But as *Stakeholder Theory: The State of the Art* indicated, Robert Ackoff pointed out that systems design could be accomplished by stakeholder participation as early as 1970 and as Freeman et al.'s Chapter on the history of the development of the idea of stakeholder theory makes clear, stakeholder "theory" resulted from the actual practices of research centers and companies who were actually managing by stakeholder theory even before they had given it that name. We did not start with stakeholder theory and then apply it; rather stakeholder theory was a way of understanding certain new management practices.[20]

It is now a natural step, I believe, to bring stakeholder engagement into the boardroom. Besides the function of the Board is governance. That is what the Board is supposed to do. This proposal is designed to enable the Board to fulfill its function of governance more effectively.

How would this proposal work? The first question to be asked is "Which stakeholders should have board positions." I find the Ronald K Mitchell, Bradley R. Agle, Donna Wood, topology useful here and will adopt it.[21] One implication of using their theory of stakeholder salience is that there is no list of stakeholders that can be given a priori either for all corporations or even a single corporation. Moreover, those stakeholders deserving of board membership can change over time. (Pragmatists should find this view congenial.) What is crucial is that the corporation identify those stakeholders that are salient. Salience in the view of Mitchell, Agle and Wood is a function of power, legitimacy, and urgency. For ease of explanation, I accept their definition of these central concepts.

It is important to note that although I accept their definitions, I use the notion of saliency differently. Whereas they use the term descriptively to identify which stakeholders that management in fact pays attention to, I use the concept normatively to determine which stakeholder groups deserve voting membership on the Board of Directors.

On the Mitchell, Agle, and Wood conception, power is "a relationship among social actors in which one social actor, A, can get another social actor, B, to do something that B would not otherwise have done." Legitimacy is "a generalized

[20] See the marvelous history of the development of the concept in Freeman, Harrison, Wicks, Parmar and DeColle, op.cit., Chapter 2.
[21] Mitchell, Ronald K., Bradley R. Agle, and Donna Wood. (1997). "Toward a Theory of Stakeholder Identification and Salience: Defining the Principle of Who and What Really Counts," *Academy of Management Review,* 22, 853–886.

perception or assumption that the actions of an entity are desirable, proper, or appropriate within some socially constructed system of norms, values, beliefs, and definitions." Finally, urgency is "the degree to which stakeholder claims call for immediate attention." For my purposes, stakeholders, which have power, are legitimate, and whose claims are urgent, should have voting representation on the Board of Directors.

Having said that, we can assume that the following stakeholder groups will almost always be found salient and thus deserving of Board membership: stockholders, employees, customers, suppliers, and the community. One might note here that the notion of salience allows for a broader range of stakeholder representation than one would get if one stayed with a narrow definition of stakeholder that limited stakeholders to those groups necessary to the survival of the firm. However, my list of stakeholders that would almost always be included on the Board fits rather closely with those stakeholders that are listed under a traditional narrow definition. The primary stakeholder groups should almost always have a voting membership position on the Board of Directors.[22]

The Composition of a Stakeholder Board

My first innovation here is to add an official representative of the shareholders as a voting member of the Board. Under the status quo, it is presumed that the traditional Board speaks for the shareholders. Of course the unrelenting scandals over the past 12 years give the lie to the conventional wisdom. To start, I propose that the largest, or one of the largest, institutional investors have Board representation. Since I do not want boards with token stakeholder membership, large boards should have more than one representative from shareholders. This proposal should find support from followers of finance based capitalism of Milton Friedman's ilk. However, I note the tremendous resistance to proposals for more shareholder involvement and say in board elections and board policies. Resistance to board representation for shareholders will be even more fierce.

As in Germany and some other European countries, labor would have official representation. Even in the US, which is so hostile to labor, some companies have won cooperation from unions in times of financial distress by putting representatives from labor on the Board. The suggestion that employees be represented on the Board is not a radical idea. Of course many publicly held companies do not have a labor union, so who would represent those non-union employees? Since I am a union advocate, perhaps a reform of Board governance that provided for stakeholder representation from labor would encourage corporations to think about unions in a new light and see them as partners in the enterprise. I think having labor

---

[22] In what follows mentally add "almost always" to "should."

represented on the Board might help reduce the animosity that one often finds between management and labor. In the absence of a union, some mechanism-perhaps an election-would determine who sits on the Board to represent labor. However, it is important that the determination not be made by management. In the context of current U.S. management/labor relations, the appointment of the representative of labor by management would undermine the legitimacy of the labor representative. Also it is important to note that I am not recommending that labor's representation be limited to one person. I do not envisage a Board with a large number of management representatives and then a token representative for each salient stakeholder. However, the actual number for each stakeholder group will be a function of the size of the corporation and its board. Also in corporations with both unionized and non-unionized employees, it will be important to have representation from both groups.

Customers should have representation. Depending on the type and size of the business one of the larger customers could serve as a board member. However, for many businesses the number of customers is diverse and extremely large. Which customers should be represented on Wal-Mart's Board of Directors for example? Rather than have management pick a customer or a few customers, I would suggest that a representative of a NGO representing customers could serve. When I think of an advocate for consumers, I think of *Consumer Reports*. Perhaps someone from that organization would be an appropriate representative. If more than one customer representative is required, then other NGO's could contribute.

Suppliers present some similarities and some differences from customers. With respect to suppliers, size matters. The larger the supplier account, the greater the salience and thus the greater claim for that supplier to be a representative on the board. If there are a large number of suppliers of roughly the same size, there are a couple of suggestions that I would make. If there is a NGO that could represent the suppliers, I would recommend that as I did in the case of customers. In the absence of an appropriate NGO, I would suggest a random assignment based on a drawing or some such device. However, I wish to emphasize that I am not committed to one selection method for this supplier stakeholder or any other stakeholder group. What is important is that the selection criteria or criterion be seen as legitimate by the stakeholder group under consideration. That always or almost always means that management should not be making the choice.

The local community, listed as a stakeholder by Freeman and most stakeholder theorists, presents some challenges. When a corporation is located in a single community or a few communities in geographical proximity, the choice is somewhat easier. A representative from a local charity like the United Way, or a local political official such as the mayor might be an obvious choice. However, I think the representative should not come from a business organization such as the local Chamber of Commerce. Remember I am trying to dilute the overwhelming dominance of managers on current Boards of Directors.

With respect to large international companies, e.g. General Motors, that have plants or business facilities in many communities, what is to count as the local community? To help resolve this issue we need to use the notion of salience. The adjective "local" may not be appropriate for many corporations when it comes to determine how the community should be represented.

Perhaps we need to move to the abstract level and discuss briefly the notion of corporate social responsibility. For American corporations the socially responsible corporation is one that helps address environmental and other social problems often through corporate giving, corporate volunteer programs, or a corporate foundation. In practice what social problems a corporation seeks to address is determined by the business they are in. The Target Foundation supports education and the arts. Target believes that educated citizens are a good business investment for Target as are investments in the arts since Target is in part in the fashion industry. (It is no accident that Target hired the artist Michael Graves to design its line of kitchen appliances,) Corporate practice in this instance is in line with academic recommendations. In choosing a social problem to attack, the choice should fit with the corporation's overall strategy. This type of investment goes by the name "strategic philanthropy" With that in mind, for large companies like Target they should get board representatives from NGO's or other institutions that are involved in or promote the good works that the corporation is trying to achieve. A high profile educator and the CEO of a museum or symphony makes sense for a corporation like Target. Other corporations should pick representatives that fit their peculiar corporate mission.

Procedures for a Stakeholder Board

With respect to procedure, the Board needs to be reminded that the traditional stakeholder map with management at the center is not the appropriate mental model for stakeholder governance. Rather the operations of the Board should function as a stakeholder alliance in the way that has been outlined by Werhane. The Board of Directors should not be conceived of hierarchically but rather as a committed group of equals seeking the corporate good. Perhaps something like Rousseau's "general will" would be the right mental model. Another way of putting this is that the stakeholder board should strive for consensus. Such a board would present greater challenges, especially to strong CEO's who prefer compliant boards. Stakeholder boards would certainly be less compliant. However, I would argue that the greater independence that would come with a stakeholder board is a good thing and not a weakness. Besides the stakeholder board would perform the same basic functions as a traditional board. The chief change from the status quo is the composition of the board members although I concede that such a board does have implications regarding the power of the CEO.

In defending the notion of a stakeholder board, I am taking issue with some of those who maintain that there are arguments for employees to participate in the governing of the corporation, but these arguments do not work for other primary stakeholders. In other words, some argue that the case for putting representatives of employees on the board is stronger than it is for putting representatives of any other stakeholder group on the Board. Contrary to that position, I find the arguments of

Jeffrey Moriarity in "Participation in the Workplace: Are Employees Special?" to be convincing.[23] Toward the end of that article, Moriarity suggests that those who defend a special right to participation for employees should follow where the logic of their arguments leads them and extend a right to participation to all primary stakeholders. My suggestion is that a practical way to implement a right to participation for all primary stakeholders is representation on corporate Boards of Directors.

A Test Case: Executive Compensation

One of the most vexing problems in business ethics today is excessive executive compensation. Executive compensation is the responsibility of the Board of Directors and it is widely perceived that the Board has not acted responsibly here. Lots of suggestions, many of which come from finance and agency theory, have been tried. The goal of each is to align the incentives for management with the interests of the stockholders. Stock options were perhaps the most famous-or now infamous.[24] It is widely agreed that such aligning devices have not succeeded.

Suppose the Compensation Committee of the Board consisted of representatives of labor, customers, and investors. These representatives all have an interest in keeping executive compensation reasonable enough to attract and retain good managers but they also have an interest in not providing a cookie jar. Rather than align the interest of the CEO with the shareholders, a stakeholder board would have the incentive to oppose inordinate financial interests of management when they conflict with the interests of other stakeholders who have a stake in the game. Does anyone doubt that executive compensation would be lower and thus more fair and equitable under this kind of arrangement? That's how to address the specific governance issue of executive compensation. My proposal is that other governance problems can be most effectively addressed in the same way. The god-like supposedly "objective" perspective of the traditional Board is replaced by flesh and blood representatives of the conflicting stakeholder interests. The good for the corporation is forged through dialogue and compromise rather than discovered by a supposedly objective Board.

Section Four: Objections and Replies

Pragmatic Objections: The foremost pragmatic objection is that stakeholder governance would paralyze Board operations. Board meetings would resemble faculty meetings. Stakeholder representatives would insist on supporting their own

---

[23] Moriarity, Jeffrey. (2010). "Participation in the Workplace: Are Employees Special?" *Journal of Business Ethics,* 92, 373–384.
[24] See Harris and Bromiley, op.cit.

groups and no one would take the point of view of the corporation as a whole. In other words there would be no Rousseau's General Will in the corporate setting. Board meetings would be overly long, extremely contentious, and unable to reach consensus or even compromise for the good of the corporation as a whole.

The problem with this type of objection is that it is not empirically borne out. The same kind of objection was made in the debate between those who uphold a Friedmanite stockholder view of the purpose of the firm and those who hold a stakeholder view. Michael Jensen is the most influential of the critics of the stakeholder view arguing that it is impossible to maximize two different criteria[25] Of course advocates of the stakeholder view were not advocating maximizing but balancing. Even so critics of the stakeholder view argued that stakeholder management was management by paralysis.

Nonetheless, as we saw in "Section Three: Stakeholder Governance", major international companies including some of the largest in the world now practice a stakeholder strategy that includes stakeholder dialogues. Stakeholder concerns expressed through stakeholder dialogues influence corporate strategy. Corporations report that NGO's need not be adversaries. Indeed in my trips with Minnesota MBA's to Europe, I was struck by the number of times major corporations pointed out that they learned from NGO's, that NGO's had expertise and thus possessed information that was not available to corporate management. If stakeholder dialogues work now as an effective management tool, why should stakeholder Boards of Directors fail? (As an aside, despite the common notion that faculties paralyze universities, universities seem to be one of the best run institutions in the country right now. In the language of business, there are plenty of customers all over the world that want the products universities offer.)

Normative Objections: The chief normative objection centers on rights. By what right would stakeholder representatives be voting members of the Board of Directors? It is tempting to take a Friedmanite line here and argue that the firm should be managed for the benefit of the stockholders and the job of the Board is to see that management operates the business for the benefit of the stockholders. One might even cite Oliver Williamson's argument[26] that all the other stakeholder groups can write contracts with the firm to cover agency risks and as a result the stockholders, who cannot write such a contract, are entitled to the residual-namely profits.

Even if one adopts this line of argument, one cannot avoid noting that the current system of Board oversight is a failure. Management, with the approval of the Board, has feathered its own nest over and over again at the expense of the stockholders. In way too many cases, the Board has not protected the stockholders. Under my suggestion, the stockholders would have formal voting representation on the Board. My plan gives the stockholders real voice in corporate governance and the opportunity to protect their own interests.

---

[25] Jensen, Michael. (2002). "Value Maximization, Stakeholder Theory, and the Corporate Objective Function," *Business Ethics Quarterly*, 12, 235–256.

[26] Williamson, Oliver. (1984). "Corporate Governance," *Yale Law Journal*, 93, 1197–1230.

Second, one can take the Friedman approach and still argue that stakeholder Board representation is the best means for increasing shareholder wealth. In other words if employees are treated fairly, if customers receive high quality products, if suppliers are loyally rewarded for high quality on time delivery, and if the relevant communities believe that business is in fact contributing to the health of the community and indeed if the interests of any salient stakeholders have representation, then the business and the stockholders will profit. This is a familiar story: Companies that do well by their stakeholders will do well for their stockholders.

The problem is that management far too often has not bought into the story. As my colleagues in organizational behavior and human resource management point out, there is a literature that goes back more than 50 years that shows that enlightened human resource policy increases profits, yet management has consistently failed to practice what the literature shows will work. Jeffrey Pfeffer[27] with a colleague has just published another book in which he argues for evidence based management-management by social science evidence and not management by the gut. Given this failure by management and by the Board that has oversight responsibility, how can management be made to do what is in the interests of the stockholders? My answer with respect to the human resource issue is: give formal Board voting rights to employees. In other words, if treating stakeholders well is the best formula for profitability, then we need a governance mechanism that will ensure that management treats stakeholders well. Giving those stakeholders voting rights on the Board will increase the likelihood that management will take their interests seriously. Note that Board voting rights for stakeholders, on this argument, protect stockholder interests, which is traditionally what the Board is supposed to do.

Often then there is no conflict between Board voting rights for the stakeholders and stockholder wealth. My proposal for governance and Milton Friedman can live in harmony. But what of those cases where the interests of the stockholders and the interests of one or more of the other stakeholders are in conflict, not just in the short run but in the long run as well? In such cases the harmony of my stakeholder governance proposal with the Friedmanites is broken. And when it is broken, don't the stockholders have the right to have the conflict resolved in favor of them?

Not necessarily. First there is a pragmatic argument. If an essential stakeholder group believes that its interests will always be compromised whenever they conflict with the interests of the stockholders, why should they remain loyal to the firm? In other words, a rule, which always favors the stockholders in time of conflict, is ultimately self-defeating.

Second, R Edward Freeman and William Evan's paper[28] that points out the failure of Williamson's argument regarding contract writing, leads one to ask why does ownership in the firm give the stockholders the right to have their interests prevail

---

[27] Pfeffer, Jeffrey and Robert I. Sutton. (2006). *Hard Facts, Dangerous Half Truths, and Total Nonsense: Profiting from Evidence-based Management*. Boston: Harvard Business School Press.
[28] Freeman, R. Edward and William M. Evan. (1990). "Corporate Governance: A Stakeholder Interpretation," *The Journal of Behavioral Economics*, 19, 337–359.

in cases of conflict? This model of governance assumes that each stakeholder group represented on the Board is essential to the long run well being of the firm. Look again at Freeman's original definition-in the narrow sense- stakeholder groups are those groups necessary for the firm's survival. If each stakeholder group on the Board represents a group necessary for the survival of the firm, why should the interests of one of these groups, the stockholders, always trump when there is a conflict? I submit there is no good answer to that question. The essentialness of stockholders is not more essential than the essentialness of other stakeholders and thus there is no moral argument for its predominance.

Some might argue that using the notion of salience to determine Board representation will mean that some stakeholders who have moral claims against the corporation will be left out since they will not be represented. Specifically those who have moral claims and thus pass the test of legitimacy, may have neither power nor urgency. What about them? I agree that those stakeholders would not have Board representation but that does not mean that their legitimate moral claims should be ignored. Stakeholder groups that do not have power or that do not have urgency may lose their right to Board representation, but they do not lose the right to have their moral claims addressed. If a corporate action causes harm to any stakeholder, it is the obligation of the corporation and its management to address that issue and see if the harm can be avoided and, if not, whether the corporate action that causes the harm should cease. All I am arguing is that the existence of a moral claim against a corporation is not sufficient for Board representation.

Conclusion

A Board of Directors in a publicly held corporation has as its most important function a governance function. One of its most important jobs is to keep management honest. Over 10 years of unremitting scandals show that it has not done this job well. I suggest that the Board of Directors will do a better job of governance if it consists of representatives of the corporate stakeholders, narrowly defined according to the concept of salience, who have voting rights on the Board. In most cases the stockholders will benefit from such an arrangement and in those cases where there is conflict between the interests of the stockholders and some other stakeholder groups narrowly defined, the stockholders have no moral right to always have their interests trump those of the other stakeholders narrowly defined.

Chapter 11
Organizational Integrity and Moral Climates

Introduction

Organizations have personalities that many refer to as a "culture." Some organizations are perceived as having an ethical culture, while others are perceived as having an amoral or unethical culture. Organizational cultures do not change easily. In this chapter the following questions will be addressed about these cultures: What are the marks of an organization that has integrity? What factors are important? What ostensibly important factors turn out to be less so? What factors hinder organizational integrity?

In his book *Competing with Integrity*, Richard De George says, "Acting with integrity is the same as acting ethically or morally."[1] De George chooses the word "integrity" rather than "ethics" because of the negative connotations that "ethics" has in some business circles. For example, "integrity" does not have the connotations of moralizing that words like "ethics" and "morality" have for some people. I follow a similar approach here.

For the purpose of this chapter, I assume that an organization with integrity is an organization with a certain sort of moral climate. Detailing the characteristics of a moral climate for an organization is a goal of this chapter. Some features we associate with individual integrity are also characteristic of organizational integrity. For example, both individuals and organizations with integrity are steadfast in their commitment and actions to moral principle. However, I will argue that an organization with integrity has several characteristics that distinguish it from individual integrity (i.e., personal moral integrity) and that some central characteristics of individual

---

This article was originally published in *The Oxford Handbook of Business Ethics*, George G. Brenkert and Tom L Beauchamp, (eds.) Oxford University Press, 2010, 501–724. Reprinted with the permission of the editors and Oxford University Press. There have been some minor changes in the original in order to make this Chapter consistent with other Chapters in the book. Also some of the information in the original has been updated.

[1] De George, Richard. (1993). *Competing with Integrity*. New York: Oxford University Press, 5.

N.E. Bowie, *Business Ethics in the 21st Century*, Issues in Business Ethics 39,
DOI 10.1007/978-94-007-6223-7_11, © Springer Science+Business Media Dordrecht 2013

integrity are less important for organizational integrity. Individuals with integrity are individuals who accept responsibility for any negative consequences caused by their actions. On the other hand, achieving organizational integrity may require that managers de-emphasize or even, in certain situations, ignore issues of personal responsibility. Also, an organization with integrity must have certain kinds of organizational structures or organizational incentives. This language does not apply to individuals with integrity. Indeed the key notion of organizational integrity, "moral climate," cannot be meaningfully applied to individual integrity.

In this chapter, I begin with the central idea of organizational integrity: moral climate. I then identify the norms and values that contribute to a moral climate, including a commitment to stakeholder management, a commitment to seeing the purpose of the organization as a cooperative enterprise, and both substantive and procedural norms of fairness. Finally, I consider the role of incentives as they support or inhibit organizational integrity, identify conditions that work against moral integrity, and conclude by considering whether for-profit organizations can instill organizational integrity and remain profitable.

The Importance of a Moral Climate

Moral climate can be construed as comprising "shared perceptions of prevailing organizational norms established for addressing issues with a moral component."[2] A moral climate involves ethical commitments that are value-based and are embodied in the character of the organizational members and the organization's routines and incentive structures. One of the characteristics of an organization with a moral climate is that the organization takes the moral point of view with respect to organizational actions.

An essential characteristic of taking the moral point of view is to consider the interests of those impacted by actions. For individuals, taking the moral point of view is straightforward; it requires that one consider the impact of one's actions on others. With respect to an organization, matters are a bit more complex. For an organization to take the moral point of view, it must have leaders and a decision-making structure that allow it to consider the interests of those it affects, with special emphasis on those it wrongs or harms.

An organization with a moral climate has two different attributes. It has both shared perceptions as to what constitutes moral behavior as well as processes for dealing with ethical issues. Some of these shared perceptions are core values that guide the organization. In an organization with integrity, core values govern corporate activity. A full picture of what constitutes a moral climate requires a lengthy discussion of the norms and values that constitute a moral climate—the task to which we now turn.

---

[2] Victor, Bart and John B Cullen. (1988). "The Organizational Basis of Ethical Work Climates," *Administrative Science Quarterly*, 33, 101–125.

Stakeholder Management

One feature of an organization with a good moral climate is that its behavior is consistent with its purposes, which also must be morally justified. There is a close analogy here between individual integrity and organizational integrity. An individual has integrity when he or she exhibits good character and is steadfast in the face of adversity or temptation, and an organization displays integrity when it is true to its goals or purposes, especially when there are obstacles impeding them or temptations to deviate from them.

Strict consistency with and adherence to the organization's purpose is not sufficient for a good moral climate. The purpose must also be morally appropriate or at least not inconsistent with morality. For instance, the standard view of the purpose of a for-profit public company in the United States is the creation of shareholder wealth. Stockholders are the owners, and managers are the agents of the owners. It is the manager's responsibility to provide financial returns to the owners because that is what the owners want. This view is often attributed to Milton Friedman and is the standard view taught to students in American business school classes. This view is a *moral* position in that owners have moral rights and managers have moral obligations to them.

Business ethicists generally do not regard this classic position as the best account of a corporation's purpose from the moral point of view. Many business ethicists think that something like R. Edward Freeman's account of stakeholders is closer to the mark: Business ought to be a value-creating institution, and it should be managed to promote the interests of the various corporate stakeholders. The creation of wealth is a critical value, but it is not the only one. For example, employment that provides meaningful work and income for a decent standard of living are other pertinent values. I endorse Freeman's account of the purpose of the corporation although I will not defend it here. This defense has been well articulated in the business ethics literature, but stakeholder theory remains controversial and there are business ethicists who believe that the traditional Friedmanite view is superior. Defenders of Friedman's view acknowledge that stakeholder theory is instrumentally correct, meaning that managers who believe their moral obligation is to increase shareholder wealth must still manage from a stakeholder perspective. These managers realize they can only increase shareholder wealth if the interests of all corporate stakeholders are taken into account and promoted.

By endorsing stakeholder theory as the goal or purpose of the corporation, I am also accepting it as a correct normative position of how the firm ought to be managed. Managers may sometimes be morally required to put the interests of other stakeholder groups ahead of the interests of the stockholders. The managers of an organization with a moral climate recognize that the interests of various stakeholders have intrinsic value. Of course, we need to elaborate further on the nature of a moral climate. However, stakeholder theory provides the basic moral framework for organizational integrity.

Seven Substantive Moral Principles

I have argued elsewhere and will here assume that morality requires that a business organization be viewed as a moral community and not simply as a set of economic relationships.[3] I will now argue that how we look at and understand the purpose of an organization affects how we will behave in it. If the individuals in an organization view it purely instrumentally, these individuals are predisposed to behave in ways that harm organizational integrity. John Rawls's insight that organizations are social unions constituted by certain norms is useful here. Organizations are not mere instruments for achieving individual goals. To develop this notion of a social union, Rawls contrasts two views of how human society is held together[4]: In the private view human beings form social institutions after calculating that it would be advantageous to do so; in the social view human beings form social institutions because they share final ends and value common institutions and activities as intrinsically good. In a social union, cooperation is a key element of success because each individual in a social union knows that he cannot achieve his interests within the group by himself. The cooperation of others is necessary as it provides stability to the organization, enables it to endure, and enables individuals both to realize their potential and to see the qualities of others that lead to organizational success.

In an organization with a moral climate, the organization should be managed in ways that benefit the interests of the stakeholders. This can be accomplished only if the stakeholders in control do not treat the organization merely instrumentally, but rather as a cooperative enterprise or social union.

How should cooperation be achieved in an organization characterized as having a moral climate? An organization with an effective moral climate must be governed by a set of substantive moral *principles* and be characterized as having certain *processes* (or procedures) for decision-making. In short, there are both substantive and procedural elements required for organizational integrity. The following outline reflects a Kantian theory of what the business firm should be. It provides a foundation on which to build and to discuss other, non-Kantian approaches:

1. The firm should consider the interests of all the affected stakeholders in any decision that it makes.
2. The firm should have those, or representatives of those, affected by the firm's rules and policies participate in the determination of those rules and policies before they are implemented.
3. The interests of one stakeholder should not take priority over the interests of all other stakeholders for all decisions.

---

[3] Bowie, Norman E. (1991). "The Firm as a Moral Community" in Richard M Coughlin (ed.), *Morality, Rationality and Efficiency: New Perspectives on Socio-Economics*, Armonk: M.E. Sharpe Inc., 169–183.
[4] Rawls, John. (1999). *A Theory of Justice*, rev ed. Cambridge, MA: Harvard University Press, 58–60.

4. When a situation arises in which it appears that the interests of one set of stakeholders must be sacrificed for the interests of another set of stakeholders, that decision cannot be made solely on the grounds that there is a greater number of stakeholders in one group than in another.
5. No principle is acceptable if it is inconsistent with the principle that we should never treat a person merely as a means to our own ends.
6. Every profit-making firm has an imperfect duty of social beneficence (benefit to society).
7. Each business firm must establish procedures to insure that relations among stakeholders are governed by the rules of justice.[5]

These principles can be easily accepted by all who work within Rawls's or Kant's ethical theory. I recognize that many business ethicists work from a different normative ethical theory. However, I believe these principles are consistent with the conclusions reached in many other ethical theories as well. My interest here is in building on these principles by pointing to the norms that managers who view an organization as a social union might use to help create a moral climate.

Norms of Fairness

I now move from the seven moral principles for creating a moral climate to norms of fairness. Insights from both moral philosophy and organizational theory are useful here. Both ethicists and many social scientists working in organizational theory recognize the importance of fairness. Some economists such as Robert Frank have used the sense of fairness to explain why people sometimes complete transactions that are not in their short-term interest.[6] A principal concept of economics is that economic transactions are free actions in which each party perceives that he or she will benefit from it. If I am willing, for instance, to sell my house for $500,000 and someone is willing to pay $520,000 for it, each party will benefit if we make the deal. But for what price should the house actually sell? In real estate, the selling price is determined by negotiation. Our intuitions seem to suggest that a 50/50 split is most fair. With that in mind and without negotiation, the fair price is $510,000. With respect to the surplus of economic value generated by an economic activity, Frank argues that fairness requires that the surplus be divided equally.

Frank's principle cannot be applied directly to organizations because we need to consider not only the fairness in the distribution of an organization's outputs, but also the contributions that each individual makes to the organization. Recently Robert Phillips has argued that fairness in an organizational context requires that benefits be distributed on the basis of the relative contribution to the organization

---

[5] Bowie, Norman E. (1999). *Business Ethics: A Kantian Perspective*. Malden: Blackwell Publishers.
[6] See Frank, Robert. (1988). *Passions Within Reason*. New York: W.W. Norton.

(the equitable proportionality condition).[7] Phillips's principle is that benefits derived from organizational activity should be distributed according to the level of contribution that individuals have made to the organizational activity. Thus if Jones contributes twice as much as Smith, Jones should receive twice the benefits of Smith. Both Frank's egalitarian principle and Phillips's proportionality principle have an intuitive appeal and can be reconciled as a combined principle of fairness: Where contribution can be measured, the reward should be proportional to the contribution made. Where there is a surplus as a result of cooperative endeavor in which contribution cannot be measured, those cooperating should share the surplus equally. For managers of a firm with organizational integrity, the question is, how should the rewards of a cooperative enterprise be distributed in a firm with a moral climate? The appropriate principle is that the rewards should be distributed fairly as a function of productivity. Where productivity cannot be measured, the surplus value that results from cooperative economic activity should be equally distributed.

Issues of fairness in an organization are not limited to the internal distribution of profits. One of Frank's major contributions to economic theory has been to show the power and moral importance of perceptions of fairness in many economic transactions. Issues of fairness arise in many of the relations that an organization with integrity has with its various stakeholders. Organizations that violate widely held norms of fairness in their stakeholder relations do so at great peril, including a cost to their perceived status as an organization of integrity. One instance of this is the Coca-Cola soft drink dispenser that can adjust the price of a coke to temperature.[8] When Coca-Cola's CEO at the time reported the existence of this machine his announcement was met with outrage because people perceived that changing the price of a coke in response to changes in temperature was unfair. Thus, a Coca-Cola dispenser that adjusts the price of a coke to temperature was never manufactured. Other companies, though, have similar campaigns, such as the use of frequent flier miles as a means for priority boarding that are accepted by consumers. This demonstrates that while human reasoning is often inconsistent, any violation of strongly held norms of fairness will lead to the perception that an organization lacks integrity.

Procedural Norms

In addition to the substantive principle of fairness, notions of procedural fairness are important in achieving a moral climate. Rawls believed that his account of justice was basically procedural. With respect to the principles of justice for the basic structure of society (i.e., society's most basic institutions and forms of organization)

---

[7] Phillips, Robert. (2003). *Stakeholder Theory and Organizational Justice.* San Francisco: Berrett Koehler Publishers Inc.

[8] See Coca-Cola's New Vending Machine A. (Harvard Business School Case 9-500-068).

a fair procedure would result in principles that were just. Rawls's emphasis on the importance of fair procedures has parallels in the organizational behavior literature. From that literature we learn that perceptions about the justice of the procedure affect perceptions about the justice of the outcomes. This finding has led some in the organizational behavior field to develop the concept of "organizational justice."

One of the more important empirical findings in organizational justice is that people are more inclined to accept an adverse result—a result that does not benefit them—if they have had a role in determining how decisions are to be made. In other words, input into the design of the process increases acceptance of adverse decisions. This finding is especially important in employee evaluations because if employees have had input into the evaluation process, then a negative evaluation of any employee will likely be accepted by that employee. What the organizational justice literature shows is that an organization is more effective if the procedures are just. Decisions regarding reward and task support will be more often accepted if everyone affected has participated in the development of the procedures.

Of course, the fact that people will likely accept adverse results if they believe they have been involved or consulted in setting the procedures does not mean that their acceptance is justified. Here we need to relate social science accounts of how organizational justice is perceived and its effects on efficiency with normative ethical theory on just procedures. An obvious key to a just procedure is impartiality. The procedure cannot be biased in a direction that shows self-interest or that uses criteria unrelated to merit.

To achieve organizational integrity, the procedures for decision-making in the organization need input from all organizational stakeholders. Moreover, the procedures must not be biased against or merely reflect the self-interest of one group of stakeholders.

One way to solidify this discussion of justice, both substantive and procedural, is to examine a particular instance of remuneration, namely the remuneration of CEO's and other high executives in a for profit business. Many journalists and business ethicists believe that executive compensation is too high and that executives are being rewarded unfairly at the expense of the rest of the employees and perhaps also at the expense of the stockholders. In terms of our discussion above, these executives receive an unfair share of the surplus generated by profitable businesses.

Some defend the current level of executive pay by appeal to the market. They argue that markets set executive compensation, and therefore they are procedurally just. However, critics deny that markets set executive compensation. They point out that compensation committees composed primarily of other CEOs set the compensation. This process creates an obvious bias in favor of CEOs because people have a cognitive bias toward overvaluing their personal contributions and of blaming their shortcoming on either others or impersonal forces beyond their control. CEOs are not exempt from cognitive bias and consequently will tend to over-reward CEOs. Having other CEOs set CEO salaries contributes to what Garrison Keillor of the Prairie Home Companion refers to as the Lake Wobegon effect, a situation in which all the children are above average. In this case, it is the CEOs who are all above average.

Many sorts of wrong procedures have an adverse effect on organizational integrity. To continue the point about setting executive compensation, I turn to agency theory. Agency theory has been used by researchers in a wide range of organizational fields, such as economics, sociology, marketing, accounting, political science, and organizational behavior. Much of the scholarly literature on executive pay is grounded in agency theory and is accompanied by suggestions that may solve the agency problem. The "agency problem" is the tendency of the agent to choose his or her interests when they conflict with the interests of the principal. Within management theory, the typical application of this framework is to shareholders as principals and managers as agents. In management, the agency problem exists when the managers put their own interests, especially their financial interests, ahead of the interests of stockholders.

Agency theorists have a long history with incentive systems. A central issue for agency theorists is how to monitor or create incentives so that the agent acts not on his or her own behalf, but rather on behalf of the principals. With respect to corporate managers, including the CEO, the issue was aligning the incentives of the organization so that managers would work to the shareholders' benefit, rather than for their own benefit. Business history presents many cases in which CEOs have promoted their own interests at the shareholders' expense. This seemed especially prevalent at the beginning of the twenty-first century.

One device for aligning the objectives of top-level managers with stockholders that became increasingly popular was the use of stock options. However, in pathbreaking research already referenced in Chap. 3, Jared Harris and Philip Bromiley examined the effect that certain compensation schemes, especially the granting of stock options, had on the likelihood of a firm having an accounting restatement as a result of misrepresentation.[9] Using a matched sample data set, they found two similar companies in which one had experienced an accounting restatement due to an accounting irregularity and one that had not. The U.S. General Accounting Office provided the data on the accounting irregularities. What might explain the difference between two similar companies? Harris and Bromiley showed conclusively that granting of a large amount of stock options significantly increased the likelihood of accounting misrepresentation, whereas the comparatively smaller bonuses did not have that affect.[10]

What lessons for organizational integrity can we extract from this? As pointed out in Chap. 3, there has been a tendency for agency theorists and others who work with incentive systems to ignore the dark side of human nature–the possibility that those responding to incentive systems will not always behave ethically. They assumed that because people behaved in a self-interested way, it did not mean that people would cross the line and behave unethically. This oversight seems unrealistic

---

[9] Harris, Jared and Philip Bromiley. (2007). "Incentives to Cheat: The Influence of Executive Compensation and Firm Performance on Financial Misrepresentation," *Organization Science,* 13, 350–367.

[10] Additional variables affecting misrepresentation are discussed briefly in Chap. 3.

as the Harris/Bromiley research shows. Incentives to motivate behavior are a key part of the management of any organization, but under what conditions do they become morally suspect? In Harris and Bromiley's research, bonuses were not correlated with accounting irregularities, but stock options were. What differentiates stock options from bonuses in influencing managers to commit accounting irregularities? One answer is that bonuses are usually much smaller than stock options. People are less likely to cheat when the gains are small. Executives who manage for organizational integrity need to be knowledgeable and realistic about human nature. Organizational integrity cannot be achieved by assuming that people will do the right thing.

Many have reacted to the recent wave of corporate scandals by saying that executives are overly greedy: a character flaw. But why have some executives become greedy? The explanation is in the distinction between viewing an organization as merely an instrument to satisfying one's individual needs and seeing an organization as a social union. If the organization is seen as a means to personal enrichment and not seen as a cooperative enterprise of all those in the organization, it should come as no surprise that the executives of such an organization feel entitled to the rewards. Psychological theorists have shown that people tend to take credit when things go well and blame bad luck or circumstances beyond one's control when things go badly. Thus a CEO takes all the credit when an organization performs well but blames the general economy or other factors when things go poorly. This human tendency is predictable when executives look at organizations instrumentally.

I have been arguing that the key to organizational integrity is the existence of a good moral climate. In summary, the following elements are essential for a good moral climate: (1) commitment to a moral purpose for the organization, (2) a view of the organization as a social union rather than merely a means for achieving individual goals, and (3) management in accord with a set of substantive moral principles (including those of fairness) and in accord with a set of procedures that at a minimum avoid bias and give the employees a voice in the rules governing the organization.

Considerations That May or May Not Contribute to Organizational Integrity

The Perspective of Ideal Theory

A common criticism of philosophical ethics is that philosophers tend to write about ethics from an ideal standpoint, meaning that they tend to think that the task of ethical thinking is to discover the right thing to do free of conflicts and practical impediments. Once the right thing to do is determined, then people will have a blueprint of what should be done and will follow that blueprint. As John Rawls once wrote, "The other limitation on our discussion is that for the most part I examine the principles of justice that would regulate a well ordered society. Everyone is presumed to act justly and to do his part in upholding just institutions."[11]

Approaching organizational integrity from an ideal standpoint is not an adequate practical perspective for those managing for organizational integrity. Nobel laureate Amartya Sen—in a keynote address on the occasion of the 20th anniversary of Harvard's Safra Foundation Center for Ethics—noted that research in professional ethics could not be based on what he called "transcendent ethics." Such an approach to ethics will be of some but not much help in pinpointing moral integrity in organizations. Since organizations are composed of people, we need to take the findings of psychology, sociology, and economics into account in order to achieve organizational integrity.[12] Ethical theory always exists in tension: On the one hand, ethics should tell us what ought to be the case; on the other hand, what we ought to do cannot be so demanding that it requires what we cannot do or cannot reasonably expect to be done. What we can or cannot do is often an empirical question best addressed by the social and biological sciences. In managing for organizational integrity, executives must balance the ideal, the practical, and the possible. They must take account of legal requirements, cost considerations, risk/benefit analyses, community standards, and the like.

In business ethics, it is vital to keep ethical requirements of a theory close to what is known about human behavior. When I developed a Kantian account of business ethics, I tried to balance being faithful to Kant with Kantian prescriptions that were consistent with what we know about human behavior. As noted earlier, people will accept adverse decisions if they have a role in deciding the rules that govern how decisions are made. With this in mind, Kant's demand that persons not be treated as a means merely, but as ends, takes on a concrete reality. To respect persons in a business organization, we arguably do not have to find a way to end up with a win/win every time. In certain situations, giving stakeholders voices in the rule-making and decision-making process may be all that is required to respect them as persons.

Assessing the Characteristics of a Workforce

Another step in structuring a realistic and practical account of organizational integrity is to understand how humans respond to incentives, which helps establish appropriate and inappropriate incentives. Organizational theory has much to tell us here. Over 40 years ago, Douglas McGregor published *The Human Side of Enterprise*, in which he contrasted two theories about human nature known as theory X and theory Y. Theory X assumed that people had an inherent dislike of work

---

[11] Rawls, op.cit, 7–8.
[12] Richard Brandt excelled in using the insights of the social sciences including psychology and anthropology.

and would avoid it if possible and that they seek to avoid responsibility. Theory Y assumes the opposite: Employees like work, but prefer it when self-directed. They want to act imaginatively, creatively, and are willing to assume responsibility. They also act morally much of the time and can be trusted. Theory Y people are less susceptible to the agency problems mentioned earlier, in which agency theorists assume that workers would rather do something instead of work, thus suggesting that workers would under perform in their jobs. The more theory Y people an organization has, the greater the likelihood that the organization will exhibit organizational integrity, since theory Y people do not view either their jobs or the organization instrumentally. Rather, theory Y people extract meaning from their work. Thus, it is easier to align individual goals and the conditions for organizational integrity when you have a large number of theory Y people. This conclusion does not mean that organizational integrity is impossible in an organization composed mostly of theory X people, but it is more difficult because theory X people view the organization instrumentally.

People are not purely theory X or theory Y, but this broad categorization is nonetheless useful. The first task of management is to assess accurately whether theory X or theory Y persons dominate one's labor force and then to manage in ways that increase the predominance of theory Y employees. Accurate knowledge of the characteristics of one's work force will help manage for organizational integrity. The second task of management is to find ways to convert theory Xs into theory Ys. If a person stubbornly remains theory X, it is probably in the best interest of organizational integrity to terminate the person.

The Importance of Incentive Structures

If incentives are structured to promote self-serving or even unethical behavior, then an increase in self-serving or unethical behavior is to be expected. Mere exhortations to be moral are of limited value. Management scholars and managers know this and when employees accept structured incentives and then do something that is self-serving or unethical, management must take some, and perhaps most, of the responsibility. This point can be illustrated with two much discussed Harvard Business School cases.

First the Sears Auto Centers case concerns allegations that surfaced in June of 1992. The charge was that Sears Auto Centers had been performing unnecessary repairs on customer vehicles.[13] Many believe that changes in the compensation system were part of the problem. Mechanics had always been under a production quota, but on January 1, 1992, the production quota was raised by 60%. In addition, compensation changed from strictly an hourly wage to an hourly wage equivalent to

---

[13] Sears Auto Centers, Harvard Business School Case 9-394-009.

83% of former earnings plus a variable on work actually performed. This increased pressure on mechanics to speed up work and to surpass minimum production quotas. The California Attorney General at the time said that the structure "made it totally inevitable that the consumer would be oversold."

Second, a case from the 1970s involved the H. J. Heinz Company (the Administration of Policy case)[14]: Certain Heinz divisions, including the Star Kist division, had engaged in accounting irregularities. Expenses were recorded in 1 year, but the good or service was not received until the following year. The result was a decrease in income in the former year and an increase in income during the latter. In addition, sales were recorded in one fiscal period that should have been recorded in an earlier one. Why do that? If you have met your numbers for the year and the next year is uncertain, there is an incentive to increase expenses this year and lower them next year. The conclusion of an investigating audit committee focused on "poor control consciousness." The committee said, "World headquarters senior management apparently did not consider the effect on individuals in the [divisions] of the pressures to which they were subjected."[15] Other factors cited included the lack of an effective code of ethics, an effective compliance procedure, a monitoring process, competent personnel at world headquarters including those competent in finance, and an electronic data processing manager.

Incentives are a key part of the management of any organization, but when are incentives and goals permissible and when are they morally suspect? Recall Harris and Bromiley's research in which bonuses were not correlated with accounting irregularities, but stock options were. An important task of those seeking organizational moral integrity is to think creatively about incentive structures. Managers need to think about what unforeseen consequences on ethical behavior or lack thereof the incentives might produce. The devising of incentive systems requires what Patricia Werhane refers to as moral imagination.[16]

In addition, as we see in the Heinz case, one needs competent people in the right places, effective monitoring, and an effective compliance program. These conditions are essential for organizational integrity. In her discussion of the Sears case, Lynn Sharp Paine argues that the incentive structures must be made to fit into an organization that already has integrity. Incentives can be helpful, but they can also be abused. In diagnosing the problem at Sears, an ethical climate did not pre-exist. Quality control and audit systems were absent and there were inadequate guidelines on what was to be considered legitimate preventive maintenance. In a telling comment, Paine says, "There is no evidence in the case that Sears has encouraged professionalism, integrity, or self-restraint.... Problems arise when companies

---

[14] Harvard Business School Case 9-382-034.

[15] Goodpaster, Kenneth E., Laura L Nash, and Henri-Claude de Bettignies. (2006). *Business Ethics, Policies and Persons*. Boston: Irwin McGraw Hill, 121.

[16] Werhane, Patricia. (1999). *Moral Imagination and Management Decision Making*. New York: Oxford University Press.

introduce such compensation programs without insuring that quality controls, audits, cultural values, and disincentives for abuse are sufficiently strong to counter this potential."[17]

Codes of Ethics

In the public arena people concerned about organizational ethics, especially if moral problems have arisen, often ask, "Does the organization have a code of ethics?" Many people think that codes of ethics are important for the creation of a moral climate and for the maintenance of organizational ethics. However, my view of codes of ethics used in this chapter is more nuanced. Codes of ethics by themselves are not a good indicator of an organization's commitment to ethics. For a code of ethics to be effective, it needs to be part of a broader moral climate. If the moral climate is absent, a code of ethics is likely to be window dressing. Enron, for instance, had one of the best codes of ethics of any corporation, yet the ethical climate at Enron was seriously degraded even before its collapse. A code of ethics is useful only if the other factors that contribute to organizational integrity are present. As we saw in Chap. 3 a powerful argument for this position is provided by transaction cost economics.[18]

Recall in Chap. 3 that I used the distinction between high and low asset specificity to establish my claim that a code of ethics alone is not a good indicator that a company is ethical. In the language of this Chapter, I would say that a good code of ethics is not necessarily a good indicator of a good moral climate or of an organization with integrity. Codes of ethics have low asset specificity and are easily copied. Even a company with a bad moral climate can have a good code of ethics as the Enron example illustrates. Thus, a good code of ethics is not a reliable indicator of whether an organization has high ethical standards or low ethical standards. However, when a code of ethics is supported by a pervasive moral climate, it can be a useful device for guiding employee and even management conduct, especially if the code is quite specific in its norms. As was mentioned in Chap. 3, perhaps the best-known example of a code of ethics that has made a difference in management decision-making and that does legitimately contribute to organizational integrity is Johnson and Johnson's Credo (J and J Credo), which is not simply a document on which all employees must sign off. It is a living, pervasive, and enforced document. The Credo is evaluated periodically to determine if it still reflects the values and vision of the company and if it is still useful as a tool for helping resolve ethical

---

[17] Paine, Lynn Sharp. (1997). *Instructor's Manual: Cases in Leadership, Ethics, and Organizational Integrity.* Burr Ridge: Irwin, 80–81.

[18] The development of transaction cost economics is primarily attributed to Oliver E Williamson. See his (1975). *Markets and Hierarchies.* New York: The Free Press, and his (1985). *The Economic Institutions of Capitalism.* New York: The Free Press.

issues or dilemmas the company might face. Thus there is a symbiotic relationship between the ethical climate at J and J and the J and J credo. This is a worthy goal for every business organization.

Determining Individual Responsibility

To achieve organizational integrity and a pervasive moral climate, one cannot assume that solving moral issues within the organization is always a matter of focusing on individual responsibility. Determining individual responsibility is part of what is required to create an appropriate moral climate, but sometimes trying to determine who is responsible for a moral failure obstructs and retards necessary organizational reform. Moral imagination is required to decide when to focus on individual responsibility, to ignore issues of individual responsibility, and to focus on technological fixes or structural organizational reform.

As we saw in the California Sears Auto Centers case, the incentive system encouraged Sears auto repairmen to do unnecessary repairs. From the paradigm of individual responsibility, it seems strange to blame the incentive system. The incentive system is not an intentional actor, yet much literature in business and business ethics suggests that the incentive system is to be blamed. However, an incentive system is established by individuals, and they must assume responsibility for adverse ethical effects of the system they initiate. Contending that the incentive system is responsible for the behavior should be understood as shorthand for saying that the individuals who created the incentive system are responsible for consequent unethical behavior. At Sears it seems that it was the managers who were responsible for the overcharging by the Sears repairmen, not the repairmen.

This determination is not quite right, however, because the problem is one of shared responsibility. Being *influenced* by incentives to act unethically does not absolve one of all responsibility. It is appropriate to place some responsibility on those who created the incentive system and some on those who acted on the incentives. Both are responsible for the moral climate that results. Of course, in many cases we must decide how to distribute greater or lesser responsibility to different individuals when all bear some degree of responsibility.

Sometimes an effective moral climate results from balancing responsibilities, but in other circumstances determining individual responsibility is not important at all. Focusing on individual responsibility can even detract from organizational integrity. One example is the problem created by medical mistakes in hospitals. In the late 1990s it was estimated that medical errors caused 100,000 deaths per year. Organizational integrity requires that medical organizations do everything possible to eliminate such mistakes. Evidence shows that rather than blaming individuals each time something goes wrong, the best approach is having an organizational system that searches for and implements technical fixes and related ways of reducing medical error.

To make this point, I use an extended example. In 1996, a 2 month old baby boy named Jose Eric Martinez died after being given the wrong dose (ten times the recommended amount) of the drug Digoxin. An investigation established the causal sequence that resulted in the accidental overdose as follows[19]: The first step in the sequence was the determination of the appropriate amount of Digoxin to be administered. The attending physician and resident did the calculations and determined that the correct dose was 0.09 mg. However, when the resident wrote the order on Jose's chart, he made a slip of the pen and entered 0.9 mg—a dose that was ten times too high. When the physician checked the chart, the mistake went unnoticed.

The Digoxin order was faxed to the pharmacy. The pharmacist thought the amount too high, so he placed the order on the coffee pot-the location of the unofficial important pile and then paged the resident to discuss the order. However, the resident had left for the day and did not receive the page. A back up copy of the order that had been sent by messenger arrived and was filled by a technician. The technician filled a vial with 0.9 mg of Digoxin and left it for the pharmacist to check. By the time the pharmacist checked the dosage, he had forgotten his original concerns. Since the order and the dosage in the vial matched, the pharmacist sent the prescription out.

That was not the end of the opportunities to correct the error. The nurse who received the vial thought that the dosage was incorrect, so she approached the resident on call who was not the same resident who made the initial error. This resident redid the math and got the correct dosage of 0.09; but when he looked on the vial he failed to notice that the decimal point was in the wrong place and the dosage on the vial actually read 0.9.

There is a clear causal chain here, but which individual was responsible for the death of Jose Martinez? Are all the individuals who contributed to the mistake in some measure responsible for it? If one is concerned about organizational integrity, these questions may not be the right ones to start with. This suspicion is supported when a few more facts of the case are added. The pharmacy was one person short the night the order was filled. A policy existed that the phone must be answered within four rings and that visitors should be greeted within 5 s–a policy that put pressure on an understaffed unit. The nurse who questioned the order was from a country in which women rarely confront men and in which women rarely confront doctors. Cultural practices and some well-intentioned policies played a role in the events that occurred.

Hermann Hospital (as it was known in 1996[20]) in Houston, where this tragic mistake occurred, did not try to improve organizational integrity by investigating who was responsible. No one was fired, and no new rules for individuals to follow were introduced. Rather, technological solutions were instituted. The hospital's computer would automatically flag questionable orders for the most dangerous drugs, and the hospital looked for a paging system that would alert a caller when the person being paged had his pager deactivated.

In a 1995 hospital case at Martin Memorial Hospital South in Stuart, Florida, a 7-year-old boy died when he was given the wrong medication. Instead of receiving lidocaine as prescribed, the syringe contained a highly concentrated dose of

---

[19] Belkin, Lisa. (1997). "How Can We Save the Next Victim?" *The New York Times Magazine*, June 15.
[20] After a 1997 merger the merged hospitals were referred to as Memorial Hermann.

adrenaline that was suitable for external use only. The procedure, which was common in hospitals throughout the U.S., was to put the lidocaine into a cup and then empty the contents of the cup into the syringe. Instead, the syringe was filled from the wrong cup. By putting a cap on the vial of lidocaine, it could be drawn directly out of the bottle into a labeled syringe. The cup, and thus the possibility of that kind of error, was eliminated.[21]

In these cases the search for individuals responsible for the medical mistake appear to do more to inhibit organizational integrity than to advance it. What was needed was a reassessment of procedures and an honest and transparent discussion of what happened and what needed to be changed. If the focus was on identifying and punishing the individuals involved, the parties would have been trying to protect themselves rather than change procedures. In these cases, not looking for those responsible wound up helping to improve both the quality of the operations and moral climate.

Sometimes even the fear that individuals will be held responsible inhibits the introduction of technology that would improve safety. This is especially true in a litigious society like the United States. Fear of lawsuits and civil punishment created some resistance to an open discussion of the issues in the medical error cases discussed previously. To use another example, it is my understanding that a technological innovation can track all the actions of pilots on commercial aircraft. Using this device, mistakes or tendencies that might lead to disastrous mistakes can be discovered and possibly corrected before a tragedy occurs. It is my understanding that the system is apparently operative on British Airways. However, it is also my understanding that union pilots in the United States have apparently resisted this technology on grounds that it will be used to "punish" them. A litigious society like the United States may make organizational integrity more difficult under such circumstances.

Organizational integrity is thus not simply a matter of having a mechanism for holding individuals responsible. It is the result of a myriad of complex factors that are both individual and institutional. Sometimes it is important to resolve problems of a lapse of ethics by holding individuals responsible, but often it is most important to solve a crisis of organizational integrity by changing procedures or creating a technological fix.

Elements That Inhibit the Development of a Moral Climate

Groupthink

One of the biggest dangers in the path of achieving a high level of organizational integrity is the danger of groupthink. The concept of groupthink was first introduced by William H. Whyte in an article in *Fortune*. In his construal, groupthink referred

---

[21] The details of this case are in Belkin op.cit.

to open use of group values to achieve expedient and right outcomes. Later the term took on a negative connotation, especially at the hands of its major discussant, Irving Janus. Janus thought of it as the thinking of a cohesive in-group often driven by a desire more for unanimity rather than for realistic appraisal. Janus regarded it as a faulty decision procedure resulting from group pressures that lead to a deterioration of "mental efficiency, reality testing, and moral judgment."[22] Psychologists have identified a number of factors that lead to groupthink. These factors include (1) overestimation of the group, (2) close-mindedness, (3) pressures toward uniformity and unanimity, (4) the stereotyping of outsiders, (5) self-censorship, (6) direct pressure on dissenters, (7) mindguards,[23] and (8) the illusion of invulnerability.

It has been argued that a paradigm case of groupthink occurred among those involved in deliberations and conference calls surrounding the Challenger Launch in January of 1986. The Challenger exploded shortly after liftoff. The launch was initially scheduled 6 days earlier, but mechanical problems caused a delay. The O-rings in the booster rockets became an engineering concern. A recommendation by Martin Thiokol engineers not to launch because the safety of the O rings could not be guaranteed in the predicted cold weather was belittled and eventually overruled, in large part because NASA was eager to get the mission underway. Some have argued that groupthink at NASA was the chief explanation for the flawed decision to proceed.

It is widely believed that it is difficult to change a corporate culture. Approximately 7 years later on February 1, 2003, the Columbia was lost as it exploded on reentry over Texas. Subsequent investigation showed that requests to photograph the tiles that had been damaged during takeoff were denied. The report on the Columbia disaster had a disconcerting similarity to the official report on the Challenger disaster. Again groupthink may have been a primary cause.

Groupthink can be seen as the dark side of teamwork. Given that teamwork is important for organizational success, how can groupthink be avoided? The quality and character of the team leader are key considerations.[24] The most important factor in avoiding groupthink is an environment in which different opinions and questioning is encouraged. The group's leader will have to avoid being too directive. Sometimes it may be necessary to appoint critical evaluators with the specific responsibility to raise questions or challenge consensus. The more the members of a team think alike, the more groupthink is likely to occur. Moral failure often occurs when the leader of an organization surrounds himself or herself with "yes men," who are those who tell the boss only what he or she wants to hear. Moral failure can also result when meetings are seen as inefficient and brain storming or other activities designed to encourage a multiplicity of ideas for solving a problem or achieving

---

[22] Janus, Irving. (1972). *Victims of Groupthink*. New York: Houghton Mifflin, 9.

[23] Mindguards occur when members protect the group and the leader by withholding information that is problematic or contradictory to the group's cohesiveness.

[24] This chapter has not emphasized leadership as an ingredient in organizational integrity. This is not because the quality of the leader is unimportant.

an organizational goal are discouraged. Commentators have pointed out how John F. Kennedy instinctively followed all these suggestions during the Cuban missile crisis. He was sometimes absent during the discussions so that he would not stifle them. He sought the advice of people with different points of view including some with unpopular opinions. Kennedy's behavior here is in contrast with George W Bush who did just the opposite in deciding to go to war in Iraq. Whereas Kennedy's strategy proved successful, Bush's did not.

Of course analysis paralysis must be avoided but so must group think. As with so much in organizational ethics, balance is important. However, groupthink is clearly a very serious threat to organizational integrity.

Teleopathy

Another error in decision-making to be avoided has drawn the attention of Kenneth Goodpaster in his work in business ethics.[25] This error, known as teleopathy, is defined as "the unbalanced pursuit of purpose in either individuals or organizations." The principle components of teleopathy are fixation, rationalization, and detachment. Goodpaster shows how many important cases in business ethics can be explained as instances of teleopathy. Consider shareholder theory–the theory that the obligation of the manager is to increase shareholder wealth. If organizational integrity requires stakeholder management, then the single-minded focus on only one stakeholder–the shareholder–will lead the organization astray by ignoring the interests of other stakeholders. The most common criticism made by critics of public corporations is that they are slaves of Wall Street and focus entirely on making the quarterly numbers so they can maximize profits for shareholders. A number of failures to achieve organizational integrity have resulted from this single-minded focus on shareholder profit. Even if a manger is single-minded about profit, as Friedman, Jensen, and others recommend, the manager will only succeed if he or she does not always give priority to what is most profitable. To increase shareholder wealth, the manager must often give special attention to other stakeholders whose support is vital to the success of the firm. Avoiding teleopathy is both good business and necessary for organizational integrity.

If a corporation is to be single-minded, it should be so in pursuit of creating value for corporate stakeholders. However, being single-minded here does not make the manager guilty of teleopathy, since the single minded goal requires balancing the goals and interests of all stakeholders. Being single-minded in that respect requires great flexibility with respect to the management of a public corporation.

---

[25] For example, see his (2007). *Conscience and Corporate Culture.* Malden: Blackwell Publishing.

Conflicts of Interest

Another significant danger for an organization—especially when the organization is viewed instrumentally rather than as a social union or cooperative enterprise—is the possibility that the members of the organization will permit conflicts of interest. A standard definition of a conflict of interest is the following: A person has a conflict of interest if (a) he is in a relationship of trust with another person or institution requiring him to exercise judgment in that other's service, and (b) he himself has an interest that tends to interfere with the proper discharge of responsibility to the other party.[26]

If members of an organization see the organization solely as a means to their own private interest, it should come as no surprise that when the opportunity arises for them to put their own interests ahead of the interests of others in the organization, they will be tempted to do so. This situation is represented in the classic agency problem discussed earlier. The accounting scandals at the turn of the twenty-first century sparked a renewed discussion of conflicts of interest in business. None was more notorious than the relationship that existed between Enron Corporation (an American energy company) and Arthur Andersen LLP, a "big-five" accounting firm. Andersen had huge consulting contracts with Enron, and questions arose about how objective they could be when they performed as auditors. In addition, some of Andersen's personnel functioned as internal auditors at Enron—a clear violation of generally accepted accounting principles and a clear case of a conflict of interest. Moreover, a virtual revolving door existed between Andersen and Enron in which employees who worked for one would end up working for the other.

On Wall Street the mergers of investment brokerages and banks created another example of conflict of interest. Investment analysts such as Henry Blodget and Jack Grubman would hype the stock of firms that provided IPO (Initial Public Offerings) funds and merger and acquisition business to the banking side of the business. The projections on stock growth given to investors were not based on an objective analysis of the future value of the firms, but rather were designed to increase artificially the value of the stock to the benefit of the bank and its client.

To see more precisely why the examples above constitute a conflict of interest we must ask to whom the auditors and the investment analysts properly owed their allegiance. The client of public auditing firms is the investing public (the idea behind the notion of "certified public accountant"). The investing public is also the client of investment advisors. In both cases the allegiance should have been to the investing public, but instead the personal interests of the investment advisors and the interests of Arthur Andersen and the banking side of such corporations as Citicorp were given priority. The auditors of public companies are in a position of trust with respect to the investing public, as are investment analysts. However, in these cases this trust was violated because personal or institutional interests prevented the

---

[26] Davis, Michael. (1982). "Conflict of Interest," *Business and Professional Ethics Journal*, 1, 17–28.

objective professional analysis that was required. Emails show that Grubman disparaged stocks in private that he publicly recommended.[27]

Even if one takes a Friedmanite view about the purpose of a public corporation–namely, that it should be managed in the interests of the stockholders–the activities described above are wrong and indicate a lack of organizational integrity. These individuals and firms violated a number of the conditions required for organizational integrity that have been enumerated and defended in this chapter. The events provide additional evidence that the agency theorists who postulate a cynical psychological egoism may not have been cynical enough. They assumed that the manager's self interest would stop at the point of illegality or blatant immorality. The widespread existence of conflicts of interest—both financial and non financial conflicts—within organizations stands as a significant impediment to organizational integrity.

Why Firms with Organizational Integrity Should Be Successful

Business people will want more than the account of organizational integrity in this chapter. They will want to know if business organizations with integrity can be financially successful. Ideals of organizational integrity must be shown to be practical and affordable. The starting point of the argument that organizations with integrity can be successful is the claim made by some corporations that their reputation as organizations with integrity gives them a competitive advantage in the marketplace. Their reputation for organizational integrity is part of their brand. Marketing theorists and finance theorists know that a brand can be highly valuable even though it is intangible. Firms such as Johnson and Johnson have organizational integrity as part of their brand and believe that their brand gives them a competitive advantage.

We need an argument to show that there is some reason to accept what Johnson and Johnson takes to be true–that their reputation as an organization of integrity gives them a competitive advantage. Transaction cost economics–the theory we used to show why codes of ethics by themselves are not good indicators of a moral climate–is the theoretical basis for the argument. The argument from Chap. 3 is worth repeating in this context. Key to the argument is the fact that organizational integrity is grounded in the values and routines of the firm, an idea that is evident in the list of items I have identified as characterizing organizational integrity. Those values tend to be knowledge-based, embodied in individual employees or firm routines, and characterized by high asset specificity. Assets characterized by high asset specificity are difficult to copy

---

[27] One of the most complete and best accounts of this era is Charles Gasparino's. (2005). *Blood on the Street*. New York: Free Press. If Arthur Andersen's decline and fall is of interest, see Barbara Ley Toffler's. (2003). *Final Accounting*. New York: Broadway Books.

because they are unique or nearly unique to the firm that possesses them. Experience confirms the theory that moral climates are difficult to copy.

What evidence backs this claim? Both scholarly literature and business experience suggest that it is difficult to change moral climate once it has become part of the corporate culture. A good example is the contrast between Ashland Oil Company and Exxon-Mobil. When Ashland Oil was involved in an oil spill in January of 1988, the CEO and other corporate officers quickly went to Pittsburgh, admitted fault and directed the clean-up. This action was wise from both an ethical and a business perspective. Ashland oil had its fines reduced and suffered less litigation as a result of its behavior. Executives also gained respect as an ethically responsible company. In March of 1989, Exxon, as it was known then, experienced the Exxon Valdez oil spill in Prince William Sound off the coast of Alaska. Exxon's CEO never visited Alaska and belatedly sent a taped message of apology. Exxon has stayed in an adversarial mode since the beginning. Exxon apparently had learned nothing from the Ashland Oil incident and thus was subjected to much litigation and a serious blow to its reputation. The courts awarded $287 million dollars for actual damages and (on appeal) punitive damages of $2.5 billion dollars.[28] Exxon did not learn from Ashland's successful handling of the crisis and thus suffered both financially and in terms of its reputation. Why did Exxon behave as it did? To use our earlier language, the answer is that corporate culture and specifically a moral climate have high asset specificity and—unlike codes of ethics—are not easily copied.

In strategic management, a competitive ideal is to occupy a position in which the firm has an asset that is difficult to copy and gives it a competitive advantage. An organization that has integrity is in that position. Because of this competitive advantage organizations with integrity should be successful. However, there are some disturbing recent trends in corporate America showing that the argument mentioned thus far is not sufficiently persuasive.

A Pessimistic Concern and a Topic for Future Research

Although the moral climates of organizations with integrity are difficult to copy, they can be lost. That is, an organization that has integrity can lose it. That seems to be happening. Let's look at some of the companies that business ethicists have held up as shining examples of organizational integrity over the past 35 years in order to see how integrity can easily be lost. The "Hewlett-Packard Way"- the credo that had guided the firm for generations- was exemplary, but after its merger with Compaq

---

[28] This decision of the 9th U.S. Circuit Court of Appeals has been appealed by Exxon to the U.S. Supreme Court. On the last day of its term in 2008 the Supreme Court reduced the 2.5 billion dollar damage award to just over 500 million.

HP ran into trouble. The HP Board became dysfunctional, and corporate officials engaged in illegal activity to determine who was leaking information about Board deliberations to the public. There were massive layoffs as a result of the merger, and morale plummeted. The Hewlett Packard Way became ineffective. There is general consensus in the literature that HP lost critical dimensions of its integrity—or at least that it was severely tarnished.

Merck and other companies supply similar examples. Merck had achieved acclaim for manufacturing a drug to cure river blindness, but its reputation became tarnished by the Vioxx scandal. Merck was accused of promoting Vioxx while knowing of its dangerous side effects. Likewise, British Petroleum, which established the motto "Beyond Petroleum," and after much fanfare and success in communicating its corporate social responsibility, was found negligent for a refinery explosion in Texas and then in April of 2010 the Deepwater Horizon oil rig exploded in the Gulf of Mexico causing the greatest oil spill in American history. Finally the HB Fuller Company, which originally provided a model of the enlightened corporation under the leadership of Elmer Andersen followed by his son Tony Andersen, became just another company focused on quarterly returns. The company that resisted Wall Street came to pay it homage.

Good research is necessary to help us understand what happened to so many of our shining examples of organizational integrity. One thing is clear. Achieving organizational integrity is difficult and once achieved is characterized by high asset specificity. Thus, it is difficult to copy. On the other hand, these examples tell us that departures from organizational integrity can have an immediate impact on the reputation of the firm and that once a reputation is lost, it is difficult to regain. If these generalizations are correct, one has reason to be pessimistic about the future. Are firms with organizational integrity an endangered species?

Conclusion

I have argued that organizational integrity exists when an organization has a moral climate. This culture exists only if the organization adheres to certain substantive ethical norms. Other features of a moral climate include fair procedures and the existence of incentive structures that support moral conduct rather than incentive structures that are perverse with respect to moral conduct. Groupthink, teleopathy, and conflicts of interest must be avoided. Corporate codes of ethics are no substitute for a moral climate, but once embedded in an organization with integrity, such codes can be useful as general guides. In an organization with integrity, the organization is not viewed as a mere instrument for individual personal advancement, but rather is seen as a cooperative endeavor of those within the organization that provides value to its corporate stakeholders. Organizational ethics is the set of norms and actions that create a moral climate, but these must be embedded at the highest level and constantly monitored. The managers, especially top executives, should show leadership with respect to organizational ethics. Sadly we still have a great deal of work to do in creating organizational integrity, but at least many are now seriously engaged in the endeavor.

Part V
Teaching Business Ethics

Chapter 12
Crucial Decisions for the Teaching of Business Ethics

Some Important Historical Background

Every person teaching business ethics faces a number of challenges. Contrary to the beliefs of some, teaching business ethics is extremely difficult. I first taught business ethics in the fall of 1978 in the Department of Philosophy at the University of Delaware and continued to teach business ethics through the spring of 2012-a total of 34 years. Those 34 years included teaching business ethics to undergraduates, full time MBA's, part-time MBA's, Executive MBA's and international Executive MBA's such as the one in the Warsaw School of Economics. Along the way I have been fortunate to win some teaching awards and also had more than one business ethics class "blow-up." The reflections in this final Chapter reflect my thinking about the teaching of business ethics as I look back over a variety of experiences spanning those 34 years.

One reason I introduced a business ethics course at the University of Delaware was a commitment I had made to the National Endowment for the Humanities (NEH). I had been Executive Secretary for the American Philosophical Association (APA) where I had obtained a grant from the National Endowment for the Humanities to develop curriculum materials for a course in business ethics. The committee to develop these materials consisted of three businessmen, three business school professors, and three philosophy professors.[1] As a condition of the grant, each university agreed to the offering of a course in business ethics during the grant period. This period was referred to as the Trial Teaching Phase.

---

[1] The complete list of participants with their academic association or business association were as follows: Business School Faculty, Thomas Dunfee, Wharton, Henry Eilbert California State Long Beach, Gene Lavengood, Northwestern University; Businessmen Franklyn Judson, Sr. Vice President and General Counsel (retired) I-T-E Imperial Corporation, Elliot Lehman, President, FEL_Pro Corporation, Lionel Wernick, Vice President, Batten Barton, Durstine and Osborn; Philosophers Kurt Baier University of Pittsburgh, Norman E. Bowie, University of Delaware, and Peter French, University of Minnesota at Morris.

N.E. Bowie, *Business Ethics in the 21st Century*, Issues in Business Ethics 39, DOI 10.1007/978-94-007-6223-7_12, © Springer Science+Business Media Dordrecht 2013

The Committee evaluated the six courses and came to the unanimous agreement "that the traditional ethical theories were unsuccessful as pedagogical devices for achieving the aims of the course."[2] More than 30 years later incorporating the traditional ethical theories into business ethics remains a challenge and how it is done involves the first crucial decision those teaching business ethics face. That challenge will receive considerable attention later.

What is significant is that in the late 1970s and early 1980s the APA in partnership with the NEH was an early player in the development of business ethics. Unfortunately that interest waned and today support for the teaching of business ethics on the part of the APA is virtually non-existent. There is, for example, no newsletter on business ethics as there are for a number of other applied disciplines. However, the report of the Committee addressed a number of important issues in the teaching of business ethics at the very beginning. It seems appropriate to start with some of those issues and the conclusions that the interdisciplinary team reached regarding the teaching of business ethics.

In addition to the NEH grant, one other initiative in the teaching of business ethics deserves mention. Roughly in the middle of the 1980s Arthur Andersen committed five million dollars to introduce the teaching of ethics into the business schools. Arthur Andersen started by inviting representatives from departments of finance, accounting, marketing, management, and economics to their education center in St. Charles Illinois to learn how to introduce ethics into the curriculum. (After 1 year Arthur Andersen eliminated economics because those representing that discipline seemed unable to grasp what counted as an ethical issue.) The underlying belief was that business ethics should be taught across the business curriculum and not limited to a single business ethics course. In addition, we developed written cases and video (VCR) cases for use in each of the disciplines. Attendees in this program received lectures on ethical theory taught by Manny Velasquez, Patricia Werhane, and me. The three of us served on the 15 person Advisory Board. The terrible irony is that Arthur Andersen ceased to exist after the firm's actions as the auditor of Enron. Unfortunately, the efforts of Arthur Andersen to have business schools adopt ethics across the curriculum failed to survive as well. I am unaware of any business school that has the extensive ethics curriculum that Arthur Andersen recommended. Although most people believe that the best approach to the teaching of business ethics is to integrate the teaching of ethics throughout the business school curriculum, I am not aware of any major business school that has tried to do that.

Another aspect of the ethical failure of Arthur Andersen and thus of its business ethics initiative was the fact that the failure contributed to the growing cynicism about business ethics-the notion that business ethics is an oxymoron. That cynicism is fairly universal. For example, teaching in the Executive MBA program at the Warsaw School of Economics was one of my hardest assignments. The Poles were especially cynical about ethics since there had been so much government corruption under Communism. Bribery in business had been a way of life. With respect to

---

[2] Report of the Committee for Education in Business Ethics, 1980, p. 6.

cynicism, not much has changed since that first course in 1978, nearly 35 years ago. How to deal with student cynicism is yet another crucial decision in the teaching of business ethics.

Let us turn to these first two crucial decisions I have mentioned and after an extended discussion of them I will address a number of other crucial decisions that arise in the teaching of business ethics.

Crucial Decisions

Decision #1: What Is the Role of Ethical Theory in the Teaching of Business Ethics?

Since the difficulty of introducing ethical theory into the course was recognized at the outset, it might be useful to start with the NEH Report of the Committee for Education in Business Ethics. First the committee needed to identify what went wrong with the introduction of the theories. Those teaching the experimental courses found that most students could understand the essentials of the theory, but as the committee reported, they then applied the theory very simplistically. In a complicated case, the students might simply say, "Calculate the greatest good" or alternatively, "Respect people." My own way of expressing this is that the students consider ethical theories as basic tools in a tool box. If a problem looks like a problem of determining consequences as with environmental issues, then the students grabbed for utilitarianism. If the problem seemed one of human relations as in organizational theory or in human resources, then they grabbed for Kant's respect for persons principle. By the way this problem existed in courses taught in philosophy departments as much as in courses taught in business schools, despite what you might expect. As the Committee Report indicated, "The application of theory to practice is one of the most difficult tasks in the teaching of business ethics."[3]

This problem was exacerbated by the fact that we as philosophers criticize the theories. As a result the students in those first NEH courses thought that each theory is equally bad and that ethical theory is therefore not helpful. As the Committee Report put it, "The standard critical approach can leave the students with a kind of moral nihilism..."[4] My own experience is that this problem is worse in business schools, where students want and expect answers to ethical questions. Students who expect answers present another critical decision in the teaching of business ethics. The more business students with an engineering background that you have in a course, the greater the difficulty of explaining that the interesting ethical issues in business do not have clear answers.

---

[3] Ibid.
[4] Ibid.

We have not completely overcome this issue of how to introduce the traditional ethical theories into business ethics courses, although some suggestions will follow. The Committee itself recommended that those teaching business ethics needed to spend more time on the teaching of central ethical concepts and that these concepts be introduced before the theories are introduced. The concepts the Committee had in mind were the following: "Honesty", "Fidelity", "Loyalty", "Obligation", "Autonomy-Dependence-Paternalism", "Freedom", "Justice", "Self Respect", "Dignity", and "Rights". I sometimes referred to concepts like these as bridge concepts because they bridge theory to application. For example, "honesty", "fidelity", "justice", "self-respect" and "rights" are all concepts that serve to bridge Kantian moral theory to problems in business. Of course these bridges will not help one of my Wharton Students, taught in the fall of 2010, who said that "There is no such thing as justice."

I think those initial insights of the Committee are correct although as time has gone on, the list of bridge concepts has changed somewhat. Most courses in business ethics will discuss conflicts of interest. My strategy colleagues showed me the importance of "trust", which can serve as both a strategic concept and a moral concept. By the time I finished teaching at Minnesota, my way of dealing with the use of ethical theory was as follows. First, I never started with theory. I started with cases that raised ethical issues in a dramatic fashion. One case was from the Arthur Andersen project discussed earlier that shows how easy it is to fall into an ethical issue. The case is especially realistic and helped me establish some rapport with the students. Second, I only introduced a theory when it fit naturally with a business topic. My second class discussed the relation between ethics and profits and emphasized the importance of building trust in a successful organization. Kantian theory fit in perfectly here. Utilitarianism fits naturally with business's responsibility to the environment. Virtue theory was a natural for the last class in "Ethical Leadership." Third, I made liberal use of bridge concepts. For example for the Marketing Ethics class, I used the Coca-Cola case that discussed the failure of the idea to have a coke machine that changed price according to temperature. This case raised the question of fairness. So did our discussions of marketing to the vulnerable in the same class. And conflict of interest was a natural for discussions of the financial crisis. Fourth, I pointed out successful management required an understanding of theory. Business thinking with its notions of risk assessment, cost/benefit analysis etc. is quite utilitarian in its orientation. Managers often think, talk and act like utilitarians. However, a substantial subset of employees think like Kantians, especially when a decision made "for the sake of the company," has a negative impact on employees. Last in the later years, I simply spend less time on the intricacies of the theories than I used to. For example, I used to spend time distinguishing act from rule utilitarianism, By the end when all my teaching was in the business school, I left that issue to the reading assignment and never really emphasized it in class. I was not especially happy with the trend to less theory but students had become so impatient with theory. Student impatience with theory has increased along with the tendency not to read. In the world of YouTube and iPhones, getting students to pay attention to the written word is a challenge.

Decision #2: Dealing with Cynicism

I find dealing with student cynicism to be the most difficult issue in the teaching of business ethics to overcome. The cynicism comes in a number of different forms. Inevitably there will be some students in the class who do not believe in things like fairness and are more than willing to say so-surprisingly. You cannot be gentle with such students. You might simply announce that you will give such a student a C and then when they complain simply argue that as they pointed out there is no such thing as fairness. Practically, of course, you cannot do that since in most universities a student could appeal the grade and win when the grade is patently unfair. (Of course, the instructor might argue that a student who says there is no such thing as fairness really deserves a C-or worse.) Moreover the successful student appeal would prove there is such a thing as fairness after all but this is probably not the way to win the argument.

Another tactic is to ask the student if he or she is willing to publicly announce that position in their business activities. After all, it is one thing to say there is no fairness in the safe confines of a classroom and quite another to announce such an opinion to those with whom you do business. Publicly stating that one does not believe in fairness in a business context is self-defeating. People will not want to do business with you. Of course, some people in business may say they believe in fairness but ACT as if they do not believe in fairness and the unsuspecting person who is engaging in business finds out that the person on the other end of the deal does not believe in fairness after the fact.

A more common expression of cynicism is the view that business is amoral at best and frequently immoral at worst. This view is a version of what my colleague Ed Freeman calls "the business sucks story." Regrettably the practice of business gives lots of evidence that "the business sucks" story is true or at least true enough. What is especially disconcerting is that the examples of business ethics heroes have become tainted over the years. We business ethicists used to point with pride to the behavior of Merck in providing the drug to cure river blindness free forever to the affected regions of the world. But then came Vioxx. We lauded Johnson and Johnson's Credo and their performance in the Tylenol poisonings. But then in 2011 came all the quality control problems with 50 product recalls in 15 months including the especially embarrassing recall of Children's Tylenol. In addition to these reports in the media, many students have experienced unethical behavior in the workplace. Put this all together, and students believe that the ethics course is something they have to do to look good and that business ethics professors, especially those trained in philosophy, are simply naïve about how business really works. It's no wonder we business ethics teachers get discouraged. However, the only remedy to this problem that I can think of is to keep finding new examples of exemplary business ethics behavior. Fortunately those stories still exist.

A final issue around cynicism comes when the ethics course challenges the model that nearly all students are taught-the purpose of business is the maximization of profit. Nearly all business ethics courses contrast the Milton Friedman/Michael Jensen model of stockholder finance based capitalism with stakeholder theory. In those discussions, ethics looks like an add on and an expensive one at that since the assumption by most students is that being ethical is a cost that subtracts from the bottom line.

So what can a business ethics professor do? First you can point out that being unethical can surely be costly as well and even lead to bankruptcy. In my first class, I have a case that I let run to the end so the students can see the credits. The case was prepared by Arthur Andersen as part of its five million dollar contribution to integrate business ethics into the business schools that I discussed earlier. I make the point that no one would have believed in 1995 that in 2012 I would exist and Arthur Andersen would not. That gets their attention.

Second, I try to attack what Ed Freeman describes as the separation thesis. Just the way we talk about business ethics makes it seem as if a business decision is one thing and an ethics decision is another. But business decisions have impacts on stakeholders and once a decision has impacts on people you have an ethical issue. You cannot separate one from the other. It is not a matter of deciding on business grounds and then deciding whether or not to be ethical. You can make a good business decision that is unethical, or a good ethical decision that is a poor business decision or ideally a good business decision that is also simultaneously a good ethical decision. We call that a win-win and I try to get students to aim for that. By the way a bad business decision that is also unethical is really stupid. But it happens. Sometimes it is useful to show some examples of them.

Third, I try to show that as a practical matter there may not be that big a difference between Friedman's stockholder wealth maximization theory and stakeholder theory. As I mentioned in Chap. 6, even Michael Jensen seems now to accept the fact that if you are to maximize shareholder wealth, then you need to take care of your stakeholders. In other words Jensen is willing to accept stakeholder theory as an instrumental theory about how to create stockholder wealth. Of course, I want more than an instrumental theory, but at least instrumental stakeholder theory has an appeal that helps blunt the skepticism of a lot of students.

Fourth, I try to make the case by using Kantian Ethics and Transaction Cost Economics that good ethics can be good business. I show both through theory and by example that ethics enables companies to reduce transaction costs, reduce self-serving behavior and monitoring costs, and build trust among the corporate stakeholders.

However, even in doing all that some students will never give you a chance and if those students happen to be perceived as leaders in the class you are in for a long semester.

Decision #3: How Different Should Business Ethics Courses Be for Undergraduate Students, Liberal Arts Students, Executive MBA's, Part-Time MBA's and Full-Time MBAs'?

For 15 of my 20 years at Minnesota, I had a joint appointment in both the Philosophy Department and the Carlson School of Management so I taught undergraduate business ethics philosophy courses, required business ethics courses in all the MBA programs and a PhD seminar in business ethics in the business school. Obviously, the PhD seminar was very different from all the rest. In the Executive MBA course I used my co-edited text *Ethical Theory and Business* along with Harvard cases and a few other articles or non Harvard cases. The Director of the Executive MBA program encouraged me to use my text even though large sections of it were not used in the course. She pointed out that students liked having a text by the instructor and there was no extra expense to students because all texts were included in their tuition. On those occasions where I taught full time or part time MBA's I used a course packet consisting of cases and articles. In the undergraduate philosophy business ethics course I used my co-edited text without the Harvard cases. Since the undergraduate course was a full semester I could use much more of the material in the text.

All the topics covered in the MBA courses were also covered in the undergraduate philosophy business ethics course. However, there were lots of differences between the MBA courses and the undergraduate course. First the undergraduate course met twice a week for 90 min. The Executive MBA class had eight meetings of 4 h each. The undergraduate students had little business experience beyond summer work or entry level jobs. The executive MBA's had management positions and in many cases senior management positions. Experience-or lack thereof- blended well with the scheduled classroom time for these courses. The undergraduate course was primarily lecture with a generous amount of video and some discussion. Except for discussion the classroom situation might be described as passive. However, with the Executive MBA's we had an opportunity for student team presentations and for much more discussion. Those classrooms were much more active. In both cases, the course was generally well received.

The full time and part time MBA course presented more of a challenge since, like the undergraduate philosophy course, I had two 90 min sections per week. I cut down the amount of reading for those courses and continued with the in class case study presentations. Those presentations took up half the class. I never felt I had enough time. It was tempting to eliminate the team in class presentations, but I have discovered that students often learn better when they are actively engaged in team projects. These team projects enabled students to apply the concepts in the reading material. Additionally, the Carlson School administration actively encouraged team projects.

Reflecting on the variety problem, I think you can discuss the same topics but that you need to modify the readings and the amount of discussion to account for differences in the length of the class and in the work experience of the students. Undergraduate classes are usually not as much fun since many are taking the course simply to meet a requirement and it is often clear that a number of students in the class are not genuinely interested no matter how many rabbits you pull out of a hat. The MBA classes are much more lively but we philosophers are always in danger of being ignored because we have no business experience. My advice to philosophers who teach MBA's is that they read widely in the business press, cultivate friendships in business, and have loads of business examples ready for lecture and discussion.

Decision #4: What to Do When Students Want Answers and There Aren't Any

A common criticism of my course is that it does not provide answers. Students from an engineering or natural science background are especially troubled by the lack of answers. The more humanities courses a student has had the easier it is to overcome this problem. For many years at the very end of the course I provided what I called a framework for ethical decisions. But concluding with advice such as "Don't do anything you do not want to see on the front page of the *Wall Street Journal*" seemed quite trite especially after a semester of heavy theory-and I don't mean just ethical theory- and tough cases. I tried pointing out that focusing on cases or issues with clear answers is a waste of time. You do not need a business ethics course to know that stealing is wrong and that what Bernie Madoff did was wrong. Simply in terms of a valuable use of student time, it makes sense to focus on cases and issues that are not obvious. The last few years I taught I discovered, or more accurately rediscovered, Billy Joel's "Shades of Gray." I played that at the beginning of every class to emphasize the point that my course focused on the gray areas of business ethics. "Ain't no rainbow shining on me, shades of gray are all that I see." Student response to this technique varied. Especially the first few times I used it, students really got into it. One class had some talented musicians so they even made up a graduation skit based on the song. Some classes really liked the song on day one but were or seemed bored by day five. At Wharton, I knew my message was not getting across when a student in one section insisted that we have a song from Bombay Millionaire rather than the Billy Joel song. Perhaps in my late 60s I could not find the right music. Nonetheless, a good business ethics course needs to look at tough cases that do not have easy answers.

Decision #5: How Should Business Ethics Course Be Graded?

Grading an ethics course raises a host of difficult questions. Problems in grading are exacerbated by the fact that my course, and I think most business ethics courses, do not have right answers. So the students think that there are no standards upon which they can be judged. Everyone ought to get A's or so the students think.

Lately a number of business schools have begun to address the issue of grade inflation. When I first started teaching we did not give a lot of A's. Grade inflation is now a real issue. However, I think the problem is more serious at the undergraduate level. Graduate courses have always had a high percentage of A's. I think Wharton's policy of a 20 % limit on A's is too strict although one wonders if their policy really matters because the students always vote to not have their grades released to potential employers. The only effect of the 20 % rule is to increase tension between the faculty and the students. The real problem with grade inflation-that potential employers have no way of distinguishing the most able students from the less able-is not helped by a 20 % limit on A's if the employers do not see the grades. Some schools like Maryland are trying to obtain a 50/50 split on A's and B's. I actually prefer Minnesota's system which has a higher limit on A's for undergraduate courses in business than it does for MBA courses. I think Minnesota even has different limitations on A's for different types of MBA courses. The Executive MBA had the most permissive limit. The average for the class was expected to be A- However, for an increasing number of business ethics faculty a limitation on the number of A's that you can give is a reality and you don't have any other choice except to follow school policy.

One of the effects of attempts to deal with grade inflation through limitations on the number of A's given is that such restrictions create a forced curve. I have always thought that forced curves were unfair. All sections of a course are not the same. And the quality of students in a course varies from year to year. Sometimes it might be appropriate to give 80 % A's while at other times 50 % or even fewer might be the right number. If the percentage of A's given by an instructor really does vary across sections and among years, that is prima facie evidence that the instructor is taking grading seriously and making distinctions among the students' work. What I think is unacceptable is an instructor who gives all A's. However, I also think it is wrong for an instructor to try to prove he is "a tough guy" by giving a lot of low grades. In some schools this game of tough guy is played by whole departments that want to show how hard their courses are. Departments whose courses are highly quantitative are often tempted to play this game. That kind of gamesmanship makes grading in ethics courses even harder. If a business ethics professor does not adopt the tough guy approach then the view that business ethics is a soft easy course is only confirmed in the mind of the tough guys.

A good business ethics course has some characteristics that make it more difficult to grade than standard business courses. One task of a business ethics course is to get students to see an event as an ethical issue. A good business course sensitizes students to ethical issues. It has been amazing to me to see how students simply do not see a conflict of interest situation as a genuine conflict of interest and thus as a genuine ethical issue. Getting finance majors to see that Goldman Sachs had conflicts of interest during the financial crisis was very challenging. I had the same experience with marketing majors with respect to the issues of marketing to the vulnerable. Most students think that the fast food companies have no responsibility for or even need to be concerned about obesity. Even when I transform it into a strictly management issue, many students do not see it. I put the issue this way. Should the CEO of McDonalds do anything in response to criticism that McDonalds is contributing to the obesity crisis. The standard response of many students and most marketing majors is that people are free to choose what they want to eat and they ought to be free to so choose. A student that reasons that way is not as good as a student who reasons as follows: Whatever my personal opinion about free choice, I need to ask the strategic question of how I should deal with my critics. Ignoring them may be a bad strategy simply on business grounds. By this point in my course a good student should remember the Royal Dutch Shell in Nigeria case and the Royal Dutch Shell Brent Spar case to see that ignoring one's critics can be a bad business decision. I

ought to give the first student a B and the second student an A. However, I can assure you that the first student will then complain that I am giving him or her a B because I do not like their political opinion. Sensitizing students to see ethical issues, even if only as management issues, often does not sit well with grading them especially when the number of A's you can give in a course is limited.

I have found one way to get a number of B's without resorting to "objective tests" such as multiple choice, fill in the blank, or true/false. I assign a case, "The Sarah Strong" case authored by Diana Robertson and the late Tom Dunfee. This international case is due on the day that we discuss international business ethics issues in class. In the instructions I say something like, "Defend your answers using relevant course material." You will always find students who do not use any course material at all. And you will find others who are behind in the reading so they will use course material but not relevant course material. I always get my B's. It never fails.

To avoid arguments about the case, I always get permission to post a few of the A cases online. I make sure that I post A cases from both sides of the issue. Thus I would include an A answer from the Milton Friedman perspective and an A answer from the Ed Freeman stakeholder perspective. In that way an aggrieved student cannot say that the only reason he or she got a B was because I didn't agree with their political opinion.

Finally since most business ethics courses include a lot of class discussion, how can you grade discussion? The problem becomes especially critical when you have, as I did, classes of 60 or more. The first thing I do is to concentrate only on those who speak frequently and well and those who do not speak at all. The other thing I do is give a class grade usually A- or B+ depending on the quality of the class discussion and any limitations I have on the number of A's I can give. In that way, especially at the end of 6 or 7 weeks, it is easy to pick out the limited number of students who performed better than average and also those that did not speak up at all.

However, one must be very careful not to get overconfident here. At Wharton I had the luxury of having a student assistant whose sole job was simply to keep track of who spoke and how many times. I then tested my own impression from memory against her records and I was wrong more often than I would like to admit. Keeping track of discussion and grading it fairly is one of the major challenges in grading. Yet I have had few if any students challenge my discussion grades. Go figure.

Decision #6: Should a Business School Have a Required Course or Should It Try to Get Ethics in All Functional Areas?

As we saw from the discussion of the Arthur Andersen initiative, almost from the beginning there has been an argument about whether you should have a stand alone business ethics course or try to integrate ethics into the entire business curriculum. Nearly everyone agrees that integration would be best, however, it is impractical. I do not know of any program that has successfully integrated ethics across the business curriculum. Indeed the people who talk most about integrating are at business schools that do little if anything in the way of business ethics. So let's agree on second best-the stand alone business ethics course. To be effective, it needs to be a full course like other courses in the curriculum. However, getting a full course on a par with other courses in the curriculum is a difficult assignment.

On another topic, teaching business ethics before the regular school year starts is a mistake because it signals that business ethics is not part of the regular curriculum and is analogous to some of those remedial finance courses you need to take before you get to the real curriculum. If a business school is serious about business ethics it will have at least one full required graded course as part of the regular curriculum. Anything less signals that business ethics is a second class citizen.

Having defended that full stand alone course as the only practical way to have business ethics in the curriculum, there are some things that can be done to integrate ethics into the general business curriculum. If the person teaching business ethics in the MBA program is a philosopher, he or she must become conversant in the functional areas of business so that there can be frequent tie-in to the functional curriculum. Also one need not assume that only a philosopher can teach the course. Many of my colleagues have considerable expertise in topics that they may not even consider ethics but which clearly are. In human resource management, a key topic is "How should employees be treated.?" In finance, agency problems can be construed as problems in ethics. And strategy professors who talk about building trust as a strategic necessity are talking ethics. Marketing professors who study the impact of advertising on children are doing ethics. Philosophers should look for colleagues who have an interest in topics that have ethical connotations and build relationships with those colleagues. Perhaps there could even be some team teaching. Building these kind of relationships may be the closest we can come to integrating business ethics across the business curriculum.

Decision #7: Should You Invite Business People to Help Teach Your Business Ethics Course?

There is no question that students love to have business people teach a class or team teach a section. Having business people team teach was specifically recommended by the NEH committee. For several years running one of my best classes in my Minnesota Executive MBA course was team taught with Jim Hale, Chief Counsel of the Target Corporation. Jim was present in 1987 as Target fought off a take-over attempt of Dayton Hudson (later Target) by the Hafts of the Dart Corporation.

There are dangers, however. MBA students have a tendency to think that professors without business experience are not as credible as those with business experience. The good news in this bad news is that they hold that opinion of all business faculty-not just business ethics faculty. This is an issue that is not often discussed openly among business faculty.

The decision about whether to involve business people in teaching business ethics courses becomes more serious when business people are hired as adjuncts to teach an entire section or sections of the course. Some business guests have a tendency to tell war stories. I have been rather reticent to use outside business people to teach my class because of this tendency for business people to tell war stories or to tell the students how ethical they and their companies are. Often the ethics presented is fairly simplistic. My own way of navigating this problem is to rely on the business experience of my MBA's especially my Executive MBA's and part-time MBA's. Since all my classes have a very strong discussion base, it is fairly easy to get students to show how what I am teaching is (or is not) relevant to what they experience in the business world. If I do use a business person, it is in the context of joint teaching rather than simply having a guest lecture. After a couple of years Jim Hale and I were able to play off against each other in a way that was effective in teaching. With undergraduates I am more willing to have a guest lecture by a business person. After all the actual experience base of most undergraduates is usually more limited. Ironically it is much harder to get guest lecturers for an undergraduate class. Business people are more interested in access to MBA's than they are in undergraduates.

Decision #8: How Prominent Should the Use of Cases Be?

I start with the assertion that all business ethics courses should include business cases and I do mean "All." It does not matter whether the course is taught in the business school or in the philosophy department, the course is for undergraduates or graduates, the course is taught to a US audience or is taught abroad. It gets more interesting when one asks if teaching business ethics should be done entirely by the case method as is done at the Darden School, University of Virginia and at Harvard. Frankly I think that decision should be up to the institution or, where there is no institutional policy, up to the instructor. I always felt comfortable with a combined approach-some lecturing and some case analysis. However, in my Executive MBA course at Minnesota the "final exam" was a team produced written case as might be found in the Harvard or Darden list of cases. My students did an excellent job with that assignment. A couple of their cases were actually published in the Darden case-book series.

The NEH Committee had extensive discussions about the use of cases in business ethics courses. The Committee actually wrote 16 cases ranging from three pages in length to one paragraph. These cases, or at least some of them, were used by the six faculty during the trial teaching phase. Reaction to the cases was mixed on the part of both students and the participating faculty. The one principle the Committee endorsed was that cases should not simply make an obvious ethical point. Personally I do not think any of the 16 cases developed for the courses were guilty of that.

The cases were all very short in length as are many of the cases in most of the business ethics anthologies. MBA's are used to lengthy cases along the Harvard model. The NEH Committee cases and many cases in the textbooks are simply too short for the kind of analysis MBA's typically give a case. The shorter cases are more effective in undergraduate courses and in philosophy departments where there is less need perhaps to include extensive financial information. Some faculty use both a business ethics text and a business ethics casebook.

An even more common approach is for the instructor to put together a series of Harvard (perhaps with some Ivy and Darden cases added) cases that meet the specific topic requirements of the course. I always took this approach for my business school course graduate course. When I taught undergraduate philosophy courses in business ethics, I was more sparing in my use of Harvard like cases and more inclined to stick with the cases in my own co-edited text, *Ethical Theory and Business*. It may be interesting to note that as we have worked through the various editions of our text, we have tried to include some longer cases although none have ever approached the length of a standard Harvard case.

Teaching a case requires a number of special skills. Several of my colleagues like Ed Freeman, Ken Goodpaster, and Tom Donaldson are very skilled at it. I always had good luck at getting lively discussions and getting the issues out. However, I was not always as successful at getting closure so that students could have a "takeaway" or several "takeaways." After leaving Minnesota, I actually would email a list of "takeaways" to the students in my Wharton course and Maryland courses once the class was over. The Maryland students seemed to appreciate that-the Wharton students much less so. Although the "takeaways" were based on my perception of what transpired in class discussion, there was always the danger that since I produced them, the students did not own them even though they had evolved from the class discussion. Anyone teaching a business ethics course who was not trained in the case method is well advised to read one of the excellent descriptions on how to teach cases in the business schools.

Decision #9: Should You Try to Measure Student Performance and if So How?

Toward the end of my teaching career there was a movement in education to try to determine empirically and objectively whether students learned anything in their courses. In principle, I think that is a good question to ask. I often wondered whether even after the best discussions the students really learned anything. We had a good discussion but were there genuine takeaways that they would remember? Would the course really make a difference in their business lives?

I really never had to come up with these measures so I do not have any good advice to offer. Given that part of a business ethics course is to sensitize students to ethical issues so that they can recognize ethical issues when they face them, I do not know an easy way to see if the students are more sensitive to ethical issues after the course is complete. One thing that might be done is to have the students analyze a case at the beginning of the course and then analyze the same case at the end of the course. If the course has been successful, there should be marked improvement in the later essays. However, if this device supplements other course requirements, it might involve a lot of extra work on the part of the students. Also for instructors, especially those with large classes, where there is a lot of extra reading and evaluating to be done. I leave the ultimate solution as to how to prove that your students really learned anything to the next generation.

Decision #10: Student Laptops

When I started teaching business ethics there were no laptops and even after they came on the scene most classrooms were not equipped to facilitate their use. I remember when the new Carlson School of Management building opened everyone was proud of the fact that each seat had a place to plug in a laptop. Of course in a couple of years wireless technology made those plug ins obsolete. At first everyone welcomed the use of laptops in the classroom. Then the dirty secret got out. Students were using their laptops to check their email or the latest football scores rather than taking notes and listening to the case presentation or class discussion. I know that the response of many faculty to this problem is to ban laptop use. I never thought that was the right approach so I told students that they should use the laptops to aid in the class discussion but not for personal use. Obviously just saying that was not going to change behavior. What I did was ask questions that required lap top use. For example, I would ask students to get the financials on a certain company or to check a stock price or to go to an advertisement on the internet. Did that end all using the computer for personal email and the like? Certainly not, but it did lessen it and it set up expectations that laptops were to be an integral part of the learning experience. It seems to me that is how new technology should be handled. We should use it; it should not use us.

Decision #11: How Far Should a Business Faculty Member Go in Using the New Technology?

That decision is an easy one for a young faculty member starting his or her career. These young faculty are comfortable with the new technology and use it in their personal and other areas of their professional lives. The older you are the more difficult it is to keep up. Nonetheless keep up you must. I noticed that in my syllabus for the sections of my Maryland Executive MBA course, I was using YouTube in class and assigning YouTube events. I assigned the Academy Award winning movie *Inside Job.* Some of the items in my required reading list sent students to websites. I also had several VCR videos to show although these are now a relic. The Executive MBA classrooms at the Carlson School of Management no longer have the equipment to shows VCR tapes. I retired just as this change went into effect. Of course I do have traditional cases and even some traditional reading assignments. However, as you can see I made the effort to use the technological devices and tools that my students were comfortable with.

What does concern me, however, is the decline in reading that students do. My MBA students at the end of my career read much less than my undergraduates when I started out. It seems to me that less reading is correlated with less critical thinking. However, this issue of whether the new technology has some serious adverse consequences on the ability of people (not just students) to think critically and recognize fact from opinion extends far beyond issues in the teaching of business ethics so I leave that for others. One "big" issue does concern me, however. Does the teaching of business ethics have a future?

A Concluding Worry

In the beginning business ethics had a hard time gaining legitimacy in the business schools. I had hoped that after 30+ years business ethics would be accepted as a legitimate discipline and business ethics courses would have the same status as other courses in the business curriculum. Alas that has not been the case. Indeed as I write this chapter in 2012, we seem to have regressed in that regard despite an uninterrupted series of scandals and crises during the entire first decade of the twenty-first century. Notre Dame decries the fact that it cannot hire a permanent chair in business ethics, but I know that they have turned down several of the most important people in the field. Georgetown University's failure to make a chair appointment cost them that chair and the ambitions for business ethics at Georgetown were never fulfilled. Villanova has eliminated its required business ethics course. Some Catholic institutions have done well with and by business ethics-St Thomas, Loyola of Chicago, and DePaul come to mind.

Among non-Catholic universities, I would only give high marks to Virginia's Darden School and perhaps the University of Washington. Wharton probably has the most distinguished set of business ethics scholars in any university, but the 9 h required course is insufficient. The University of Maryland instituted a business ethics requirement for all business programs, but with the exception of Accounting, has no trained faculty to teach it and recently has admitted that is trying to figure out what to do with ethics. And my biggest disappointment is with my own institution, the University of Minnesota, which has not replaced me as Andersen Chair and has allowed a number of programs I created to languish (although a new undergraduate requirement in business ethics has just been approved).

Perhaps the problem is, in part, one of methodology. All my colleagues at Minnesota were social scientists. Much of ethics is not science. When it is taught as a normative discipline, it uses the methodologies of the humanities. Increasingly business schools are insisting that business ethics scholars publish only in A business journal outlets. Books are not respected. A philosophy journals are not respected. Even journals that focus on business ethics are sometimes not accepted. This situation is not tenable. Unless the situation changes, the future for the teaching of business ethics and for normative research in business ethics does not look bright. At the end of a long career in the field, this state of affairs is depressing.

References

Arnold, Denis G., and Jared D. Harris (eds.). 2012. *Kantian business ethics: Critical perspectives.* Cheltenham: Edward Elgar Publishing.

Bowie, Norman E. 1988. Accountants, full disclosure, and conflicts of interest. *Business & Professional Ethics Journal* 5(3/4): 59–73.

Bowie, Norman E. 1990. Money, morality, and motor cars. In *Business ethics and the environment*, ed. W.M. Hoffman, R. Frederick, and E.S. Petry, 89–97. New York: Quorum Books.

Bowie, Norman E. 1991. The firm as a moral community. In *Morality, rationality and efficiency: New perspectives on socio-economics*, ed. Richard M. Coughlin, 169–183. Armonk: M.E. Sharpe Inc.

Bowie, Norman E. 1998. A Kantian theory of meaningful work. *Journal of Business Ethics* 17: 1083–1092.

Bowie, Norman E. 1999. *Business ethics: A Kantian perspective.* New York: Blackwell.

Cohen, Marc A., and John C. Dienhart. 2012. Citizens, Kant and corporate responsibility for the environment. In *Kantian business ethics: Critical perspectives*, ed. Denis G. Arnold and Jared Harris. Cheltenham: Edward Elgar Publishing.

Commission of European Communities. 2001. GREEN PAPER promoting a European framework for Corporate Social Responsibility, Brussels, July 18.

Donaldson, Thomas. 1989. *The ethics of international business.* New York: Oxford University Press.

Donaldson, Thomas, and Thomas W. Dunfee. 1999. *Ties that bind.* Boston: Harvard Business School Press.

Dubbink, W., and J. Smith. 2011. A political account of the corporation as a morally responsible actor. *Ethical Theory and Moral Practice* XIV(2): 223–246.

Dubbink, W., and L. van Liedekerke. 2009. A neo-Kantian conceptualization of CSR. *Ethical Theory and Moral Practice* XII(2): 117–136.

Duska, Ronald. 2007. The why's of business revisited. In *Contemporary reflections on business ethics*. Dordrecht: Springer.

Dworkin, Ronald. 1977. *Taking rights seriously.* Cambridge, MA: Harvard University Press.

Evan, William M., and R.Edward Freeman. 1988. A stakeholder theory of the modern corporation: Kantian capitalism. In *Ethical theory and business*, 3rd ed, ed. Tom L. Beauchamp and Norman E. Bowie, 97–112. Englewood Cliffs: Prentice Hall Inc.

Frank, Robert H. 1988. *Passions within reason.* New York: W.W. Norton & Co.

Freeman, R. Edward, and William M. Evan. 1990. Corporate governance: A stakeholder interpretation. *Journal of Behavioral Economics* 19: 337–359.

Freeman, R. Edward, Jeffrey S. Harrison, Andrew C. Wicks, Bidhan L. Parmar, and Simone DeColle. 2010. *Stakeholder theory: The state of the art.* Cambridge: Cambridge University Press.

Friedman, Milton. 1970. The social responsibility of business is to increase its profits. *New York Times Magazine*, September 13.

Friedman, Milton. 1982. *Capitalism and freedom*. Chicago: University of Chicago Press.

Friedman, Thomas L. 2006. *The world is flat, updated and expanded*. New York: Farrar, Straus and Giroux.

Goodpaster, Kenneth E., Laura L. Nash, and Henri-Claude de Bettignies. 2006. *Business ethics, policies and persons*. Boston: Irwin McGraw Hill.

Harris, Jared D., and Philip Bromiley. 2007. Incentives to cheat: The influence of executive compensation and firm performance on financial misrepresentation. *Organization Science* 18(3): 350–367.

Herman, Barbara. 2007. *Moral literacy*. Cambridge: Harvard University Press.

Jamal, Karim. 2004. After seven decades of regulation, why is the audit profession in such a mess? *Business and Professional Ethics Journal* 12(1/2): 65–92.

Jensen, Michael C. 2002. Value maximization, stakeholder theory, and the corporate objective function. *Business Ethics Quarterly* 12(2): 239–255.

Kant, Immanuel. 1785, 1990. *Foundations of the metaphysics of morals*. New York: Macmillan Publishing Co.

Kant, Immanuel. 1798, 1991. *Metaphysics of morals*. Cambridge: Cambridge University Press.

Koehn, Daryl. 2004. What form of business regulation is workable? *Business and Professional Ethics Journal* 12(1/2): 43–63.

Korsgaard, Christine. 2009. *Self-constitution: Agency, identity, and integrity*. Oxford: Oxford University Press.

Mitchell, Ronald K., Bradley R. Agle, and Donna Wood. 1997. Toward a theory of stakeholder identification and salience: Defining the principle of who and what really counts. *Academy of Management Review* 22: 853–886.

Moriarity, Jeffrey. 2010. Participation in the workplace: Are employees special? *Journal of Business Ethics* 92: 373–384.

Partnoy, Frank. 2003. *Infectious greed*. New York: Henry Holt and Co.

Rawls, John. 1999. *A theory of justice*, rev. ed. Cambridge, MA: Harvard University Press.

Reynolds, Scott J., and Norman E. Bowie. 2004. A Kantian perspective of the characteristics of ethics programs. *Business Ethics Quarterly* 14(2): 275–294.

Rorty, Richard. 1989. *Contingency, irony and solidarity*. Cambridge: Cambridge University Press.

Rorty, Richard. 2006. Is philosophy relevant in applied ethics. *Business Ethics Quarterly* 16(3): 369–380.

Sagoff, Mark. 1981. At the shrine of our lady of Fatima, or why political questions are not all economic. *Arizona Law Review* 23: 283–1298.

Sagoff, Mark. 1988. *The economy of the earth*. Cambridge: Cambridge University Press.

Smith, Jeffery. 2012. Corporate duties of virtue: Making (Kantian) sense of corporate social responsibility. In *Kantian business ethics: Critical perspectives*, ed. Denis G. Arnold and Jared D. Harris, 59–75. Cheltenham: Edward Elgar Publishing.

Smith, Jeffery, and Wim Dubbink. 2011a. Understanding the role of moral principles in business ethics: A Kantian perspective. *Business Ethics Quarterly* 21(2): 205–231.

Smith, Jeffery, and Wim Dubbink. 2011b. Understanding the role of moral principles in business ethics: A Kantian perspective. *Business Ethics Quarterly* 21(2): 205–231.

Thaler, Richard H., and Cass R. Sunstein. 2008. *Nudge: Improving decisions about health, wealth, and happiness*. New Haven: Yale University Press.

Vaaler, Paul M., and Norman E. Bowie. 2010. Transaction cost economics, knowledge transfer and universal business norms in multinational enterprises. *International Journal of Strategic Change Management* 2(4): 269–297.

Velasquez, Manuel. 2000. Globalization and the failure of ethics. *Business Ethics Quarterly* 10(1): 343–352.

Victor, Bart, and John B. Cullen. 1988. The organizational bases of ethical work climates. *Administrative Science Quarterly* 33: 101–125.

Werhane, Patricia. 1999. *Moral imagination and management decision making*. New York: Oxford University Press.

Werhane, Patricia H. 2000. Exporting mental models: Global capitalism in the 21st century. *Business Ethics Quarterly* 10(1): 353–362.

Williamson, Oliver E. 1975. *Markets and hierarchies*. New York: The Free Press.

Williamson, Oliver E. 1985. *The economic institutions of capitalism*. New York: The Free Press.

Wood, Allen W. 2008. *Kantian ethics*. Cambridge: Cambridge University Press.

Index

N.E. Bowie, *Business Ethics in the 21st Century*, Issues in Business Ethics 39,
DOI 10.1007/978-94-007-6223-7, © Springer Science+Business Media Dordrecht 2013

CPSIA information can be obtained at www.ICGtesting.com
Printed in the USA
LVOW10*0315310713

345489LV00007B/43/P